Edinburgh Studies in English and Scots

edited by
A. J. Aitken
Angus McIntosh
Hermann Pálsson

LONGMAN

LONGMAN GROUP LIMITED LONDON
Associated companies, branches and representatives throughout the world

© **Longman Group Ltd 1971**

All rights reserved. No part of this publication may be reproduced,
stored in a retrieval system, or transmitted in any form or by any means,
electronic, mechanical, photocopying, recording, or otherwise,
without the prior permission of the copyright owner.

First published 1971
ISBN 0 582 52230 7

Made and printed in Great Britain by
William Clowes and Sons Limited London and Beccles

This volume is dedicated in affectionate and grateful remembrance to O. K. Schram (1900–1968), for thirty years teacher of English Language in the University of Edinburgh

Contents

Phonetics

Scots

Acknowledgments

We are grateful to the following for permission to reproduce copyright material:

The Trustees of the British Museum for Reproductions A and B (*pp.* 30 and 31), and for an extract from an unpublished transcript by A. J. Aitken; Victor Gollancz Ltd and Curtis Brown Ltd for extracts from 'Voice of Authority' and 'Against Romanticism' from *A Case of Samples* by Kingsley Amis; Victor Gollancz Ltd and Harcourt, Brace & World Inc for extracts from *Take a Girl Like You, That Uncertain Feeling* and *I Like It Here*, all by Kingsley Amis; The Scottish Text Society, Edinburgh, for an extract adapted from *The Poems of James VI of Scotland* edited by James Craigie, Vol I, 1955, and an extract from *The Maitland Folio Manuscript* edited by W. A. Craigie, Vol II, 1927.

Abbreviations

AfdA	*Anzeiger für deutsches Altertum*
Archiv	*Archiv für das Studium der Neueren Sprachen*
AL	*Archivum Linguisticum*
BM	British Museum
Bodl	Bodleian Library
CUL	Cambridge University Library
DEPN	E. Ekwall, *Concise Dictionary of English Place-Names*
DOST	*Dictionary of the Older Scottish Tongue*
EDD	*English Dialect Dictionary*
EDG	J. Wright, *English Dialect Grammar*
EETS ES	Early English Text Society, Extra Series
EETS OS	Early English Text Society, Original Series
FL	*Foundations of Language*
JEGP	*Journal of English and Germanic Philology*
JL	*Journal of Linguistics*
MED	*Middle English Dictionary*
OED	*Oxford English Dictionary* (previously *New English Dictionary*)
PBB	*Beiträge zur Geschichte der deutschen Sprache und Literatur* (H. Paul und W. Braune)
PGr²	*Grundriss der Germanischen Philologie*, second edition, Strassburg, 1900–9
SND	*Scottish National Dictionary*

SHR	*Scottish Historical Review*
SHS	Scottish History Society
STS	Scottish Text Society
TPS	*Transactions of the Philological Society*

Du	Dutch
Flem	Flemish
Goth	Gothic
LG	Low German
MDu	Middle Dutch
ME	Middle English
MFlem	Middle Flemish
OE	Old English
OF	Old French
OFris	Old Frisian
OHG	Old High German
ON	Old Norse
OS	Old Saxon
WS	West Saxon

Old and Middle English

M. L. Samuels

Professor of English Language, University of Glasgow

Kent and the Low Countries: some linguistic evidence

1

Linguistic correspondences between England and the Continent have hitherto been interpreted as due to (*a*) pre-invasion tribal connections, or (*b*) post-invasion trade and other contacts, or (*c*) pure coincidence. Chadwick in 1906[1] favoured (*b*) or (*c*) as against (*a*), and despite the evidence given in the same year by Jordan[2] and the fuller evidence since presented by Schwarz,[3] recent opinion still favours Chadwick's view. It is expressed most forcibly by D. DeCamp:

> . . . the origins of the English dialects lie not in pre-migration tribal affiliation but in certain social, economic and cultural developments which occurred after the migration was completed. . . . Only those influences which were felt after the migrations were relevant to formation of the English dialects; . . . these dialects originated not on the continent but on the island of Britain.[4]

Involved here are questions of principle beyond what is suggested by the title of this paper, but some preliminary discussion of them is necessary. Linguistic correspondences between Kentish and Frisian are denied any relevance for the invasion period because 'the most obvious Kentish features can be observed gradually making their appearance in documents of the ninth century',[5] and therefore 'can hardly prove a common ancestor in the 5th century'.[6] This argument must be carefully examined. If the features in question were lexical or syntactical, it could hardly apply at all, for the absence of such features from early documents must in any case often be accounted for by differences of register. But they are in fact phonological (*e* as the reflex of both earlier *ў* and earlier *ǣ*, and *ia* as the reflex of earlier *ěo*); and the explanation of their absence from the earliest Kentish texts as due to dialect mixture[7] is rightly dismissed by DeCamp, for, even in dialectally mixed texts, at least some hint of them might be expected.

Nevertheless, there are two further possibilities of which this argument takes no account. The late appearance of correspondences does not prove that there was no original connection. Phonetic change is determined largely by the suprasegmental features of juncture, stress, pitch and intonation, which are never recorded in early writings. The same change may appear, therefore, centuries after the two groups of speakers have separated, yet be the result of the same conditioning factors that have been operating ever since the separation. How else are we to explain the radical distinction between north and south in three different areas – England, the Netherlands, and Germany, seen especially (*a*) in the loss of the *ge-* prefix and the earlier loss of unstressed syllables generally in the north of each area, compared with their retention in the south;[8] and (*b*) in the retention of the original [uː] as in *hūs* in the north of each area (Northern English, Frisian, Low German) compared with the diphthongisation in English *house*, Dutch *huis*, German *haus*?

Secondly, there is the possibility of wide allophonic variation. The use of ⟨æ⟩ and ⟨y⟩ in early Kentish writings tells us only that they represented phonemes distinct from that represented by ⟨e⟩; it tells us very little about their phonetic realisations, and certainly cannot disprove either (*a*) that the /æ/ of Kentish and Frisian was, throughout the earlier period, of a more raised variety than those of West Saxon or Northumbrian, or (*b*) that the /y/ resulting from *i*-mutation in Kentish and Frisian was of a lower and less rounded variety than elsewhere, irrespective of the chronology of *i*-mutation.

In short, what is postulated here is no more than the normal transmission, from one generation to another, of suprasegmental features (whether distinctive or not) and of allophonic and other non-distinctive features of the spoken chain. Such transmission is assumed to be purely environmental, not genetic, though there seems to be no valid objection to the term 'inherited'.

It is perhaps not surprising that, until recently,[9] scholars have tended to neglect these possibilities. The portmanteau label 'inherited tendencies' was discredited largely because its users either omitted to define it or – worse still – gave it a specifically biological interpretation.[10] But if the transmission is one of suprasegmental or subphonemic features and is environmentally conditioned, there are surely no grounds for objection. It is supported by the evidence of modern regional and class dialects where, for example, a paralinguistic feature like unusual voice-quality is found to accompany an unusual phonetic system, and appears to have conditioned the antecedent changes in that system.[11]

The significance of this is that the dialect distributions of periods much later than the invasion must always be considered as potentially relevant to the invasion period. The early evidence, confined as it is to phonemic and segmental representation, is often insufficient to tell us the precise age of a correspondence: that, so far as it can be gauged at all, must be judged from other evidences and probabilities – historical, demographic, sociological and the like. In assessing these, too much importance is sometimes attached to negative evidence. For example, the argument, based on archaeological finds, that the invaders were of mixed origins and that any linguistic correspondences with the Continent that occur are therefore irrelevant,[12] is a circular one. It implies merely that, from the archaeological evidence, we ought not to expect to find any linguistic correspondences, and that, if found, they are to be ignored.

Against this argument, the linguistic evidence agrees with Tacitus, Ptolemy, Bede and vernacular English traditions. Indeed, if we had no conventional historical sources concerning the early home of the English, and we attempted to 'place' the Old English invaders according to the principles of linguistic geography, we would have no alternative to the area from Jutland to Schleswig-Holstein. For, as has long been recognised,[13] the correspondences usually associated with the groupings 'West Germanic', 'Ingvaeonic' and 'Anglo-Frisian' must be considered together with those between Old English and North Germanic, and admit of no other arrangement than that shown in the accompanying figure. To say that the correspondences with Old Norse and Gothic are merely coincidental[14] is no more justifiable than saying that the correspondences between, say, present-day northern and midland English are the only relevant ones, and that those between northern English and Scots are coincidental.[15]

All dialect maps of the past are necessarily hypothetical, but the validity of this pre-migration map is confirmed by its details, which are of the type found in modern maps. It is an axiom of linguistic geography that every dialect that is not isolated constitutes, *for some of its features*, a 'border area' to its neighbours, and for those features com-

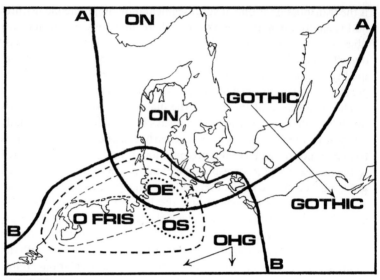

The lines denote the following correspondences:

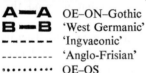 OE–ON–Gothic
B — B   'West Germanic'
------   'Ingvaeonic'
----------   'Anglo-Frisian'
··········   OE–OS

NOTE The terms ON, OE etc refer here not to the later languages but to
the early dialects of Germanic corresponding to *pre*-ON, *pre*-OE etc.

bines the two different forms of its neighbours in free or conditioned
variation. It is of interest, therefore, that Old English possessed some
of the very pairs of variants that would be expected of its geographical
position on the Continent, notably both *eom* and *beo*,[16] *hwæþer* and
hweþer.[17]

Within this framework, it is difficult to see why the views of Möller,
Siebs, Jordan[18] and Schwarz[19] concerning Anglian and Saxon have
been questioned. The correspondences listed by them between Anglian
and Old Norse or Gothic on the one hand and between West Saxon and
Old Frisian or Old Saxon on the other[20] provide unassailable evidence
that some of the differences between Anglian and West Saxon go
back to a period on the Continent when the Angles dwelt north of the
Saxons. To postulate this does not, of course, imply the transplant-
ation of tribal units intact. It means simply that, amidst all the mixtures

suggested by the archaeological evidence, there must usually have been preponderances that determined the preference for one linguistic variant to another; and, significantly, it must have been some of those same preponderances that determined the names of the earliest English kingdoms.

2

If such obvious features of their continental origin distinguish Anglian and West Saxon, why should this possibility be rejected for Kentish? Admittedly, the problem of the Jutes is more complicated, for the historical evidence suggests wider earlier migrations. The linguistic evidence must therefore be interpreted in the light of the historical evidence, which suggests an original home in Jutland, north of the Angles, and then a migration to a position in which there was contact with Frisians to the west and north-west, Saxons to the east, and Salian Franks to the south, *ie* probably in southern Holland, north of the lower Rhine. This placing does not rest exclusively on the evidence of *Eotena* in *Beowulf*, nor necessarily on the theory of the identity of the two Hengests,[21] but is confirmed by the letter of the Frankish King Theudebert, which, on any interpretation, presupposes the Eutii as occupying a buffer-area between Franks and Saxons.[22] Finally, we have also to reckon with the possibility of Salian Franks among the fifth-century settlers south of the Thames.[23]

The linguistic evidence fits this framework. We should not expect the earliest stage, in Jutland, to be more than faintly reflected. There are no lexical or grammatical connections with Old Norse, but there are some purely mechanical phonetic survivals. Neckel, in 1927,[24] pointed out that a feature common to Old English and Old Norse is Back-Mutation (Old Norse 'Breaking'), and it is found most extensively in Kentish, less in Anglian, and least of all in West Saxon. This distribution mirrors exactly the varying degrees of connection between North Germanic and the Jutes, Angles and Saxons that might be expected from the historical evidence for their original positions. Of still greater interest is the parallel development of rising diphthongs in Old Norse, in Middle Kentish, and to a lesser extent in Old Frisian (Old Norse *-ju-*, *-jo-*, *-ja-* etc; for Middle Kentish spellings *cf* below, page 9).[25]

But it is the second continental position of the Jutes that is most clearly confirmed by the linguistic features of Kentish. As has been shown above, it is permissible to reconstruct for that period isoglosses

of phonetic significance only (not phonemic), and these fit the historically recorded position exactly. Firstly, there are the striking affinities
between Kentish and Frisian already mentioned,[26] and secondly, there
is the more southerly trait not shared by Frisian – the voicing of initial
[f, s, θ] to [v, z, ð]. Since, in Old English, [f, v], [s, z] and [θ, ð] were allophones of the phonemes represented by ⟨f⟩, ⟨s⟩ and ⟨þ, ð⟩, no hint of
the voicing is to be expected from the spelling until later.[27] The *Kernge-
biet* for this voicing appears to have been Franconian, for in the other
dialects of Germanic it either did not take place at all or was only partial
(as in High and Low German). Bennett's theory[28] that the Jutes and
Saxons acquired the habit from the Franconian area before the invasion is borne out by the large area in Middle English and modern
dialects showing the feature.[29] It could also, in part or whole, be attributed directly to Salian Franks among the invaders,[30] and that would
not invalidate the hypothesis that many of the invaders had had close
connections with Frisia.

   Whichever view is accepted, it should be clear that the theory of complete 'linguistic anonymity' for the invaders of Kent is unlikely. However, it is not the purpose of the present article to insist on pre-invasion
inheritance as the explanation of all correspondences, but rather to
argue against the currently accepted dogma that they are all due to
post-invasion contacts. Obviously both kinds of influence must be
reckoned with, but in varying proportions according to what is being
considered – language, archaeology, social and legal institutions,
agrarian systems. Of these, the main problem of any substance – the
similarity of the Kentish field system to that of the Ripuarian, not the
Salian, Franks – remains a problem on any view, and it does not radically affect the present discussion whether there could have been Ripuarian Franks of influence among the invaders,[31] or whether both
Ripuarian and Kentish systems are isolated relics of Celtic or Romano-
Celtic practice.[32] For the rest, much of the profusion of artefacts of
Frankish origin found in Kent must be due simply to its position as the
channel for English trade with the Continent, and the similarities in
social and legal systems can be explained by either pre- or post-invasion
influences (more probably the former)[33] from Salian Franks or Frisians. Whatever the proportions in any given sphere, the language of
the settlers cannot be discounted as something wholly transient, as has
been seriously proposed by those who regarded Kent as settled by
Ripuarian Franks who gave up their own language.[34] At least one of
the correspondences with Frisian is no mere transient fashion, as may

be seen from the modern Dutch and Flemish dialect distributions of *reg, rek* 'back' and *pet* 'well'.[35] But later in the medieval period, as we shall see, the balance of continental influences on South-East England tended to shift still further from Frisian to Franconian. Frisian influences in the Old English period are known to have been strong,[36] but, for such well-established features it is reasonable to assume a pre-invasion basis, strengthened by later contacts.

3

In Middle English, the only area in which the Old English centring diphthongs were preserved in any quantity was Kent: they survived as rising diphthongs with a palatal on-glide, as is evident from the spellings *ia, ea, y(e)a, ie, ye*, which are a prominent feature of Dan Michel's orthography.[37] Not only were they preserved, but they were re-integrated in the system of that dialect by new parallel rising diphthongs in the back series, /wo/ and /wɔ/, as in *guod(e)* 'good', *guos* 'goose', *guo* 'go', *buon* 'bone', *buoþe* 'both'. Since some scholars have denied that *uo* here represents a diphthong,[38] and others claim that it occurs in no other Middle Kentish texts,[39] it may be as well to examine the evidence here:

1 The spelling *guod* in the version of the *Southern Legendary* in Bodl MS Laud 108 must be excluded from the discussion, since its scribe used *gu* as a digraph to distinguish the plosive (as in *leggues, kingue*) from the affricate (as in *segge, ligge*), and simply extended the use to distinguish 'good' from 'God'.

2 Besides the *Ayenbyte*, spellings occur in two other localised texts: Cambridge Univ Libr Addit MS 6845, *ff* 12ʳ–14ʳ (Ordinances of St Lawrence, Canterbury), in which occur *gwod(ys)* 'good(s)' and *gwo* 'go'; and a letter (1432) of William [Moldash], Prior of Christ Church, Canterbury,[40] containing *guode*. In the former text, ME /u/ has its normal spelling *u* and *o*; no case can be made for the use of *w* as a diacritic, and it therefore follows that *wo* in this and other texts listed below confirms the diphthongal nature of the sound represented by *uo* in the *Ayenbyte*.

3 Although the three localised texts all have Canterbury associations, there is reason to believe that the area covered by the feature included southern as well as eastern Kent. It does not occur in the two main texts that have associations with North-West Kent,[41] but it does occur in the following unlocalised texts:

(a) Trinity College Oxford MS 57 (*Southern Legendary* and other religious verse):[42] *guod(e)*, passim.
(b) Lambeth Palace MS 216, *f* 111^{r-v}: *gwode*.
(c) BM Sloane 3285 (Medica), *f* 55^r: *guod*.
(d) Bodl Douce 84 (Medica), *f* 47^v: *guod*.
(e) Burton MS (Verse Confession):[43] *ygwo* 'gone'.

Apart from some spellings that survive from exemplars, the language of all these is south-eastern,[44] and casts further light on the phenomenon. Firstly, MS Lambeth 216 has *good wyf* but *þe gwode man, in gwode waye*, which suggests a prosodic distinction similar to that between [guəd] and [gwodlək] in modern Frisian dialects.[45] This is further evidence that Middle Kentish *uo, wo* represent features of the spoken language.

Secondly, the language of the Trinity College Oxford MS is of special interest in combining with its south-easternisms[46] a rounded vowel in the predominant forms for 'yet', 'thither', 'since' and 'did' (*ʒut, þuder, suþþe, dude*). These forms are not connected with the fact that the greater part of the MS is of the *Southern Legendary* and probably derived from a south-western exemplar, for they extend through the other parts of the manuscript which can be shown from relict forms to derive from non-western exemplars.[47] Thus the scribe's own forms[48] can be deduced from a comparison of his treatments of the varying originals. They form a dialect complex that differs from both the *Ayenbyte* and localised West Sussex texts,[49] and can hardly be assigned elsewhere than to the sparsely-documented area of South-West Kent and East Sussex. Once this assumption is made, it is confirmed by the evidence of two further manuscripts[50] which share features with the Trinity College Oxford MS on the one hand[51] and with localised West Sussex texts on the other.[52]

There is, therefore, strong circumstantial evidence that the diphthong represented by *uo, wo* was current in southern as well as eastern Kent. The same diphthongisation was a prominent feature of many continental dialects, both Germanic and Romance, in the medieval period. The subject has been surveyed by Frings,[53] who finds two main areas of occurrence: (a) sporadically in the dialects of modern Frisia and medieval Jutland, and (b) extensively as a result of the Frankish and Old High German diphthongisations of *e* to *ie* and *o* to *uo*. This latter, according to the most likely theory, had spread from Romance to Frankish during the Merovingian and Carolingian periods,[54] and it is of special interest that an outcrop of it has existed since medieval times in West Flanders.[55] At the nearest point across the channel, in the coastal strip of South and East Kent alone of all ME dialects,[56] the system of diphthongs was amplified to the same pattern by inclusion of the same change and word-group as in one of the two continental diphthongisations. It is difficult, therefore, to escape the conclusion that the Kentish development was due to influence from the Continent. We cannot rule out the possibility of 'inheritance' (in the sense already defined) from earlier Jutish, Frisian or Frankish sources,[57] but, in this instance more than in any of those from the Old English period discussed above, a spread from the Continent through trade and other contacts seems likely, particularly in view of the close relations with Flanders in the twelfth and thirteenth centuries.

It might be objected that the development of a diphthong is an untrustworthy criterion,[58] but the hypothesis is confirmed by another feature of south-eastern Middle English – the replacement of /ð/ by /d/, as in *de* 'the', *dykke* 'thick', *dis* 'this'. Medially, this can occur sporadically in fifteenth-century texts from all parts, often as a reverse spelling due to the opposite change of /d/ to /ð/ in words like *together*, *whither, mother*. But there is evidence that in Kent, East Sussex and to some extent East Surrey it had taken place in all contexts by the early fifteenth century. It survives, in demonstrative forms only,[59] in the modern dialects of part of the area,[60] but, since doubt has been expressed regarding its exact scope in later Middle English,[61] I list here some twenty-six texts in which it occurs, with representative examples from longer texts and total occurrences from shorter ones. Reverse spellings with *þ/th* for original /d/ are also included.

A *Localised texts (mostly documents)*:

1 Canterbury Cathedral Ch. Ant. *c* 1232:[62] *dey* 'they', *dese* 'these', *dys* 'this'; *-yth(e)* past part, *sythe* 'side'.
2 Register of Horton Priory, Kent, Will of William Finch, 1443 (BM Addit 5516, *f* 15ᵛ):[63] *thoght(h)er* 'daughter'.
3 Public Record Office, Early Chancery Proceedings 15/32 (fifteenth century), Yalding, Kent: *wolthen* 'would', *Yalthyng* 'Yalding'.
4 *Ibid*, 26/61ᵇ (fifteenth century), Sutton, Kent: *-ith* past part.
5 *Ibid*, 13/76 (fifteenth century), West Hoathley, Sussex: *sesith*, *requireth* past part.
6 Priory of St Pancras, Lewes, English document of 1469 on the

Latin court rolls of the manor of Langney:[64] *de* 'the'; *-yth* past part.

7 CUL Gg.I.6 (Speculum Devotorum), Sheen, Surrey:[65] *neuyrdeles* 'nevertheless', *benede* 'beneath'; *thowgthtyr* 'daughter', *elthyr* 'elder', *bothyly* 'bodily', *nethys* 'needs', *beholthynge* 'beholding'.

B *Texts for which there is some, but less certain, evidence of localisation*:

8 Will of Stephen Thomas of Lee, South-East Essex, written at Sandwich, Kent, 1417–18:[66] *dey* 'they'.

9 BM Sloane 442 (Recipes, Medica etc):[67] *dey* 'they', *der* 'there', *dorwgh/durwe/durghe/drowgȝ* 'through', *dykke* 'thick'; *þo* 'do', *unþur* 'under', *grynþe* 'grind', *syþe* 'side'.

C *Unlocalised texts, the language of which suggests south-eastern provenance*:

10 Bodl Douce 45, *ff* 30ᵛ–52ʳ (Medica and Recipes): *den/dan* 'then', *dyse/dese* 'these', *dat* 'that', *der* 'there', *dey* 'they', *de* 'the', *dow* 'thou', *dykke* 'thick' and 'the same', *dyrde* 'third', *dorw(e)* 'through', *swyde* 'very', *beneden* 'beneath'.

11 Bodl Rawlinson F 14 (Partonope of Blois):[68] *deþer/dethir* 'thither'; *clouthe* 'cloud', *sythis* 'sides'.

12 Bodl Rawlinson Liturg g.2:[69] *day* 'they'; *deþe* 'deed'.

13 University College Oxford C.188 (Partonope of Blois):[68] *do* 'those', *-ed* third sg pres indic; *-yth* past part.

14 BM Sloane 297 (Agnus Castus): *-yth* past part, *wykkyth* 'wicked'.

15 BM Sloane 3285 (Medica) *ff* 1–32: *dys* 'this', *dorn* 'thorn', *dynge* 'thing', *deþyst/þedyst* 'didst'; *-yþ/-eþ* past part, *beþ* 'bed', *heþ* 'head', *eþþer* 'adder', *unþer* 'under', *neþe* 'need', *thyrþe* 'third', *boþy* 'body'. Hand 2, *ff* 33–92: *sydes* 'times', *seed* 'boil', *-id* third sg pres indic.

16 BM Addit 11306 (Penitential psalms): *dat* 'that', *dys* 'this', *dy* 'thy', *de* 'the(e)', *der* 'there', *dey* 'they', *do* 'those', *dourȝh*, *doruȝ-* 'through', *denkyt* 'thinks'; *þon* 'done', *þoyt* 'does', *þay* 'day', *þown* 'down', *þeparte* 'depart', *þefamyt* 'defamed'.

17 BM Addit 18216 (Medica and Recipes): *de* 'the', *dykke* 'thick', *drydde* 'third', *unnede* 'scarcely', *clodyd* 'clothed'; *-yþ/-yth* past part, *syþe* 'side', *þraȝt* 'draught'.

18 CUL. Ff III.11 (Prose Merlin):[70] *dought* 'thought'; *elther*
   'elder', *-eth* past part.
19 Glasgow Hunterian V.5.13 (=443: Brut): *dys* 'this', *de* 'the',
   dee 'thee', *dy* 'thy', *dere* 'there', *dethyr/dedyr-* 'thither'; *unþer*
   'under', *þepartyth* 'departed', *-yth* preterite and past part.
20 Lambeth Palace 216, *f* 111ʳ⁻ᵛ: *-ed* plural pres indic, *hedne*
   'heathen'; *wenþe* 'wend'.
21 Trinity College Dublin A.4.4 (69), *ff* 84–124 (Prick of
   Conscience): *dulke* 'the same', *dikke* 'thick', *dridde* 'third',
   dudir/-er 'thither'; *þoʒtris* 'daughters', *þrynke* 'drink'.
22 Wellcome Historical Medical Library 405:[71] *dikke/dykke*
   'thick', *dynne* 'thin', *dridde* 'third', *-id/yd* third sing pres
   indic, *sede* 'seethe'.

D *Texts showing a south-eastern stratum of dialect mixed with one or
   more other strata*:

23 Bodl 48 (Nassyngton's *Speculum Vitae*, and the poem
   Symonye and Couetise):[72] *day* 'they', *dyng* 'thing', *dridde*
   'third'; *þo* 'do', *þraweþ* pl 'draw', *scholþe* 'should', *go(o)þ*
   'good', *fynþe* 'find', *-eþ* past part.
24 BM Cotton Caligula A.ii (mainly romances and religious verse
   and prose). For spellings, reference may be made to the article by
   A. J. Bliss.[73]
25 BM Cotton Julius D ix (Southern Legendary). The following
   may be added to the forms quoted by Bliss:[74] *dis* 'this', *dulke*
   'the same', *dridde* 'third', *blid* 'glad'; *þeþe* 'deeds', *þoʒter*
   'daughter', *scholþe* 'should', *beþ* 'prayed', *unþer* 'under'.
26 Trinity College Cambridge B.11.24 (=263: Fifteen Signs before
   Doomsday):[75] *de* 'thee', *dondyr* 'thunder', *dorow* 'through',
   swyde 'very'; *wonþer* 'wonder', *unþer* 'under'.

From the texts listed in A above, it would appear that the area in
which this feature occurred was Kent, East Sussex and East Surrey.[76]
But equally relevant is the great number of texts listed in C and D,
mostly from the early fifteenth century, which suggests that the development must have taken place over the whole of that area soon after
1400. On the Continent, it is clear that the gradual loss of the Germanic
/θ-ð/ phoneme was a matter of geographical spread, and a survey of
the dates of its stages suggests that the south-east English development was part of the last stage before it ceased, leaving only the rest of

English and Icelandic unaffected. It started in South German in the eighth century and then spread northwards, reaching Middle German in the ninth and tenth centuries, Low Franconian in the eleventh, Low German in the twelfth, Danish in the fourteenth and Swedish in the fifteenth.[77] The date of its spread from Flanders to South-East England thus exactly parallels that of the spread from Danish to Swedish.[78] Apart from the difference of /ð/ and /d/, many words had the same form in both Flemish and English (*eg: thick, thin, thorn, these, there*) and therefore provided a link for the substitution of /d/. If further confirmation is needed, there remains a significant detail of its distribution in modern English dialects: besides the south-eastern area nearest to the Continent, it was reported by Wright only from Pembrokeshire,[79] an area of enforced settlement by Flemings in the early twelfth century.[80]

In the South-East, this change took place at the last period possible before the emergence and consolidation of the fifteenth-century London standard, which presumably checked the further spread of the change, and ultimately limited its distribution to demonstrative forms only. But it was not yet limited to these in the time of Bullokar, who included *thorn* among the words still pronounced with [d] in East Sussex and Kent.[81]

The above discussion suggests the following conclusions:

1 The language of Kent may owe as much to its continental origins as to post-invasion contacts, and there is no evidence that compels us to prefer the latter to the former.
2 In any consideration of cross-channel influences on the language of Kent, Flanders in the Middle English period provides a better-substantiated source than Frisia in the Old English period. While, therefore, there is no reason to deny such Frisian influence, it may have been supplanted by that of Franconian earlier than has been hitherto supposed.

As might be expected, the result is a kaleidoscope. I have attempted elsewhere[82] to show that the retention of older linguistic features and the selection of new ones both depend on a complex of factors – inherited tradition, environment and system. Old and Middle Kentish reflects the history of its speakers over a long period, and does so more vividly than dialects less close to the Continent. There is indeed much truth in Myres' references to Kent as 'a natural channel for continental modes and fashions' and 'a cultural bridge, yet culturally unique'.[83]

But his endorsement of Hodgkin's opinion that 'the Jutish nation was . . . to all intents made in Kent'[83] need not apply to the whole linguistic evidence. It is well to remember that the transmission of linguistic features is largely unconscious, and that, although a language may change greatly in new environments, it may also on occasion reach further back than movable artefacts, laws or burial customs.

Notes

My thanks are due to Dr A. I. Doyle (Durham) and Professor Angus McIntosh (Edinburgh) for references to a number of the manuscripts listed in Part 3, and to Mr L. W. Collier (Glasgow) for advice on certain points in Parts 1 and 2.

1 H. M. Chadwick, *The Origin of the English Nation*, Cambridge, 1907, *pp* 63–7.

2 R. Jordan, *Eigentümlichkeiten des anglischen Wortschatzes*, Heidelberg, 1906.

3 E. Schwarz, *Goten, Nordgermanen, Angelsachsen*, Bern, 1951.

4 D. DeCamp, 'The Genesis of the Old English Dialects', *Language*, 34, 1958, 232. For other, more moderate, expressions of this view see F. M. Stenton, *Anglo-Saxon England*, Oxford, 1947, *p* 9, and A. Campbell, *Old English Grammar*, Oxford, 1959, § 5.

5 A. Campbell, *ibid.*

6 D. DeCamp, *loc cit*; H. M. Chadwick, *op cit*, *p* 63.

7 E. Sievers (revised K. Brunner), *Altenglische Grammatik*, Halle (Saale), 1942, § 2, Anm. 5.

8 In Northern England, the change could be partly due to Norse influence, but that follows from the fact that in Norse itself the syncope of unstressed syllables took place much earlier than elsewhere, so that the general north-south distinction for Germanic as a whole is thereby emphasised rather than distorted. See further 'The Suffixed Article in North Germanic', *AL*, 3, 1951, 23–37, especially 27–8 and references there quoted.

9 *Cf* A. Martinet, *Économie des changements phonétiques*, Berne, 1955, especially *p* 130, and also in *Word*, 8, 1952, 30–1.

10 For example, J. van Ginneken in *Tijdschrift voor taal en letteren*, 27, 1939, attributed the late appearance in both English and Flemish dialects of /f/ in words like *enough* to 'een biologisch aangeboren articulatiebasis' (*pp* 304, 306 and 316).

11 Certain of the Liverpool dialects might be cited as examples of this. *Cf* D. Abercrombie, *Elements of General Phonetics*, Edinburgh, 1967, *pp* 94–5.

12 DeCamp, *op cit*, *pp* 237–8.

13 H. Möller, review of A. Erdmann's *Über die Heimat und den Namen der Angeln* in *AfdA*, 22, 1896, 148; T. Siebs in PGr.[2], Vol 1, 1154–8; R. Jordan, *op cit*, *pp* 112–24; J. Hoops, *Reallexikon der germanischen Altertumskunde*, Strassburg, 1911–19, Vol 1, *p* 87.

14 K. Brunner, *Die englische Sprache I*, Halle (Saale), 1950, *p* 80.

15 It might be noted that Schwarz (*op cit*, *pp* 150–3) falls into this error when he insists that only the Gothic-ON correspondences are significant, and not those of Gothic and OHG. As may be seen from the map on *p* 6, *both* sets are explicable geographically, one dating from before, the other from after, the Goths' Baltic migration.

16 *Cf* ON *em*, Goth *im* with OS *bium, biun*, OFris *ben, bem, bin, bim*, OHG *bim*. The fact that *eom* and *beo* in OE were differentiated according to function is not relevant here, for the differentiation itself depends on the availability of forms and

not vice versa (*ie* it is a result of geographical coincidence). See further *TPS 1965*, 20–1.

17 With *hwæþer*, *cf* ON *hvaþarr*, Goth *hvaþar*; with *hweþer*, *cf* OFris *hweder*, OS *hwedar*, OHG *hwedar*.

18 *Cf* note 13 above.

19 *Op cit*, *pp* 228–9 and 259.

20 Some of the better known are: Anglian (*e*)*arun*, ON *eru* but WS *sindon*, *sint*, OFris *send*, OS *sind*(*un*); Anglian *in*, ON *i*, but WS and OS more commonly *on*; Anglian gen sg *f*(*e*)*adur*, ON *fǫður* but WS *fæder*, OFris *feder*, OS *fader*; and the much greater frequency of contracted negative forms like *næbbe*, *nylle* in WS and OFris than in Anglian (for this last see S. R. Levin, *JEGP*, 57, 1958, 492–501). Of special interest is the agreement of ONorthumbrian *ðerh* and Goth *þairh* as against *-o-*/*-u-* elsewhere (Schwarz, *p* 125), and with it the possibility that ON also had an *e*-form before it was replaced by the phonetically heavier *i gegnum*. Even if this latter is discounted, there remains the attractive hypothesis of a geographical relationship between the Goths in South Sweden and the Angles in Jutland, which is further supported by the more extensive survival of the reduplicated preterite in Anglian (Schwarz, *p* 259).

21 The identity was been questioned (*eg* by A. G. van Hamel in the *Klaeber Miscellany*, Minneapolis, 1929, *pp* 159–71), but it should be reiterated here that it is Hengest, the invader of England, who occupies such an important place in Frisian chronicles and folklore (*cf* Chapter IV of N. S. Aurner's *Hengest: A Study in Early English Hero Legend*, University of Iowa Humanistic Studies II, No 1, 1921).

22 Quoted by Chadwick, *op cit*, *p* 92. *Cf* R. H. Hodgkin, *A History of the Anglo-Saxons*, London, 1952, Vol 1, *p* 82; E. Schwarz, *Germanische Stammeskunde*, Heidelberg, 1955, *p* 124.

23 See Vera Evison, *The Fifth-Century Invasions South of the Thames*, London, 1965, and *cf* note 30 below.

24 *PBB*, 51, 1927, 1–17.

25 W. H. Bennett, 'A West Norse–Frisian–Kentish Parallel', *International Anthropological and Linguistic Review*, 1, 1953, 71–80.

26 To these may be added the correspondence of rising diphthongs mentioned in the preceding paragraph. The suprasegmental features favouring the development of these may be assumed to have been originally Juto-Norse, but to have been carried to Frisia by the Jutes. An alternative possibility is that the rising diphthongs of Old Frisian are to be explained by later Viking influences (as suggested by H. T. J. Miedema, *Van York naar Jorwerd*, Groningen, 1966); but this explanation could not apply to Kentish, so that the main parallel drawn above remains unaffected.

27 It is relevant to add that /ð/ has indeed remained thus unmarked to this day.

28 W. H. Bennett, 'The Southern English Development of Germanic initial [f, s, þ]', *Language*, 31, 1955, 367–71. It need not be assumed (with Bennett) that Saxons with this trait must necessarily have been from the Litus Saxonicum, since it could have spread from Franconian to the more westerly parts of the original Saxon area.

29 The main evidence in Middle English is for [v]; that for [z] is more sporadic, but modern dialects confirm that the area was the same for both (EDG, §§ 278 and 320). The evidence for [ð] rests partly on its distribution in modern dialects, which is the same as for [v] and [z] (*ibid* § 310), and partly on the further (conditioned) change of [ðr] to [dr] in the same area (*ibid* § 313). For the more restricted distribution of [d] as in [dis] 'this', see above, *pp* 11–14.
    Bennett's view was questioned by H. M. Flasdieck in *Anglia* 76, 1958, 363–4,

on the ground that the early WS spellings *antsacodon, gesuntful* show that the voicing had not yet taken place. But these spellings, as so much else in 'Alfredian' OE, could be Anglian in origin.

30 It might be questioned whether the evidence of movable artefacts should be allowed to outweigh that of Theudebert's letter. However, Evison (*op cit*) makes a strong case to the effect that many of the grave-goods that have been discovered were personal possessions of fifth-century Frankish warriors.

31 A hint of this possibility might be gathered from maps 2, 3 and 8 in Evison, *op cit*, but they are also open to other interpretations.

32 R. H. Hodgkin, *op cit*, Vol 1, *pp* 93–4.

33 It is a weakness of DeCamp's hypothesis (*op cit, pp* 238–9) that, in order to sustain his chosen dogma that none of the distinguishing features of Kentish are pre-invasion in origin, he has to assume that the similarities in social, legal and agrarian systems are also due to later transmission.

34 J. E. A. Jolliffe, *The Jutes*, London, 1933, *p* 101.

35 T. Frings, *Die Stellung der Niederlande in Aufbau des germanischen*, Halle, 1944, maps 13 and 14.

36 See the case presented by DeCamp, *op cit, p* 238. With his other main thesis – the spread of phonological innovations from Frisia via Kent to the rest of England – we are less concerned here. It is as well to note, however, that if this thesis is adopted we have then to explain why (*a*) the raising of $\bar{æ}^1$ to $\bar{e}$ is more consistently marked in early Northumbrian than in the early Kentish from which it is assumed to have spread, and (*b*) the effects of *i*-mutation are similarly greater in West Saxon than in Kentish.

37 The spellings mostly represent the reflexes of OE *ēa* and *ēo* (Old Kentish *ia, io*) as in *dy(e)ad* 'dead', *dyaf* 'deaf', *nyed* 'need', *lyeue* 'dear', but also that of Old Kentish *ē* as in *hier(e)* 'here', *hyere* 'hear', and in French words. See J. K. Wallenberg, *The Vocabulary of Dan Michel's Ayenbite of Inwyt*, Uppsala, 1923, *pp* 305–13.

38 *Ibid, p* 100.

39 *Ibid, p* 101.

40 *Christ Church Letters*, Camden Society, NS 19, 1877, *p* 10.

41 These are: the poems of William of Shoreham in BM Addit 17376 (EETS ES, 86), and the text of Bishop Sheppey's poems in New College Oxford MS 92.

42 Parts of this MS were printed by C. Horstmann in *Archiv*, 56, 1876, 404*ff* and in his *Altenglische Legenden*, Heilbronn, 1878, *pp* 124–38.

43 Printed by Carleton Brown, *Religious Lyrics of the Fourteenth Century*, Oxford, 1924, *pp* 109–10.

44 The spellings *guod(e), gwod(e)* also occur in two other MSS: BM Arundel 158 (Rolle's Psalter), and Bodl Rawlinson F 32 (Proverbs of Wisdom). The language of these would not preclude localisation in the South-East, but, since the evidence is less certain, they have been omitted from the above list.

45 T. Frings in *PBB*, 63, 1939, 25–6 and 34 and references there quoted; J. M. N. Kapteyn, *Festschrift T. Siebs*, Breslau, 1933, *p* 152*ff*.

46 *eg hy* 'she', *shel* 'shall', *þorgh* 'through', *senne* 'sin', *helles* 'hills', *neȝende* 'ninth', and *þaȝ* (beside commoner *þeȝ*) 'though'.

47 Notably the *Debate between St Bernard and the Virgin Mary* on *ff* 167–9, which contains the forms *swilk, ilk, mekel* and *er* 'are'.

48 'Scribe' here is intended to mean 'the latest scribe responsible for the particular combination of forms found in the MS'. It does not preclude the possibility of subsequent exact copying, but, since palaeographical evidence is not here invoked (*eg* for dating), that possibility can be left out of account.

49 Two are of especial importance: CUL Dd xii 69, *ff* 24–31, and University Col-

lege Oxford 142. Dr A. I. Doyle kindly informs me that in the first of these the following is legible under ultra-violet light: 'This present boke ys gevyn to the parish chyrche of Shermanbury by the hondis of John hayre'; and that the second MS has similar early associations with Chichester. In both cases the language agrees with this evidence.

50 Trinity College, Dublin A.4.4 (69), *ff* 84–124, and Wellcome Historical Medical Library 405. See texts (21) and (22) on *p* 13 above.

51 Both MSS have *þor₃* 'through' (*cf þorgh* in the Trinity College Oxford MS, and *þor₃* in *Ayenbyte*), *sigge* or *sygge* 'say', *ecche, ecchon* 'each (one)'.

52 The following agreements occur with one or both of the two West Sussex texts specified in note 49 above: *he* and *sche* (not *hy*) 'she'; *goud* 'good'; *-nys, -nis* '-ness'; *schulle(þ)*, not *scholle(þ)*; *fower* 'four'; *-our*, comparative adj; occasional *hem* 'him'. There is a further link between the Wellcome and Cambridge MSS in the spellings *chal, chale* 'shall'.

53 T. Frings, 'Germanisch *ō* und *ē*', *PBB*, 63, 1939, 1–116.

54 T. Frings, *op cit, pp* 61 and 101–4; M. Schönfeld, *Historische Grammatica van het Nederlands*, Zutphen, 1959, § 68.

55 *Cf* the names in *Guod-* and *Buoc-* quoted from tenth- and eleventh-century sources by J. Mansion, *Oud-Gentsche Naamkunde*, 's-Gravenhage, 1924, and for later development J. Jacobs, *Vergelijkende klank- en vormleer der middelvlaamsche dialecten*, Ghent, 1911, *pp* 127–37. In *Het Westvlaamsch*, Groningen, 1927, *p* 279, the same author regards the diphthongisation before dentals as a persistent feature from the ninth century to the present day. For the modern dialects, *cf* the many occurrences of [yuət, xuət] and [vuətn], *pp* 69–90 of T. Frings and J. Vandenheuvel, *Die südniederländischen Mundarten*, Deutsche Dialektgeographie, ed F. Wrede, Vol 16.

56 *wo*-spellings from elsewhere are very rare; *cf* Jordan–Matthes, *Handbuch der mittelenglischen Grammatik*, Heidelberg, 1934, § 46.

57 A falling diphthong [óə] could have existed for a long period during Old English without written representation, and achieve that only later when it became a rising [wo].

58 For example, it might be claimed that diphthongs can arise in various places and at various times, as is indeed true of [iə] and [uə] in the modern dialects of north England. But (*a*) these are secondary developments which followed on the Great Vowel Shift, and (*b*) in the hypothesis advanced above, both place and time fit significantly.

59 See note 81 below.

60 See EDG, § 311, which deals with the unconditioned change of initial [ð] to [d] as in *dis* 'this', *dat* 'that', *di* 'thee'. We are not concerned here with the conditioned (assimilatory) change of [ðr] to [dr], which covers the same area as the original voicing of [θ] to [ð] (see note 29 above).

61 Jordan–Matthes, *op cit*, § 207 quote only from the Paston Letters (*cf* below, note 80). The most recent discussion is by A. J. Bliss, 'The Spelling of *Sir Launfal*', *Anglia*, 75, N.F. 61, 1957, 275–89, who gives details of spellings from two manuscripts (*cf p* 13 above).

62 Printed in *Studies in Medieval History presented to F. M. Powicke*, Oxford, 1948, *pp* 392–404.

63 Printed in *Archaeologia Cantiana*, 13, 1880, 322–3.

64 From a transcript in Edinburgh University Library kindly supplied by the editors of the Middle English Dictionary (Michigan).

65 For its medieval ownership by the Sheen Charterhouse see N. R. Ker, *Medieval Libraries of Great Britain*, second edn, London, 1964, *p* 178 (this localisation is confirmed by its language).

66 F. J. Furnivall, *The Fifty Earliest English Wills*, EETS OS, 78, *p* 37*ff*.

67 On *f* 26ᵃ there is a copy of a document which refers to a 'parson of stābryhge', perhaps Stambridge in South-East Essex.

68 EETS ES, 109.

69 Carleton Brown, *op cit* (note 43), *pp* 220–1.

70 EETS OS, 10, 21, 36.

71 Forms are quoted from a transcript kindly lent by Mrs D. Edmar and Professor B. Danielsson (Stockholm).

72 This version of the poem was printed in *Anglia*, 75, N.F. 61, 1957, 177*ff*.

73 See note 61 above. Apart from the feature under discussion and a few others, the forms are preponderantly those of the copyist's originals and not his own. It would require exhaustive study of the whole MS to decide whether there are sufficient traits common to the whole of it for the latest stratum of its language to be localised.

74 In the article referred to above, Bliss quoted only forms occurring in the incipits in Carleton Brown's *Register of Middle English Religious and Didactic Verse*, Oxford, 1916–20, though the *Life of Edward the Confessor* was printed from this MS by Moore in 1942 (Pennsylvania University Dissertation). The orthography of the MS is by no means homogeneous; much of it derives from an original which, to judge from a comparison with the bulk of the MSS of Robert of Gloucester and of the *Southern Legendary*, must have been written in a Gloucestershire dialect. Examples are: *mony* 'many', *ʒ(h)are/ʒer* 'their', *sulf/sulue* 'self', *schost* 'shouldst', *vale* 'many', *last(e)* 'lest', *lutel* 'little', *ou* 'you'.

75 Printed in EETS OS, 24, *p* 118*ff*.

76 It is not certain whether the evidence of the two texts listed in B might justify the addition of a small area in extreme South-East Essex.

77 W. Wilmanns, *Deutsche Grammatik* 1, Strassburg, 1893–1909, § 82; O. Behaghel, PGr², Vol 1, *p* 725; A. Noreen, *ibid*, *p* 601; M. Schönfeld, *op cit* (note 54), § 50; W. Steinhauser, *Festschrift M. H. Jellinek*, Vienna and Leipzig, 1928, *p* 147.

78 In the Scandinavian languages there would naturally be fewer contexts for the shift of [ð] to /d/, and correspondingly more for that of [θ] to /t/.

79 EDG, §311.

80 Other isolated occurrences in Middle English (*eg* in the Paston Letters, *cf* above, note 61) might also be due to Dutch or Flemish influence, but are outside the scope of the present article.

81 E. J. Dobson, *English Pronunciation 1500–1700*, Oxford, 1957, § 374.

   The restriction to demonstrative forms is natural, for the phonetic distance between [d] and the Standard English /ð/ of demonstrative forms is less than that between [d] and the Standard English /θ/ of all the other words. In the latter words, therefore, [d] has been replaced by a fricative under the influence of Standard English /θ/, but it is realised as [ð], the expected fricative in the consonant-pattern of southern dialects.

82 *TPS 1965*, *pp* 15–40. *Cf* A. Martinet, *A Functional View of Language*, second edn, Oxford, 1962, *p* 138.

83 R. G. Collingwood and J. N. L. Myres, *Roman Britain and the English Settlements*, second edn, Oxford, 1937, *p* 363.

Margaret Grace Dareau

Assistant Editor, A Dictionary of the Older Scottish Tongue

Angus McIntosh

Professor of English Language, University of Edinburgh

A dialect word in some West Midland manuscripts of the *Prick of Conscience*

In a well-known passage of the *Prick of Conscience* man is compared to a tree upside-down; this runs from line 672 to 683 of Morris's edition from the northern manuscript British Museum MS Cotton Galba E ix:[1]

> ... what es man in shap bot a tre
> Turned vp þat es doun, als men may se,
> Of whilk þe rotes þat of it springes,
> Er þe hares þat on þe heued hynges;
> þe stok nest þe rot growand
> Es þe heued with nek folowand;
> þe body of þat tre þar-by
> Es þe brest with þe bely;
> þe bughes er þe armes with þe handes
> And þe legges with þe fete þat standes
> þe braunches men may by skille call
> þe tas and þe fyngers alle.[2]

At least six Central West Midland texts of the *Prick of Conscience* contain at line 678 not the word *body* but one or another form of a word which, for convenience, we shall normally cite in its commonest form – *goben*. There is reason to believe that the six manuscripts involved are all closely related and that they form part of a complex of at least eleven manuscripts, only seven of which are known to survive. The seven are:

1 Yale University, James Osborn 31
2 Trinity College Oxford 16 A
3 Holkham Hall 668
4 Manchester, Rylands English 50
5 London, College of Arms LVII
6 Trinity College Oxford 16 B
7 Bodl Douce 156

The beginning of MS 5 is defective, and the crucial passage missing. However, as we hope to show in a fuller study elsewhere, there are good grounds for assuming that some form of the word *goben* was used in this text also.

The following outline of the textual relations of the above manuscripts is based on a detailed study of about 80 lines of text, those corresponding to lines 644–87 and 1856–91 of the printed edition. For at least these portions of the six manuscripts containing them the textual relations are probably as follows. No 5, which requires fuller investigation, has not been included, but it would appear to derive, directly or otherwise, from 4. Capital letters designate postulated missing manuscripts.[3]

Forms in which *goben* appears (line 678) in the manuscripts:

1 *goben*
2 *goboune*
3 *goben*
4 *gubben*
5 (passage missing)
6 *goboon*
7 *goben*

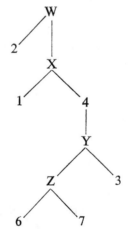

It would be premature at this stage to attempt a detailed study of the immediate antecedents to W. But since *goben* is absent in any text lying behind W and is present in all its descendants, it is clear that the word was introduced by the scribe who wrote this lost manuscript. All its surviving descendants except nos 2 and 7 reveal dialectal features characteristic of Lichfield or its immediate neighbourhood. Furthermore there is reason to believe that W descends from, or is very closely related to, another Lichfield manuscript, Harley 1205;[4] the evidence therefore points to W itself having been written in Lichfield. With the other manuscripts by the same scribe and those under separate consideration here, there is evidence for a remarkable amount of copying of northern texts in that place around 1400.[5] Of the two texts of our group which are not dialectally characteristic of Lichfield, 2 is an early offshoot from W and would seem to belong to South Shropshire, while 7 is a late derivative at least five removes away from W written in a dialect suggestive of East Warwickshire.

We must now briefly consider the work of the scribe of W, to whom we attribute the introduction of *goben*. We shall refer to him as the Lichfield Master (LM), giving him this title because he was more than a mere copyist; we shall suggest that it was not just dialectal pressure which led him to substitute *goben* for *body* at line 678. We would attribute to him numerous stylistic changes but can only exemplify here one or two types of modification made by him. Throughout he seems to be intent on clarifying and sharpening the argument of his text. Lines 652–7 illustrate his desire to make the most of the structure of the verse in the pointing of a comparison; these are at the beginning of the passage likening man to vegetable matter which culminates in the image of the upside-down tree. The removal of the earlier reading *and* from the beginning of the third line (654) in the following passage:

Of hem spryngeþ baume ful good
And oyle and wyne for monnes food;
Of þe comeþ alle foule thyngge
As urine ordure and spyttyngge

perfects the parallelism in the couplet-for-couplet comparison of *hem* (*herbes* and *trees*) and *þe* (*man*), so making the discrepancy between the two much more pointed than in Harley.

Another instance of this sort of change may be cited from line 1871 where LM replaces *mon* with *degre*:

Deþ to no degre haþ rewared –
Ryche nor pore hyȝe nor lowe.

Degre here is obviously less colourless and more pointedly appropriate than the *mon* of the earlier versions.

We turn to a second kind of change, also relevant to the problem of *goben*; this is due to LM's dislike of verbal repetition. In lines 1868–74, for example, he replaces various negatives having the form *no* a number of times by the alternative forms *ne, ny* and *nor* in order, as it would seem, to avoid the clumsy concentration of one form eight times in seven lines.

Both these types of change probably have a bearing on the introduction of *goben*. The *bely* of the original (line 679) has, in the tradition which leads to W, already been replaced by *body*, a change of some interest in itself which cannot be gone into here. This replacement gave rise to a repetition of *body* in lines 678 and 679, a repetition of precisely the kind that LM often showed a disposition to eliminate. Furthermore, in this case, the successive uses of *body* spoil the argument. For here a part of a tree is being compared with the 'corresponding' part of a man and throughout the rest of the passage *different* words are used for the arboreal and human items in the comparison (roots: hairs; stock: head, etc). The whole passage is therefore improved by eliminating the discordant pair *body: body* and replacing it by *goben: body*.

We may observe that such changes as are noted above require special understanding by textual critics. If numerous changes are purposely made by one man this can easily but wrongly suggest considerable remoteness from some antecedent text which may in fact lie very closely behind the stylistically re-worked text. Similar understanding is required of changes made by a scribe for dialectal reasons; a text directly from a northern original re-worked by (say) a West Midland scribe for local consumption may seem (and be) textually very different in certain ways from that from which it was actually copied. Certain kinds of textual remoteness are therefore no indication of any comparable distance, in terms of transmission, between one version of a text and another.

However 'stylistic' the motivation for the introduction by LM of the word *goben*, it could scarcely have been introduced had it not been comprehensible in the Lichfield area. We must now consider what further Middle English evidence there is for such a word in the kind of meaning required. It will be noted that the Latin text distinguishes between *truncus* (*þe stok*[6]) and *stipis* (*þe body*); *truncus* clearly refers to the lowest part of the trunk and *stipis* to the bole or stem from there up-

wards. *Goben* should therefore mean 'bole' and answer to the signifi-
cation of *body*[7] in antecedent versions of the poem; there is no reason
to suppose that LM did not know exactly what he was about in introducing it.

It is highly probable that *goben* (*goboune*, etc) is to be associated with
the Middle English noun *goboun* (*gobin*, *gobyn*) glossed as 'a piece,
fragment',[8] remote though such senses may seem to be from what is required in the *Prick of Conscience* passage. The Middle English word is
clearly connected with, and probably derives from, Anglo-French
gobo(u)n. There are two recorded instances of the Anglo-French word:

1 CUL Ee.4.20 *Nominale* 450: Et meynte autre gobons, And many
   other cuttynges.[9]
2 Bodl Digby 86. Si voustre oysel ad les poilles, pernez erre ki crest sus
   chene, si en fetes trois gobouns del gros . . . et de checun goboun
   fetes un auje . . .[10]

In both these passages the meaning would seem to be 'piece', 'slice' or
'lump'. The sense 'slice' suggested by the first passage is supported by
the Middle English verb *gobon*, *goben* 'to hew, cut in pieces'[11] and perhaps also by *gobbone*[12] adj 'gobony', 'divided into sections of alternate colours'.

The noun and verb are closely allied in both form and meaning to
Middle English *gobet* sb, *gobet* vb[13] (Old French *gobet*, *gobeter*). The
nouns differ mainly in that the sense '(large) lump, mass' is clearly in
evidence with *gobet*, a sense which in turn suggests a connection with
gob 'lump, mass'.[14] The *Prick of Conscience* example of *goboun* suggests however an alternative basic meaning for this word of 'mass' or
something similar. Such a basic meaning might well lead to a derived
meaning 'main mass of a tree' just as some similar base meaning for
gobet did lead to the senses 'lump of metal' and 'block of stone'.[15] A
connection between the meanings 'piece' and 'large mass' (sometimes
specified of what) seems widespread. *Cf* Old Norse *stykki* 'a piece' beside *stokkr* 'a trunk' and the parallel meanings of Old Icelandic *bútr*,
'log', 'trunk' and Modern Icelandic *bútur*, 'piece'.[16]

In view of the limited geographical distribution of the Middle English word, the provenance of the two manuscripts containing examples
of Anglo-French *gobo(u)n* is of some interest. Digby 86 contains much
material in English and the dialectal characteristics of this suggest a
South-West Worcestershire provenance. It is not easy to be so precise
about the English in the *Nominale* in CUL Ee.4.20.[17] This volume con-

sists in the main of a register of St Albans which was put together in the 1380s, and there can be little doubt about its local association with St Albans. The date of the text of the *Nominale* is uncertain but it is clearly fourteenth century and not earlier than 1340. It is not at present certain whether the part of the manuscript containing the *Nominale* must also be associated with St Albans.[18] At all events the dialectal forms in the English of this text are not typical of St Albans: if it was the work of a local scribe, he must simply have taken them over from his exemplar more or less as he found them. There is the alternative possibility that the scribe was not from Hertfordshire at all.

The English material available in the *Nominale* for assessment is regrettably scanty and is perhaps not wholly pure dialectally. But the following forms, taken together, are of considerable interest and significance: *hit* 'it'; *myche, mykul* 'much'; *aftur* 'after'; *-uth* (commonly) and *-us* (rarely) beside *-yth, -ith* etc for the third singular present indicative; *kyrke* 'church'; *sulle* 'sill'; *fuste* 'fist'. A provenance from somewhere in the region of Burton upon Trent would seem to square fairly well with these as well as most of the rest of the forms in the text. Unless this suggested localisation of the dialect of the *Nominale* is wildly inaccurate, both surviving examples of Anglo-French *gobo(u)n*, like our new instances of the English word, are West Midland.

The fact that evidence for Middle English *goboun, goben* etc in the sense 'stem of a tree' is provided exclusively by a group of West Midland manuscripts of a poem written in an entirely different part of the country is in itself curious and interesting. It suggests the importance of a careful lexicographical scrutiny of this and other 'translated' texts existing in many versions; most of these at present receive little attention and tend to be dismissed as mere debased and textually unreliable derivatives. The thoroughness with which late Middle English scribes frequently converted texts from one dialect into another is sufficient guarantee that they are capable of adding substantially to our knowledge of Middle English words and their geographical distribution.

Notes

1 Richard Morris, *The Pricke of Conscience*, Phil. Soc., 1863, *p* 19. The text has been checked from a microfilm of the MS.
2 The Latin on which this passage is based (lines 666–71) is quoted from the *De Contemptu Mundi sive De Miseria Conditionis Humanae* of Pope Innocent III, ed J. P. Migne: *Patrologiae Cursus Completus. Series Latina* Vol CCXVII, column 706.

3 We owe the working out of this tree to an approach devised by Mr Peter Buneman.

4 For information about this and other related *Prick of Conscience* manuscripts, see Carleton Brown and Rossell Hope Robbins, *The Index of Middle English Verse*, New York, 1943 (items 3428, 1193) and Robbins, R. H. and Cutler, J. L., *Supplement to the Index of Middle English Verse*, Lexington, 1965.

5 Palaeographic evidence shows Harley 1205 to be the work of the same scribe as wrote Rylands English 50, Trinity College Cambridge R.3.8 and part of Rawlinson A.389. The latter manuscript is known to have been in Lichfield from *c* 1470 to 1627 and can fairly safely be regarded as a Lichfield product. We owe the information about Rylands English 50 to Dr A. I. Doyle. *Cf* N. R. Ker, 'Patrick Young's catalogue of the manuscripts of Lichfield Cathedral', *Medieval and Renaissance Studies*, 2, 159, 166–7 and A. McIntosh, 'A New Approach to Middle English Dialectology', *English Studies* 44, 1.

6 The forms are cited from the printed northern text.

7 For the use of this word in relation to trees and plants see MED s.v. *bodi* n. sense 9b (a).

8 MED s.v. *goboun* n. *Cf* OED s.v. *gobbon* sb.

9 MED, *loc cit*. The *Nominale* is edited by W. W. Skeat, *TPS 1903–1906*, 1*–50*.

10 See G. Tilander, *Glanures lexicographiques*, Lund, 1932, *p* 134, and Tobler-Lommatzsch, *Altfranzösisches Wörterbuch*, s.v. *gobon*.

11 MED s.v. *gobonen* v. *Cf* OED *gobbon* v.

12 MED s.v. *gobbone* adj. *Cf* OED *gobony*, *gobonated* ppl.a, *goboned* ppl.a.

13 MED s.v. *gobet* n., *gobeten* v. and cpds. *Cf* OED *gobbet* sb., *gobbet* v. and cpds.

14 MED *gobbe* n., OED *gob* sb.1, especially sense 1a, b.

15 MED s.v. *gobet* n., senses 2(a) and 4. *Cf* R. E. Latham, *Revised Medieval Latin Word List*, London, 1965, s.v. *gobo*.

16 We owe this example to Mr Hermann Pálsson. Note also Scots *stove* sb. 'a cut, a slice' beside the Northern English meaning 'the stump of a tree or shrub', see *EDD* *stove* v.2 and sb.2 senses 4 and 5. Here of course the connection may be via 'something severed', but one cannot rule out a similar connection between the two meanings of *goboun*, especially in view of the gloss *cuttynges* on *gobons* in Ee.4.20 (see *p* 24).

17 See *Catalogue of the Manuscripts preserved in the Library of the University of Cambridge*, Cambridge, 1857, Vol 2, *pp* 126–30.

18 The *Nominale* immediately follows and is in the same hand as an Anglo-French treatise on heraldry (ed Ruth J. Dean, 'An Early English Treatise on Heraldry in Anglo-Norman', *Romance Studies in Memory of Edward Billings Ham*, ed U. T. Holmes (California State College Publications, No 2), 1967, *p* 21). Miss Dean has since informed us (September 1968) that the quire containing the *Nominale* cannot be earlier than 1382. The only other English material in the volume is: (*a*) an oath of obedience to the monastery of St Albans on the verso of the leaf preceding *f* 76 written in a fairly late fifteenth-century hand and in a rather standardised kind of language, (*b*) a copy of a letter from John, Abbot of St Albans, to the Bishop of Salisbury (10 January, no year) on the recto of what the Catalogue calls *f* 253 but what is now numbered *f* 282; this is in a considerably more archaic English and includes a present participle in -*ind*.

Early Modern English

Bridget Cusack

Lecturer in English Language, University of Edinburgh

Not wreton with penne and ynke
Problems of selection facing the
first English printer

In 1475 or 1476 William Caxton issued his *Recuyell of the Historyes of Troye* from the press in Bruges where he worked until moving to Westminster about two years later, and English readers were able for the first time to buy books in their own language manufactured according to the new process of printing.

The printing-house was run in collaboration with Colard Mansion, and there is some uncertainty about their partnership and the extent to which either can be said to have been principal in the business, but as their output was both French and English it is likely that each oversaw work in the language more familiar to him. Moreover, it was in the capacity of translator-printer-publisher that Caxton supplied the *Recuyell* with both an introduction and an epilogue. There is no way of telling how his readers reacted on first taking this book into their hands, but from what the printer considered worth putting in his epilogue we can reconstruct what he expected of them.

Because he has found, he says,[1] the work of translation onerous, and because he has undertaken to produce the book as quickly as possible,

> Therfore I haue practysed & lerned at my grete charge and dispense to ordeyne this said book in prynte after the maner & forme as ye may here see / and is not wreton with penne and ynke as other bokes ben / to thende that euery man may haue them attones / ffor all the bookes of this storye named the recule of the historyes of troyes thus enpryntid as ye here see were begonne in oon day / and also fynysshid in oon day /

Thus ende I this book whyche I haue translated after myn Auctor as nyghe as god hath gyuen me connyng to whom be gyuen the laude & preysyng / And for as moche as in the wrytyng of the same my penne is worn/myn hande wery & not stedfast myn eyen dimed with ouermoche lokyng on the whit paper / and my corage not so prone and redy to labour as hit hath ben / and that age crepeth on me dayly and febleth all the bodye / and also be cause I haue promysed to dyuerce gentilmen and to my frendes to adresse to hem as hastely as I myght this sayd book / Therfore I haue practysed & lerned at my grete charge and dispense to ordeyne this said book in prynte after the maner & forme as ye may here see / and is not wreton with penne and ynke as other bokes ben / to thende that euery man may haue them attones / ffor all the bookes of this storye named the recule of the historyes of tropes thus enprynted as ye here see were begonne in oon day / and also fynysshid in oon day / whiche book I haue presented to my sayd redoubtid lady as a fore is sayd . And she hath well acceptid hit / and largely rewarded me/ wherfor I beseche almyghty god to rewarde her euerlastyng blysse after this lyf . Prayng her said grace and all them that shall rede this book not to desdaigne the symple and rude werke . nether to replye agaynst the sayyng of the matere towchyd in this book / thauwh hyt acorde not vn to the translacon of other whiche haue wreton hit / ffor dyuerce men haue made dyuerce bookes / whiche in all poyntes acorde not as Dictes . Dares . and Homerus ffor dictes & homerus as grekes sayn and wryten fauorably for the grekes / and gyue to them more worshi

A *The Recuyell of the Historyes of Troye* printed by Caxton in Bruges in [1475 or 6]. Sig [Kk9r] British Museum copy (reproduction slightly reduced).

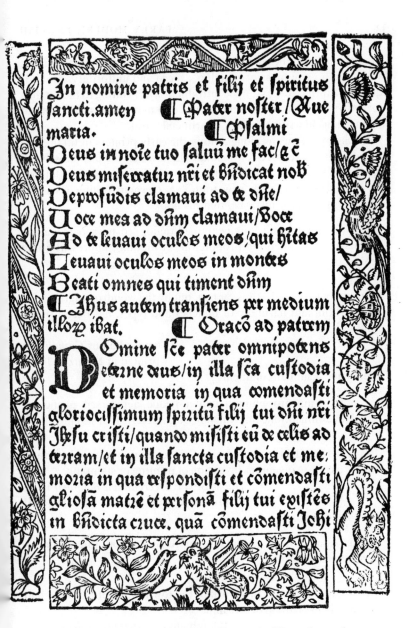

In nomine patris et filij et spiritus
sancti. amen ☞Pater noster / Aue
maria. ☞Psalmi
Deus in noïe tuo saluuū me fac / ꝗ c̄
Deus miseratuz nr̄i et bn̄dicat nob
De profūdis clamaui ad te dn̄e /
Uoce mea ad dn̄m clamaui / Voce
Ad te leuaui oculos meos / qui hn̄tas
Leuaui oculos meos in montes
Beati omnes qui timent dn̄m
☞Ihus autem transiens per medium
illoꝛ ibat. ☞ Oraco ad patrem
Omine sc̄e pater omnipotens
eterne deus / in illa sc̄a custodia
et memoria in qua comendasti
gloriocissimum spiritū filij tui dn̄i nr̄i
Ihesu cristi / quando misisti eū de celis ad
terram / et in illa sancta custodia et me-
moria in qua respondisti et comendasti
gliosā matrē et personā filij tui existes
in bn̄dicta cruce. quā comendasti Iohi

B *The Fifteen Oes* printed by Caxton in Westminster in
[1490]. Sig b5ʳ British Museum copy.

In other words, the chief advantages of this new method of making books are those of mass-production – speed and uniformity. And it is equally clear that to Caxton the introduction of printing to the English market was nothing more than the use of a new process to do an old job, mechanical writing, in fact, or artificial script.

He was by no means alone among the early printers in taking this attitude. There are not a few incunabula in which the printer writes a colophon where he discusses the business of printing, pointing out that this is writing done with new tools.[2] A German printer (possibly Gutenberg) says, for instance, that his book

> ... Non calami, stili, aut penne suffragio, sed mira patronarum formarumque concordia proporcione et modulo, impressus atque confectus est.

without help of reed, stilus, or pen, but by the wondrous agreement, proportion, and harmony of punches and types, has been printed and finished.

> [Joannes Balbus *Catholicon*;
> printed at Mainz in 1460]

Others have a similar comment:

> ... non atramento plumali canna neque aerea, sed artificiosa quadam adinuentione imprimendi seu caracterizandi sic effigiatum.

has been thus fashioned not by ink for the pen nor by a reed of brass, but by a certain ingenious invention of printing or stamping.

> [*Liber Sextus Decretalium Bonifacii VIII*;
> printed by Fust and Schoeffer in 1465]

or a shorter account:

> Petrus Adam Mantus opus hoc impressit in urbe. Illic nullus eo scripserat aere prius.

Petrus Adam printed this work in the town of Mantua. None had written there on brass before him.

> [Gambiglioni *Tractatus Maleficiorum*;
> printed by Petrus Adam de Michaelibus in 1472]

And sometimes the printer, like Caxton, mentions speed as a major advantage of print over manuscript:

Imprimit ille die quantum non scribitur anno
Ingenio:
With a machine he prints in a day even more than would be (hand)
written in a year.

[Cicero *Orationes Philippicae*;
printed by Ulrich Han in [1470]]

If, as it would appear from such opinions, printing was nothing more
nor less than a method whereby writing could be done mechanically,
and manuscripts machine produced, how did this affect the books
themselves?

It is nothing new to point out the reliance of printing on manuscript
conventions; rather, it has become a matter to be mentioned in a few
lines and then taken as read, though it is a topic deserving of further
discussion. The classic account was given by William Blades[3] more
than a hundred years ago, when he described those points in lay-out
and general appearance where the early products of Caxton's press
were clearly modelled on contemporary usage in manuscript books.

A striking instance of this is the way in which following the custom
whereby a chapter or section would be headed by an ornate large capital, added by a rubricator or illuminator for whose work the scribe
would leave a space when he laid out his lines of writing, Caxton also
left room for large initial capitals to be added by hand to his printed
text. An example of this in the *Recuyell* is reproduced in A above (*p* 30).
A second point of continuity is Caxton's following the method of
lineation in which a space is left at the end of a line when the words in it
are too few to fill it exactly, and no suitable syllable can be brought up
from the beginning of the next line. Manuscripts often had, through
this, a rather uneven right-hand edge, and so have Caxton's first books
(A). Thirdly, in the same way that scribes rarely gave their work a
separate title, or signed it by name, date or place, so Caxton left personal details unsaid (unless they came up informally in a prologue or
epilogue), and provided no title-page, beginning with an *incipit* on the
second leaf.

As he continued printing, however, Caxton moved away from this
close dependence on his predecessors in the book-trade. This happened to various degrees and in various ways. Some functions he an-
nexed to his own press, while retaining the feature itself. Ornamental
capitals, for example, were retained, but included in the printing by the
use of wood blocks, and blocks were also employed sometimes to add to

pages the decorative borders which, like initials, had at first been added by hand.[4] A particularly ornate instance of this decoration is a late production of Caxton's Westminster press, the *Fifteen Oes* (a collection of prayers in English and Latin) as shown in B (*p* 31). Similarly, it had been a not infrequent practice to sign the gatherings in manuscripts so as to help the binder arrange them in order, and this was done in printed books too. At first signatures were written in by hand, and usually subsequently lost when pages were trimmed in binding. But this too was soon included in the printing itself, the traditional position of the signature on the page being modified so as to make this possible. Thus while the *Recuyell* page in A (*p* 30) can have only a reconstructed leaf number (usually [Kk9ʳ]), the *Fifteen Oes* page in B is clearly (by the signatures on the surrounding leaves) b5ʳ.

In other cases, practices which early printers took over from manuscript style were later superseded, as when printers found how to justify their lines, forming as neat a right-hand edge as left, by spacing out the words in short lines throughout the course of the whole line (Reproduction B, except in the list of Psalms). Finally, in yet other instances, innovations were introduced which served to remove printed books even further from manuscripts, such as Caxton's later use of colophon and device to indicate himself as printer.

All these breaks with manuscript convention were gradual; Blades argues that the presence/absence of certain features can even be used for dating Caxton's books. Moreover, other printers after him took the same process further, their most notable addition being the invention of the title-page as part of the normal make-up of a book. And in a very few decades after the first English book was printed, closely modelled on manuscript style, the presses were producing books far less aligned in many respects with their handwritten counterparts.

Such matters of general presentation are, however, only secondary to a manuscript–print link of far greater import – the writing itself. For it is this rather than things such as unjustified lines or space for initial capitals that can lead the casual observer to mistake a piece of early printing for a manuscript, as the types used by the first printers were copied from the manuscript hands of the time.

As far as Caxton is concerned the only important models are the various sub-varieties of Gothic script on which his work is based. Other and later printers, especially abroad, looked to the Roman and Italic hands, but in England Gothic or Black Letter founts, inspired by Gothic hands, were predominant until the mid-sixteenth century, and survived in certain kinds of material as late as the eighteenth century. In the course of his fifteen years as a printer Caxton employed a series of founts, all describable as Black Letter, but all slightly different as to letter-shape. In his earliest type, in which the *Recuyell* is printed (Reproduction A), he is clearly influenced by the Bastard hand commonly used in fifteenth-century England and elsewhere (Burgundy, for example, where Caxton worked as a translator before taking up printing). In other of his types, especially the third, Caxton makes his letters squarer, more angular and formal, and with sharper distinction of thick and thin strokes, after the style of the classic Book hand also in contemporary use.[5] His last type (as in B) is something between these two extremes. This reflection of manuscript letter-forms has been traced in even more detail by Blades to specific models, with the suggestion that certain of Caxton's types show marked resemblances to the handwriting of the Mercers' books, and the volumes of that period in the Archives of Guildhall, and that in a similar way there is a close likeness between the Caxton–Mansion Bruges work and the manuscripts of Mansion himself, who had been a calligrapher.[6]

No one is likely to dispute that the earliest printed books were very like manuscripts; but speculation as to why this was so by no means reaches a unanimous conclusion. Some writers suggest that a deliberate attempt was being made to produce fake manuscripts to be sold at the prices handwritten material fetched: 'it was the wish of the printers that their work might be taken for that of the scribes'.[7] An anecdote which at one time was given widespread acceptance tells how John Fust sold copies of his printed Bible in Paris as manuscripts until he was forced by accusations of swindling and even of sorcery to admit that they were machine-produced. Others[8] champion the printers against charges of wilful fraud, on the grounds that neither buyers nor the printers themselves would have any conception of a book looking like anything but the manuscripts with which they were familiar. So that it was not to be expected that the first printed books should look any different from handwritten ones. What else could they look like?

That this whole question is important to any account of the history and development of printing is self-evident. It has thus been dealt with by writers on bibliography, typography, book-illustration and so on for many years. But although the linguistic repercussions of the manuscript–print continuity are also great, they have in the main been disregarded in accounts of the English of the fifteenth century. Certainly the effects on English of the introduction of printing have been discussed many times, normally in connection with the growth of standard written English, but here it is the innovations involved in printed English (particularly bulk-production of identical copies of a text which might be distributed throughout the country) which have been stressed, while the printers' conservatism has been overlooked. Moreover, where Caxton is mentioned by historians of the language, it is most often for his translations and the way he met the various lexical problems confronting him, and this would apply equally if his work had been printed by someone else.

Whereas much that is of interest to the linguist emerges from a closer examination of the work of Caxton as printer.

To draw attention to the way in which Caxton's types are modelled on the written hands of his time is only to provide the basis for a further investigation, in that not only are the shapes of the printer's letters based on those in contemporary handwriting, but his choice of what letters his founts of type are to contain is equally rooted in fifteenth-century manuscript convention.

It is not surprising that even before the printing-press made it possible to produce a large number of copies of a text in a very short time, people tried to speed up methods of manuscript production as far as the limits of handwork allowed. With this aim, among others, in mind, the *pecia* system, for instance, was evolved, whereby several scribes could work simultaneously from an exemplar split into sections. But an even more basic way of increasing output was for the calligrapher himself to work faster, running his pen on, from letter to letter to form ligatures, and abbreviating words where familiarity or expectation through the context would guarantee the reader's comprehension. This, of course, had other features to recommend it, such as the saving on vellum or paper, and the elimination of the need to be exact about the inflexions of, say, Latin words. Thus almost every letter of the alphabet might have an abbreviation sign added to it, indicating letters omitted in the vicinity, or might be joined to another letter by a connecting pen-stroke. In addition to these extensions of the normal alphabet there would be for each letter a capital form, possibly with a different shape from the small version,[9] and there might be a variant letter-shape to be used in certain circumstances, depending perhaps on position in a word, or on the surrounding letters. Moreover, two of these sub-kinds might combine: a ligature or a capital, for example, might have an abbreviation mark added to it.

All this Caxton took over, as he did the shapes of the letters, with the result that although his alphabet contained only twenty-four letters, the overall number of characters (that is, pieces of type with a distinct shape) he employed was about two hundred and seventy. If, for instance, a conflation is made of all the characters he ever used dependent on the letter *r*, twenty-eight sorts can be distinguished:

	CAPITAL	SMALL					
		Allograph I			*Allograph* II		
− A	R	r	ra	cr	2	—	b2
B			re	er			d2
B			ri	fr			o2
R			ro	ir			p2
E			ru	tr			q2
V			rr				v2
+ A	R̷	r̄	rā		2̃		
B			rē			—	—
B			rō	—			
R			rū		2̷		
E							
V			1st elem	2nd elem		1st elem	2nd elem
		−Lig	+Lig		−Lig	+Lig	

Not all these possibilities, however, are realised in every letter: *k* occurs only in capital and small form, *g* has far fewer related characters than *r*, *s* even more.

   It is, moreover, immediately clear that there was no small alteration in Caxton's usage in the course of the fifteen years or so that he was a printer. Some attention has already been paid above to the way in which the general lay-out and appearance of his books gradually changed, and it was mentioned that while Caxton employed a series of Black Letter types, each with letters of slightly different style from the others, yet there was in this change of founts no sort of development away from manuscript style of letter design, nor abandonment of an initial closeness to handwriting in favour of a more independent model. However, if the six founts of type that the printer used are compared not in respect of the shapes of their characters, but with regard to what characters there were present in each, a pattern of evolution is apparent; for many characters are abandoned in the course of time, while others are only introduced in Caxton's later types, and yet others appear only in a single fount, or are used off and on with no immediately apparent motivation. Thus of the two hundred and seventy characters used by Caxton, no fount has more than about two hundred and thirty (Type 2, following Blades' classification) and the smallest founts use about a hundred and sixty (Blades' Types 5 and 6).

The problem of choice of characters, then, the need for decision as to what selection from the possibilities offered him through manuscript use would provide a fount adequate for his purposes, comprehensive yet without redundancies, was a factor constantly confronting Caxton.

Of the various ways in which he expanded the normal alphabet the method of increase most restricted in its application is the use of allographs, distinct characters acting as exponents of the same letter under different circumstances. Thus *u* and *v* work together as allographs of a single letter, irrespective of the sound they relate to. The *v* appears initially (*voce* B7)[10] – although the capital form, occupying, of course, the same position, looks like a *V* in some of Caxton's founts, but more like a *U* in others (*Voce* B7) – and the *u* medially and finally (*haue* A1; *laude* A3; *Deus* B4; *leuaui* B8). A similar kind of practice regulates the two varieties of *s*, but the details of distribution are different here, in that *ſ* occurs initially and medially, *s* finally (*ſtedfaſt* A5; *hiſto2yes* A17; *tranſiens* B11; *ſancta* B18). With both letters this system remained in use throughout Caxton's time and beyond.

Complementary distribution is not, however, based in every case on mere position. For the letter *r* there are two allographs, the 'normal' *r* and the 2 or r-rotunda. In Caxton's earliest usage the second of these is used after *o*, the first everywhere else. That this of necessity means that *r* is always the form employed in word-initial position is only a secondary feature of the distribution. Thus *Aucto2* (A2) and *wo2ŋ* (A5), as opposed to *after* (A2) and *redy* (A7); and where this convention is not adhered to, as in *corage* (A7), there are clear reasons, which will be discussed below. The change in distribution, however, demonstrated in the later passage (B) is striking. The r-rotunda is still used after *o* (*memo2ia* B18–19) but more often the 'normal' *r* (*memoria* B15;

Oracō B12; *gloriociſſimuŋ* B16). Moreover, 2 is here extended to follow *e* (*ete2ne* B14), *i* (*ſpi2itū* B16), *u* (*miſereatu2* B5), *c* and *t*. And yet there is no consistency in this new arrangement, as *r* is equally likely in any of these places (after *e* in *miſereatu2* B5; after *c* in *criſti* B17; after *t* in *tranſiens* B11). The two allographs are, in fact, practically in free variation, even to the extent of 2 occurring (though rarely) in word-initial position.

In each of the cases described above the two allographs are of very different shapes; someone who has never seen the characters before would, on the basis of similarity in shape, be more likely to count ſ as a variant of ƒ than of *s*.[11] But in other sets allographs have a much closer similarity of form. Thus the letters *m* and *n* have each two forms, one restricted to word-final position, and the other occurring elsewhere; and in each case the word-final allograph differs from the other only in that it extends the final minim stroke below the line, as in *whoŋ* (A3) and *gentilmeŋ* (A10). The regularity with which this is done in Caxton's early work is dropped by his later books, so that although both forms are still found, with the extended one in word-final position (*ameŋ* B2; *dñŋ* B10), words can also end with what was earlier the initial and medial allograph (*medium* B11; *te2ram* B18; *in* B19 and 21 as opposed to *iŋ* B15 and 18).

A third letter which has an extended form for an allograph is *i*, with the two versions, nowadays independent letters, *i* and *j*. Here too distribution is related to position, in that where two or more *i*'s stand next to each other at the end of a word, the last of them takes the extended *j* shape. In English texts this is only likely to occur where Roman numerals are employed, as in a date; in Latin, inflexions with this sequence will not be uncommon. Perhaps because of this the *j* allograph shows no signs of the decline apparent in the use of *ŋ* and *ŋ*, and it is used consistently in Caxton's last books (*filij* B1, 16 and 20). It is noticeable that all three of the above allographs involve a series of minim strokes in word-final position, the last stroke of all being given extra length to show that it is the last; hence a final single *i* has no need to be represented as *j* (*ſancti* B2; *Pſalmi* B3).

It is possible that the word-final *m* and *n* allographs have a different origin, being reductions from earlier indications of suspension. This is a more certain explanation of the two remaining allographs employed by Caxton, that is the word-final forms for *d* and *g*. Here there is no question of distinction by a radically different shape, or by one being a slightly extended form of the other; but the word-final forms are dis-

tinguished by an outward and downward curl that one would expect to
be a mark of abbreviation, standing perhaps for a suspended termination (*transſlated*₂ A1–2; *god*₂ A2; *And*₂ A4). By derivation this is so.[12]
Scribes working with Latin texts and wanting to cut off inflexions acquired the habit of writing the stem only, with a final flourish to show
that an ending was omitted, and this became so much of a habit that
they continued it even where, as in many English words, no ending was
left off at all. So that from being a sign of abbreviation it became an
indication of the end of a word, and it is as such that Caxton uses it.
Occasionally it might be suggested that an *-e* has been omitted, but the
use of the character in words such as *and*₂ rules this out as a regular
interpretation.

By the time he was printing his last books, however, Caxton had apparently come to realise the lack of point in maintaining allographs
within either letter, and so both characters were abandoned, a single
form being used for *d* wherever it occurred in the word (*dñe* B6;
medium B11; *ad* B6), and similarly with *g*.

Because of the way they are used, it is reasonable to include some
account of capitals in a discussion of allographs, in that these too are
special forms of letters employed under specific circumstances, namely
in word-initial position when the words fulfil certain grammatical or
semantic criteria. As with the allographs already noted, capitals vary
in the degree of resemblance to their small equivalents; in some cases
size is the chief distinguishing feature (as with *c*, *o*, *p* and *ɯ*) but in
others a greater change of shape is involved (as with *g*, *q* and *r*).

Caxton's practice in regard to capitals remains fairly constant
throughout his career, but two points of change are apparent: that his
earliest fount did not contain a capital form for every letter, and that
his last founts included a second set of capital characters. Missing
from his Type 1 are capital forms of *x* and *y*; but the explanation of
this may well lie in the absence of many words demanding these
characters, in that such words would be few at any time – only, in fact,
those spelled out entirely in capitals, as a chapter heading might be,
and, with initial capital only, proper names. Capitals are by no means
constantly used for the latter (see *Homerus* A29 but *homerus* A30), and
so there is no difficulty when the *Recuyell* text mentions people or
places such as *ydumeus*, *yſaye*, *ylyon* and *ytalye*, in all of which a small
initial *y* is used without impropriety.

The second set of capitals appears in Types 5 and 6. It has already
been noted above that in his later productions Caxton took over the

illuminator's role, printing ornamental capitals and so on, where previously space had been left for a rubricator to add these by hand. These duplicate capitals that are used in his late books are an extension of this, in that they occupy the sort of positions where a rubricator might have added a little decoration, such as a vertical red line, to a capital in the body of the actual text, written the same size as the letters around it. Thus Caxton employs his 'normal' capitals in most places: proper names, beginnings of sentences, and following a large ornamental capital, for instance. But this second variety he uses where, as in the *Fifteen Oes* page in B, he wants a pattern, in this case not only a visual repetition, but also a pattern of sense, in a list of opening words of a series of Psalms. Their very shape, being far less angular than the regular capital characters (compare the capitals in *Aue* B2 and *Ad* B8) makes them conspicuous in a page of text, even when not combined with a special lay-out.

Almost all the twenty-four letters in Caxton's alphabet join with others to form the many ligatures[13] which swell the number of his characters to such a high figure. That they are not even more frequent arises from the shapes of certain letters not lending themselves to joining, and from the limitations on what letters can stand next to each other in the languages Caxton printed in. Thus although *tw* and *ſw* are perfectly possible as English sequences, to make a ligature of either pair would necessitate either a very large type-body, or else a radical modification of letter-shape. On the other hand, no practical difficulty forbids *ln* as a ligature, but as a sequence its use in English is so infrequent as to obviate any need for it.

With a few ligatures the printer can be said to have been driven to linking letters because of their shapes, as when the kern or overhanging part of an *ſ* or *f* would foul the top of any letter following it which had an ascender, such as a second *ſ* or *f*, an *l* or an *h*. But in the majority of cases it is apparent that the ligature exists because Caxton wanted it to, and because in the handwriting of the time writers did not lift their pen in sequences such as *be, ca, en, qu* and *tt*.

Although a few ligatures of three letters occur in Caxton's early types, all beginning with *ff, ſſ* or *ſc*, there are, apart from these, ligatures only of two letters. In this there is an obvious difference from manuscript practice, where if the shapes of the letters were suitable longer ligatures could be made, subject only to the correlation of the movement from left to right of hand as well as pen. In print this limitation to two letters has a curious effect on the way in which sequences are in fact realised. In general when ligatures are formed, the functions of various classes of character are strictly demarcated. The usual ligature make-up is consonant + vowel, making almost a syllabary of characters such as *fa, fe, fi, fo, fu*. But there are a few consonant + consonant characters, and others made up of vowel + consonant. And so it happens that letters which are the first element in one ligature are the second element in another. So *h* appears in *ha, he* and *ho*, but also in *ch, ſh* and *th*, and *t* in *ct* and *ſt* as well as in *ta, te, to* and *tu*. It might be supposed from this that in a sequence such as, say, *-che-* the compositor could choose how he would pair up the letters, *-ch-e-* being of equal likelihood with *-c-he-*. In practice, however, an absolutely free choice hardly ever occurs.

For in some cases one possibility was imposed of necessity by letter-shape, while the other was a purely voluntary ligature. Where *-ſhe-* occurred, for instance, the *ſh* ligature could not be abandoned, but the *he* could (as in *ſh-e* A20), and similarly with *-ſha-* (*ſh-a-ł* A24) and *-ſhi-* (*fy-n-y-ſ* | *ſh-i-d*ι A18–19). Otherwise, standard practice seems to have been simply to proceed by a rule of working from left to right, using whatever ligatures emerged from this ordering. So that in setting up the word *laboure* (A7) the compositor used ligatures for *la* and then for *bo; ur*, however, though a common sequence of letters, had no ligature that could be used, so *u* was printed alone, leaving final *re*, for which a ligature was available. Thus the make-up was *la-bo-u-re*; comparable are *la-u-de* (A3), *ſt-e-d-fa-ſt* (A5), *w-re-to-ŋ* (A14) and *p-re-ſe-n-te-d*ι (A19). That this method settled questions of ambiguity of possible pairing is clear in sequences such as *-tto-* in *attones* (A16), where it is the first chance of ligature, working from left to right, that is taken, giving *a-tt-o-n-e-s* although elsewhere (*eg: wretoŋ* A14) it is the *t* and *o* that are printed in ligature. Special circumstances too can bring variation about, as when the normal *th-e* division, as shown in *the* (A4) and *thende* (A15), is altered to *t-he* when the initial letter becomes a capital in *Therfore* (A11).

In one of the few cases where vowels can be paired up with either of two consonants in a consonant + vowel + consonant sequence, another factor is involved. In the case of *o* the letter can be second element in *bo*, *co* etc, or the first element in *o*2, a ligature ensuring that the r-rotunda allograph follows *o*. Thus in a word such as *wo*2*ŋ* (A5) the make-up is *w-o*2*-ŋ*, and, with another ligature in the same word, *Aucto*2 (A2) is arranged *A-u-ct-o*2. If, however, the *o* is preceded by a letter with which there is a ligature available, and if this is the first pair of letters in the word which can be so linked, this letter and the *o* will join. The *r*, being left a single letter, will then be printed as the r-rotunda its environment demands: thus *aco2de* (A26) is made up of *a-co-2-de*. But if a suitable letter follows, the *r* will link up with that, and it is at this point that the printer departs from one of his own 'rules'. For in all the combinations where *r* is in ligature with a following letter (*ra*, *re* etc), it is the 'normal' *r* allograph that is employed. Hence in whatever words these ligatures appear, and in whatever environment of surrounding letters, they contain this form. Thus where they follow an *o*, the rule for the use of r-rotunda is broken, and sequences such as *co-ra-ge* (A7) and *w-he-r-fo-re* (A21) result. This is in almost every instance the explanation of Caxton's apparent lack of consistency in his distribution of r-rotunda.

All these examples of Caxton's use of ligatures cited in these paragraphs have been from Reproduction A, that is, from the printer's earliest work. This was of necessity, as the reduction in Caxton's stock of ligature-characters as his work progressed is one of the clearest trends in the evolution of his founts. For where his first type has about seventy-five different combinations of letters in ligature, his last cuts this figure down by two-thirds; and although there are a few instances of sporadic use of characters which complicate the pattern, the overall shape is manifest. Examination will be made later of characters where ligature was combined with abbreviation, but considering only 'simple' ligatures, such as have been discussed above, certain patterns emerge as to what was abandoned and what kept.

The combinations of three letters were among the earliest to be discarded; those beginning in *ſc* (*ſca*, *ſce* etc) were used, in fact, only in Type 1, and after Type 2 Caxton also dropped those in *ſſ* and *ff*. Of two-letter ligatures *ſc* itself was not used after Types 1–4, and also discarded in the course of time were other *ſ* characters, such as *ſl*, and a few which seem to fall into no recognisable category, such as *ch* and *o2*. Most of the discontinued ligatures, however, follow an overall design. Thus ligatures of double letters were not retained; though the printer had begun with *cc*, *ll*, *nn*, *pp* and *tt*, these all disappeared, leaving only *ff* and *ſſ*, both of which were impossible to drop, as to set two *f*'s or two *ſ*'s side by side would necessitate an undesirable gap between them. Of the many ligatures with vowels that the printer set out with in his first fount, many were abandoned. This was done on an alphabetical basis: all ligatures with *a* and with *u* were dropped (*ca*, *fa*, *ha* / *lu*, *qu*, *ſu* etc), and the few with *i* were reduced to *li* and *fi*. This cutting down seems to have been a much later change than some (the dropping of three-letter ligatures, as already stated, was early; double letters were abandoned gradually throughout the development of Caxton's types), and the combinations with *a*, most notably, were used as late as the fifth fount the printer worked with.

It is clear that this move away from the widespread use of ligatures was not brought about by any shift in the languages Caxton was printing. The same sequences of letters which in his early types had been produced by ligatures, recur in his last books, but with a make-up of distinct single-letter characters. Thus after the dropping of *ct* (a ligature in *Aucto2* A2 and *Dictes* A29) the same pair of letters is printed in separate characters in *ſancta* (B18) and *bñdicta* (B21), and similarly the *fa* ligature (as in *ſtedfaſt* A5) is replaced by two characters in *fac* (B4). Those ligatures which Caxton retained do show a kind of coherence. The vast number of letters which were joined in his earliest books, not for any practical reason, but simply out of following manuscript habit at a point where there were no real grounds for doing so, are the ones that have been discontinued; those that the printer keeps are attributable to the shapes of the letters involved – *ff, li, ſi, ſſ, ſt* and *th* almost certainly, and probably also the combinations of consonant with *e* or *o*, such as *ce, co, he, ho, te* and *to*.

In handwritten texts the creation of ligatures was partly an *ad hoc* matter, with the scribe choosing to join two or more letters because he wished to, and partly a question of habit, with the scribe tying certain letters because he always did. When Caxton transferred this to print, as has been seen, he had to decide at the outset, when his fount of type was designed and made, which letters he would want to cast in ligature on a single type-body; and his gradual realisation that many of these conventional ligatures were, in fact, redundant can be traced through his successive founts of type. A procedure in many ways parallel to this had also to be followed when making the third kind of extension to his basic alphabet, that is, characters involving abbreviations.

With a number of exceptions which, though important, are comparatively few, the majority of manuscript abbreviations[14] were made by a very small number of actual marks and signs. Thus the customary indication that an *m* or *n* was being omitted was a horizontal stroke over (usually) the preceding letter, and, depending on the word, this preceding letter might be any of the five vowels (or *y*) or even, where a double nasal was reduced to one, another *m* or *n*. To the scribe the identical process of putting in the necessary stroke was used in every instance. With the transference to print, however, such an approach was impossible. There could be no question of a special piece of type which could be positioned so as to print a line above some other character; any additional stroke, line or curve had to be cast on the same type-body with the letter it stood nearest, forming a special abbreviation-character. Thus separate types had to be made for each of the letters after which a nasal might stand and be abbreviated, and Caxton therefore had distinct characters for *ā*, *ē*, *ī* and so on, with all the possibilities of occurrence which he would want to employ accounted for. He was then able to abbreviate as in *dīmedꝛ* (A6), *profūdis* (B6), *cōmendaſti* (B19) and *glioſā matꝛē* (B20).

In the same way calligraphers had been in the habit of abbreviating the sequence vowel + *r* to a small character more or less resembling an *r* written above or above and to the right of the preceding letter, and this convention could be used wherever wanted. But in this too the printer had to decide which letters were most likely to be followed by this sequence reduced in this way, and then cast special characters for these characters plus overwritten *r*. Caxton at various times had characters where this abbreviation mark was added to *p*, *t* and *v*.

With certain other abbreviations, however, the scribe had no such freedom of combination, so that no problem of this kind faced the printer. Thus, where a certain mark of abbreviation involved a set series of pen strokes only ever used in connection with a particular letter, Caxton's choice was simply whether to use this by casting a special type for it or not to bother. The usual form for the sequence *pro*, for example, was a *p* with a particular backwards curl added to it (*ꝓ*) which does not appear elsewhere; a parallel situation existed in the case of the *um* abbreviation, used only in the sequence -*rum*, and therefore represented by a character combining r-rotunda (because the commonest use of this would be after *o* in the Latin termination -*orum*) and a special stroke indicating the suspension (*ꝝ*).

Only rarely does a mark of abbreviation occupy a type-body of its own without some normal letter as its base, but this is the case with the two flourishes used for *con* and *us*, both written by scribes on the line and extending below and above it respectively – in the position, that is, of an ordinary letter. Thus the printer was able to treat each of these as a character in its own right. In certain sequences, however, manuscript practice made the *us* flourish a smaller superscript one, and Caxton in some of his founts maintained this usage, having a special character for -*bus* / -*bis* composed in this way (*noꝰ* B5).

An alternative for final -*us* was a mark of abbreviation shaped like the Old English letter *yog*, written on the line, but attached closely to the preceding letter. Caxton accordingly incorporated this into a series of ligatures, such as *bȝ* for -*bus*, and *lȝ* for -*lus*. This same symbol, moreover, as in manuscript convention, acted to indicate a different omission in ligatures with *q* and *ſ*.

Types were also cast for characters standing for complete words. Three of these, symbols for *the*, *that* and *thu*, involve less abbreviation than appears, for although the overwritten letter gives the impression of an omission in every case, the forms *y*ᵉ and *y*ᵘ are, in fact, full, as the *y* is acting for Old English *thorn*. Where *y*ᵗ is used for *that*, however, an *a* is omitted.

In other whole-word characters a high degree of abbreviation is present, as in the Tironian *and* sign (A12 and 13, B4), and the character where this is in ligature with *c* and a final flourish (indicating suspension) for *etcetera*.

The abbreviations so far discussed may all be said to have a stable expanded form. Moreover, apart from those representing complete words, which were hardly ever used except as such (though occasional instances of scribes employing the *and* abbreviation in words such as *hand* have been found), abbreviation-characters could be used in any word, always indicating a similar sequence of letters. There were certainly slight variations of reference possible, such as when *ū* could stand for either *un* (*profūdis* B6) or *um* (*ſpiȝitū* B16), or when an *ō* could act as abbreviation for *io*, followed by an *n* not abbreviated (*tranſlacōŋ* A27) instead of the more normal *on/om*. Some abbreviations, moreover, were based on sequences of sound rather than of letters, so that *p̄* might stand for *pre* or *pri*, and *p̣* for *pir* and *pur* as well as *per*, and also (by extension from the other pronunciation of *per*) for *par*.

When Caxton's first type was used to print English and French, these abbreviations for simple sequences of two or three letters, which were interchangeable between words, were all that the printer needed. They could be used for similar sequences in both languages, and even in Latin passages if wanted. Thus the Latin lines with which the *Recuyell* ends include the abbreviated form *pidis* for *paridis*, while the English text employs the same character in *pticuler* (*particuler*), and the French version has *p* representing the complete preposition *par*.

In the course of the previous centuries, however, the technique of abbreviation had been developed in more detail than this. Where the same terms constantly recurred in texts having common subject-matter, such as religious writings, abbreviations were made for those individual words which by their frequent use presumably presented no difficulty to the reader or writer versed in the subject and expecting certain items to appear. In such instances, unlike the sort of abbreviated sequences so far discussed, the reader would not interpret the particular character and expand it to a sequence of two or three letters, but would consider the complete word, and expand the abbreviated letter accordingly. Thus although one could assert that *r̄* stands for, say, 'omission of preceding vowel+(consonant)+*t*+vowel+*r*', and account on this basis for its use in *pr̄* (*pater*), *nr̄* (*noster*) and *igr̄* (*igitur*), yet the common ground between the three expansions is too thin to make such an approach practical; the reader of a text in which these abbreviations occurred surely expanded *pr̄* as a whole to *pater*, and so on. Similarly *ñ* meant one thing in *dñs* (*dominus*) but a different (though admittedly related) thing in *bñdictus* (*benedictus*), and *c̄* was capable of widely different expansions in different words, such as *ſc̄dm* (*ſecundum*) and *pc̄o2* (*peccato2*).

Characters to cope with abbreviations of this kind, then, were also available as part of the make-up of Caxton's founts if he wished to have them. But it is immediately noticeable about these forms that function differently in different words that they are a feature of Latin and not of English texts. They were, accordingly, of no relevance while the printer was working at English (or French) books, and it is not surprising, therefore, that they do not appear in his first fount of type.

When he later printed books in both English and Latin from one type, all the abbreviation-characters used for English texts could be made use of also in Latin books. Thus even Caxton's Type 1 could have produced spellings such as *ſaluū* (B4), *perſonā* (B20) and *exiſtēs* (B20), where the characters used for shortening words in English have been carried over into Latin with the same significance (omitted nasal). In the change to Latin, however, these forms are given a wider interpretation: so *noīe* for *nomine* (B4) and *Oracō* for *Oracio* (B12), for example, are perhaps little more free than interpretations of *ō* and *ī* in English texts, but, going beyond this, *hītas* for *habitas* (B8) involves an abbreviation standing for a sequence which it represents in probably no other word. Similarly *ū* may operate for *um/un* in a Latin word as well as an English (as was shown earlier), but in addition it will have two very different, and unique expansions in *ſpūs ſcūs ſpiritus ſanctus*.

Thus to some degree Caxton was able to accommodate his set of characters to the printing of Latin, in so far as extra interpretations could be put on existing characters. But this was insufficient to print Latin in anything like the style readers of manuscripts were accustomed to. And so when Caxton moved to his later founts new characters were included, irrelevant to the printing of English, but of great use for Latin. It is on these that forms in the *Fifteen Oes* such as *nr̃i* (B5 and 16) and *ſc̃e* / *ſc̃a* (B13 and 14) depend, and, with a different type of mark of abbreviation incorporated into a character, *noƀ* (B5). In a few cases abbreviation-characters used by Caxton as early as his first type had reference to Latin rather than English, being used in early books for such pieces of Latin as might appear incidentally, and in later founts these were, of course, retained for fuller use, as with the *-rum* sign in *illo⁊* (B12). In a few other instances, on the other hand, abbreviations that Caxton had once used became redundant, though for a reason which is both clear and interesting. Thus the character for *etcetera* was dropped; Caxton's Type 6 was, however, fully equipped to produce the same abbreviation by means of two pieces of type, the Tironian *and* sign, followed by the newly introduced character *c̃*, which had been wanting in Type 1. It is in this way that the word is made up in B4. A parallel development took place where the *-que* abbreviation, used in the Latin poem at the end of the *Recuyell* (in *absq3*) and there printed from one type-body, was superseded by the use of the letter *z* (virtually the same shape[15] as the old mark of abbreviation) to follow *q* or any other letter to which this abbreviation mark had earlier been added.

In spite of this, however, the clear pattern that emerges is that just as those characters that were abandoned as Caxton developed his craft followed a common style in being almost all ligatures, so those characters that were adopted in the course of time shared a common nature in being characters denoting abbreviation.

As a scribe might well join his letters and write in a mark of abbreviation at the same point, so too Caxton combined ligature with abbreviation to make even further characters. Thus not only does he have *ſ* and *p* in ligature, and a special character (*p*) for *per*, but he makes yet a third character for *ſper*. In the same way *ā* and the *ra* ligature combine to make *rā* for *ram/ran*, and sequences such as *ſum/ſun* and *prop* are similarly treated. The history of these in Caxton's founts is rather like that of plain ligatures: they are gradually abandoned. Of those which were used in his Type 1 some, such as *rā*, were discarded after use in this fount alone; others were continued only in a few types, the last to go being *tū*, retained until Type 4. Consequently in Types 5 and 6 characters of this sort do not appear, sequences that might earlier have been represented by them being now printed from separate pieces of type, as with the *t* + *ū* sequence in *ſpi2itū* (B16).

Though this overall pattern of the dropping of ligature-and-abbreviation characters is a valid one, it is particularly interesting to note that there are more exceptions to it than occur where other trends are concerned. The increase in the use of abbreviations, for instance, is contradicted in only a very few cases where abbreviation-characters are tried and then abandoned again (as with *s̃*, which appears only in Type 5). The decrease in the use of ligatures has, in the same way, some few exceptions (*pe*, for example, which survives to Type 6 but occurs previously only in Types 2, 3 and 4). But besides these there are a fair number of characters whose distribution in Caxton's various founts defies attempts to find a rigid pattern, many of them figuring in neither Type 1 nor Type 6, but employed on and off in Types 2 to 5. And of these erratic characters a large number are characters where abbreviation and ligature are combined, such as *cē, nū, pp, ſā* and *ēē*.

Some of the most problematic of Caxton's abbreviation-characters are those employed where there is no abbreviating to be done. The flourished forms of *d* and *g*, originally indicative of a suspended termination, but reduced in fifteenth-century manuscript and therefore print practice to word-final forms, have already been mentioned in the account of allographs above, as they were adopted consistently to allograph use. But not all cases are as straightforward. There are other characters too where Caxton has a plain letter or ligature cut through with a horizontal line through the ascender(s) that appears to denote some abbreviation. Of this type are *ħ, ſcħ, ħt, ł* and *Ħ*, and one would expect them to be abbreviation forms in contrastive distribution to normal *h, ſch* and so on, or to be in complementary distribution with their plain equivalents and used as allographs, in word-final position, for instance. Of these characters, all are in Caxton's first type, *ſcħ* and *ħt* occurring only there, the others being still in use in Type 6.

That the marked forms can indicate abbreviations is apparent from their use in Latin words with forms such as *glioſā* for *glorioſam* (B20) and *ſcła ſcło2ꝥ* for *ſecula ſeculo2um, Iħus* for *Iheſus*[16] (B11) and *Ioħi* for *Iohanni* (B21). Where they have a much more dubious status, however, is when they are used in English words.

The only way an abbreviation can be interpreted is by the occurrence of what appears to be the same word spelled in a fuller form, as *hand* to be set against *hād*, or *pater* against *p̄r*. But there is no little confusion when an attempt is made to compare other forms with those where *ħ*, *ħt* etc occur. In some instances there seems to be variation between the marked characters and spellings that add an *-e*; so that although *aħ* is found in A9, elsewhere in the same text the same word is spelled *alle*. Alternatives such as *frenfħ* and *frenfhe* also appear in the *Recuyell*, suggesting a similar role for the marked form. But as against this evidence there are as many examples of marked and unmarked forms in free alternation; thus *weħ* sometimes (A21) but *well* at others, and similarly *wyħ:wyll*, *rygħt:ryght*, *Lymbourgħ:lymburgh*, *witħ* (A6)*: wyth*. This ambiguity persists to the end of Caxton's career, as parallels are found in the *Fifteen Oes*, such as variation between *angeħ* and *angell*, and though such examples are less common in the later text, this may well be bound up with the fact that Caxton's Type 6 had no *ll* ligature, only *ħ*, so that it was less effort for the compositor to use the marked form cast on a single type-body than to set two separate *l*'s. That variants do occur, however, forbids the regular interpretation of these marked forms as the abbreviations they at first appear to be. Moreover, by the same token they cannot be regarded in the same way as the flourished *d* and *g* discussed earlier, that is as abbreviations adapted to use as allographs with a distribution based on position in the word. Yet it is evident that, irregular as their use is, there is in these characters some vestige of status as possible abbreviations, and also some link with position. So while it is unpredictable whether *ħ* or *ll* will occur at the end of *well*, yet medially and initially there is no question of choice; forms with unmarked characters, such as the *ll*, *fh* and *ht* in *naturelly*, *fhe* and *doughtir* will be found in English texts, and spellings like *illa* (B14 and 18) in Latin.

Just as printers after Caxton, either in imitation of his practice or parallel to it, followed and extended the move away from dependence on the general appearance and style of manuscripts, so too they continued to modify the make-up of the founts of type they used.

As would be expected, change was swiftest where even in Caxton's fifteen years of printing developments can be traced most clearly, notably in the dropping of ligatures, which in the course of the sixteenth century were reduced almost entirely to the more essential ones with *ſ* and *f*. With allographs, however, where Caxton abandoned only a few, his successors were similarly conservative, final *-ŋ* and *-ŋ* soon falling into disuse, but r-rotunda surviving well into the sixteenth century, and *u* and *v* behaving in complementary distribution into the seventeenth century. Most persistent of all was ſ, lasting as a possibility to about 1800.[17] Abbreviations, the one variety of character Caxton retained and even increased as he went on, survived too for a century or more, but with a gradual change of status, moving from an open alternative to a full form, to a useful device for getting words into confined space. It is noticeable, for instance, that on some sixteenth-century books abbreviations are particularly favoured at the foot of the seventh page of a gathering of four leaves; in trying to increase speed by judging the amount of material which will occupy the inner forme of the sheet and having it set simultaneously with the outer forme, the compositor has miscalculated, and found himself at the end of the last page of the inner forme with a little too much to fit into the space available, so abbreviation is used to overcome the difficulty.

No explicit account of the principles of typography was made until two hundred years after Caxton began to work out solutions to the problems of determining an adequate fount. In 1683 Joseph Moxon's *Mechanick Exercises on the Whole Art of Printing*[18] described at length the methods and procedures of book-production then in use. It is clear from this that since Caxton's time the typical fount had been cut down radically, though not completely, to dimensions much closer to the basic alphabet. In dealing with the design of type-faces, for instance, Moxon (*pp* 124–30) illustrates hardly any ligatures, and the specimen lay-out of his cases of type (*p* 32) shows a similar reduction, which is demonstrated in the printing of the text itself. Only *ct* in ligature and a few combinations with *f* and ſ occur; of Caxton's allographs only ſ appears (and r-rotunda in Black Letter), and *u* and *v* are used as distinct letters, not in complementary distribution. Characters consisting of vowels with strokes above them are found, but these are accented letters for use in printing foreign languages, and not indications of contractions. Moxon even advises the compositor to rest his galley on the part of the upper case where such characters (*Latin Sorts*) are kept, 'for those *Boxes* are seldomest used'. Abbreviations, indeed, are mentioned only as a *Botch* or shift to save space, and are dismissed not only as breaking the rules of good workmanship, but as out of date:

They have been much used by Printers in Old Times, to *Shorten* or *Get in Matter*; but now are wholly left off as obsolete.

The struggles of Caxton to discover just how much of the scribe's

stock-in-trade needed to be carried over into print to form a complete
working alphabet have been forgotten in less than two centuries. But
they determined the form of printed English.

Notes

1 The first page of this epilogue is reproduced as A (*p* 30), and a comparison of
the extract quoted here using only present-day characters with the same passage as printed by Caxton will show up many of the points discussed in the
course of the essay that follows. An edited form of the complete epilogue
appears along with Caxton's other comments on his own work in W. J. B.
Crotch's *The Prologues and Epilogues of William Caxton* (EETS OS 176),
London, 1928 (reprinted 1956). The *Recuyell* has been edited by H. Oskar
Sommer, 2 vols, London, 1894, and the introduction to this edition (*p* lxxxviii)
mentions some of the matters investigated here; the editorial policy applied to
the text by Sommer retains abbreviations unexpanded, but only some ligature
and allograph characters.

2 The examples that follow (with the translations, except for the last passage) are
taken from A. W. Pollard, *An Essay on Colophons*, The Caxton Club, Chicago,
1905, *pp* 14, 16–17, 60 and 88–9.

3 *The Life and Typography of William Caxton*, 2 vols, London, 1861 and 1863
(but also 1882 single vol edn (*The Biography and . . .* etc) for certain additional
material) especially Vol 1, Chapter 3 (*pp* 28–36), 'Scribes and Printers'. Not all
Blades' points are reproduced below. For a more recent account, with many
photographs illustrating manuscript-print continuity, see Hellmut Lehmann-
Haupt 'The Heritage of the Manuscript', *pp* 3–23 in *A History of the Printed
Book*, ed Laurence C. Wroth (The Limited Editions Club; No 3 of *The Dol-
phin*) New York, 1938. For readers wishing to get a general picture of what
printed books looked like, there are good collections of representative extracts reproduced in *Facsimiles from Early Printed Books in the British Museum*,
London, 1897; E. Gordon Duff, *Fifteenth Century English Books*, Bibliographical Society Illustrated Monographs No xviii, London, 1917; and Frank
Isaac, *English and Scottish Printing Types*, Biographical Society Facsimiles
and Illustrations Nos ii and iii, London, 1930 and 1932. Several complete
books printed by Caxton and his contemporaries have also been issued in
facsimile over the last hundred years or so.

4 It is noticeable that printers who became their own illuminators often retained
in detail the ideas on appropriateness of design for certain purposes. Thus
Beatus pages at the beginning of the Book of Psalms still appeared in print
with an initial *B* within which King David was depicted playing his harp; and
in Books of Hours the illustrations at the *Deus in adiutorium meum intende*
opening of each Hour maintained the same series of episodes as had become
traditional in manuscripts. (Compare the account of the illustrations in manuscript Books of Hours in M. R. James, *A Descriptive Catalogue of the Manuscripts in the Fitzwilliam Museum*, Cambridge, 1895, with the similar printed
items described in Edward Hodnett, *English Woodcuts 1480–1535*, Bibliographical Society Illustrated Monographs No xxii, London, 1935).

5 The fullest account of this in terms of printed books is in Talbot Baines Reed,
A History of the Old English Letter Foundries, revised A. F. Johnson, London,
1952, and R. B. McKerrow, *An Introduction to Bibliography for Literary Students*, Oxford, 1927, Appendix ii. Both these also discuss in more detail the
spread of Roman and Italic types, and the changing status of Black Letter.

For a clear sketch of the various distinctions of scripts that underlie printed work see N. Denholm-Young, *Handwriting in England and Wales*, Cardiff, 1954. The situation is not clarified by the variety of terminology used by different writers to denote the same hand or type-face. Not only are related words from different languages used (*bastard, bastarda, lettre bâtarde*) but also completely unrelated terms (*textura, lettre de forme, book hand*).

6 Blades, *op cit*, Vol 1, *pp* 31–2. For an approach to Caxton in the context of the area where he began to print, see Wytze and Lotte Hellinga, *The Fifteenth-Century Printing Types of The Low Countries*, 2 vols, Amsterdam, 1966. Illustrative specimens of Caxton's various types are given in E. Gordon Duff, *op cit*, Plates i–x, and in Blades, *op cit*, Vol 2, Plates xi–xxiv, with tables of the characters employed in each.

7 Geoffrey Dowding, *An Introduction to the History of Printing Types*, London, 1961, *p* 5.

8 Such as S. H. Steinberg, *Five Hundred Years of Printing*, London, 1955, *pp* 30–2; also Curt F. Bühler, *The Fifteenth-Century Book*, Philadelphia, 1960, who draws an analogy with the way in which the earliest American motor-cars were not only modelled on contemporary horse-drawn vehicles, but even called 'horseless-buggies' – as with 'horseless-carriages' in Britain.

9 The distinction between capital and small forms would normally nowadays be made in terms of *upper* and *lower case*; but as the basis of this is the arrangement of characters in a compositor's cases of type, to use this terminology in reference to handwriting would be inaccurate, and in reference to Caxton's press anachronistic, as his arrangement of type was not according to the later standard lay-out. See Blades, *op cit* (but in 1882 edition only), Plate x.

10 The line references that follow are to the two extracts shown in Reproductions A and B. That these differ in two dimensions (Type 1: Type 6, and English: Latin) is not intended to suggest that Caxton altered his alphabet as the result of turning to the printing of Latin at the expense of English; his output of books in the vernacular continued throughout his career. Most features in the development of his founts could have been illustrated equally well from an English page of a late book, but as one feature (the increased use of abbreviation-characters) *is* bound up with the use of Latin, it could only be shown by taking an example such as this. The *Fifteen Oes* contains, in fact, prayers in both Latin and English.

11 An interesting difference from the setting up of allophones within phonemes on a basis of complementary distribution, in that phonetic similarity is normally called in to complete such an account.

12 Hilary Jenkinson, though arguing chiefly about the hands on which early type is based, touches on this and some of the other matters discussed here, particularly 'abbreviations' such as *H*, in 'English Current Writing and Early Printing', *Transactions of the Bibliographical Society*, Oct 1913–March 1915, 13, London, 1916.

13 Blades calls such combinations of two or more letters cast on a single type-body *logotypes*. In reference to scribal usage a distinction is sometimes made (as by C. Johnson and H. Jenkinson, *English Court Hand*, Oxford, 1915) between letters simply joined (*ties*) and letters joined with a modification of size or shape being involved (*ligatures*). The use of *ligature* in the present essay follows R. B. McKerrow, who has an account of their origin and use, *op cit*, *pp* 312–15, and the majority of writers on typography.

14 There are summaries of manuscript conventions in respect of abbreviation in N. Denholm-Young, *op cit*, *pp* 64–70, L. C. Hector *The Handwriting of English Documents*, London, 1958, *pp* 28–38, and, tracing the development of various

signs, E. M. Thompson, *An Introduction to Greek and Latin Palaeography*, Oxford, 1912, *pp* 75–90.

15 Early printers not uncommonly used this same principle that approximate identity of shape was enough for the reader to understand. Thus in both *The Kalendayr of Shyppars* and *The Traytte of God Lyuyng*, English texts produced in Paris in 1503 from a fount meant for French, the printer, Antoine Verard, had to make up a *k* by printing *l* and r-rotunda as close as possible. In the *Recuyell* extract shown in A Caxton is apparently happy to allow any series of three minim strokes to stand for any sequence of letters composed in this way: thus the word *in* is twice printed from the type for word-final *m* (lines 4 and 13) and three times (lines 18, 19 and 26) from the other *m* allograph.

16 That the spelling with an *h* is the usual full form here indicates the degree of assimilation the Greek abbreviation of the *nomen sacrum* has undergone (and similar spellings such as *Iheruſalem* were an extension of this taking of a Greek *e* for an *h*). As the character Caxton employs is clearly the same as the *h*-abbreviation in *Iohi*, the argument that this is the same letter as in *hath* (A8) holds good.

17 McKerrow, *op cit*, quotes works and dates in more detail in his Appendix iii.

18 Ed Herbert Davis and Harry Carter, London, 1958. It is to this edition that the page references apply.

J. P. Thorne
Lecturer in English Language, University of Edinburgh

The grammar of jealousy:
A note on the character of Leontes

Critics have been sharply divided over the question of the dramatic effectiveness of Shakespeare's presentation of the behaviour of Leontes in Act I, Scene 2 of *The Winter's Tale*.[1] Most modern critics regard it as entirely successful, taking their lead on this (as on so many points regarding this play) from F. Tinkler who describes Leontes' speeches in this scene as presenting '. . . an almost pathological study of the birth and growth of jealousy'.[2] Earlier generations of critics, on the other hand,were equally unanimous in their criticism. Their complaints are summarised by Quiller-Couch in the following passage from his introduction to the play. 'Shakespeare weakens the plausibility of it [*ie* Leontes' jealousy] as well by ennobling Hermione – after his way with good women – as by huddling up the jealousy in its motion so densely that it strikes us as merely frantic and – which is worse in drama – a piece of impossible improbability. This has always and rightly offended the critics, and we may be forgiven for a secret wish, in reading Act I, Scene 2, to discover some break or gap to which one might point and argue, for Shakespeare's credit, "Here is evidence of a cut by the stage manager's or some other hand, to shorten the business." But the scene runs connectedly, with no abruptness save in Leontes' behaviour, which indeed confounds Camillo, on the stage, hardly less than it shocks us, in the audience.'[3]

It is unlikely that anyone who finds Leontes' behaviour implausible can be persuaded by arguments based on the text to think otherwise. The purpose of this paper is to show that at least there is evidence in the text to counter the accompanying, implicit, criticism that Shakespeare had no interest in the dramatisation of Leontes' jealousy, that he expended very little care and skill in writing Leontes' speeches, and that (like most critics) he was merely anxious to get on to the second part of the play and the pastoral land of Bohemia as quickly as possible. It seeks to show that, on the contrary, in the characterisation of Leontes Shakespeare made careful and consistent use of a sophisticated dramatic device, that of writing the speeches of Leontes in two quite distinct styles, one virtually indistinguishable from that of the other characters in the play, the other highly idiosyncratic. The grammar of Leontes' soliloquies and speeches to Camillo in Act I, Scene 2 reveals unusual features that are not to be found in the speeches of other characters, or in his own speeches elsewhere in the play. It is as if there were two characters called Leontes, both presented in quick succession in the second scene of the play: the first, the public Leontes, apparently sane, speaking to the other characters in the play, speaking like the other characters in the play, the second, the private Leontes, obviously mad, speaking at first only to himself and subsequently to his intimate friend and adviser, Camillo, in a quite distinct idiom.

Several of the peculiar characteristics of this idiom are exemplified in Leontes' first soliloquy.

> Too hot, too hot:
> To mingle friendship far, is mingling bloods.
> I have tremor cordis on me: my heart dances,
> But not for joy; not joy. . . . This entertainment
> May a free face put on; derive a liberty
> From heartiness, from bounty, fertile bosom,
> And well become the agent: 't may; I grant:
> But to be paddling palms and pinching fingers,
> As now they are, and making practised smiles
> As in a looking-glass; and then to sigh, as 'twere
> The mort o'th'deer; O, that is entertainment
> My bosom likes not, nor my brows . . .

                                                      [I.2.108–19][4]

The first point to notice here is that while not actually incorrect the syntax is at several places (to say the least) extremely awkward. Take the line 'To mingle friendship far is mingling bloods.' Sentences with a nominalisation on either side of the verb *to be* are, of course, well-formed, but it is unusual to find such a sentence where one nominalisation is an infinitive and the other a participle. That is to say, what one would expect to find is either, 'To mingle friendship far is to mingle bloods,' or, alternatively, 'Mingling friendship far is mingling bloods.' But either emendation destroys the dramatic point of the line. As it stands the awkwardness of the syntax serves to underline the absurdity of the claim Leontes is making. The asymmetry of the phrases on either side of the copula draws attention to how forced is the identification that Leontes is making in this identity statement.

Equally awkward, but in a different way, is the next sentence but one, 'This entertainment / May a free face put on,' etc. The word order makes the sentence irresolvably ambiguous. The occurrence of the second noun phrase between the modal and the main verb makes it impossible for one to decide whether it is the subject or the object of 'put on'. Nor – as far as the dramatic effect of the speech is concerned – does it matter. What does matter is that Leontes is capable of producing sentences so ambiguous that it is impossible to assign a single interpretation to them. This tells one much more about Leontes than could be learnt from either of the two possible interpretations of this sentence.

But perhaps the most characteristic feature of Leontes' sentence construction in his first soliloquy is the use made of conjunction. The next part of the sentence just discussed, '. . . derive a liberty / From heartiness, from bounty, fertile bosom' (with the typical, infelicitous omission of the preposition in the last phrase) and the subsequent sentences 'But to be paddling palms and pinching fingers, / As now they are, and making practised smiles / As in a looking-glass; and then to sigh, as 'twere / The mort o'th'deer . . .' both exemplify Leontes' tendency to turn his sentences into lists. In many cases these are little more than lists of synonyms or near synonyms.

> Come, captain,
> We must be neat; not neat, but cleanly, captain:
> And yet the steer, the heifer, and the calf,
> Are all called 'neat' . . .
>
> [I.2.122–5]

and

> Go to, go to!
> How she holds up the neb! the bill to him!
>
> [I.2.182–3]

and

> They're here with me already; whisp'ring, rounding:
>
> [I.2.217][5]

Leontes' fantasy is built up word by word. The words of one sentence expressing his morbid imaginings suggest the words of the next, thus extending and elaborating his delusion; the effect on Leontes himself being to convince him that he has a mass of objective evidence. Any word can trigger the process, almost any word can suggest to him a *double entendre*

> *Camillo*   To satisfy your highness, and the entreaties
>   Of our most gracious mistress.
> *Leontes*   Satisfy?
>   Th' entreaties of your mistress? satisfy?
>
>   [I.2.232–4]

All except the last quotation are from soliloquies. The first and third, together with the list of similes for feminine falseness:

>   ... women say so
> (That will say any thing!) but were they false
> As o'er-dyed blacks, as wind, as waters; false
> As dice are to be wished, by one that fixes
> No bourn 'twixt his and mine ...
>
>   [I.2.130–4]

are all asides occurring in the middle of speeches addressed to other characters (Mamilius and Camillo). Once one has noticed this tendency to turn his sentences into lists as characteristic of the 'private' Leontes, one does not need the help of stage-directions or punctuation to tell one that at these points Leontes has lapsed into soliloquy.

Leontes' second extended soliloquy reveals another characteristic stylistic feature:

> Affection! thy intention stabs the centre:
> Thou dost make possible things not so held,
> Communicat 'st with dreams – how can this be ? –
> With what's unreal thou coactive art,
> And fellow 'st nothing: then 'tis very credent
> Thou mayst co-join with something, and thou dost
> (And that beyond commission) and I find it,
>
>   [I.2.138–44]

The last three lines contain what, from this point on, are the words Leontes uses most frequently in this scene; *nothing* (negative indefinite pronoun), *something* (positive indefinite pronoun) and *it* (positive definite pronoun). Apart from the features *animate/inanimate* pronouns are semantically empty. The rules governing pronominalisation require either that the pronoun occurs in the deep structure of the sentence or that the deep structure contains two identical noun phrases, in which case a transformational rule re-writes one of them as a pronoun in the surface structure. In this second case the pronoun in the surface structure is related to a noun phrase in the deep structure and, therefore, to the semantic interpretation assigned to that noun phrase.[6] This seems to be the analysis required to account for the *it* at the end of the last sentence. But notice a striking peculiarity in Leontes' use of pronouns. In analysing this sentence, looking back along the sentence to find the basis of the interpretation of the final *it*, one discovers that the noun phrase to which it is related is itself a pronoun – *something*. That is, the semantically empty *it* derives from a form that is also semantically empty. Hence no interpretation attaches to *it* in this sentence. But clearly Leontes is under the impression that there does. He is convinced that he has made a meaningful statement about the grounds for his jealousy, that he has identified as actually happening what only exists as an unidentified subconscious fear. The way Leontes uses pronouns is an essential clue to what, at this point in the play, is his most important characteristic; the tragic capacity to take his own expressions of jealousy as reports of states of affairs actually existing in the outside world.

One finds a similarly odd use of the pronoun *it* in the lines

It is a bawdy planet, that will strike
Where 'tis predominant; and 'tis powerful . . . think it . . .
From east, west, north, and south! be it concluded,
[I.2.201–3]

The word *it* occurs altogether five times in these three lines. (In the eight lines 200–8, all part of a soliloquy, *it* occurs nine times.) But notice particularly the use of *it* in the first line – 'It is a bawdy planet,'. No amount of searching through the context will reveal what this *it* refers to. Once again the point is not that we should try to supply a reference but notice that it is characteristic of Leontes' speech that one is not supplied.[7]

Another striking, and characteristic, use of the pronoun *it* occurs in one of the first of Leontes' speeches to Camillo:

> *Leontes* ... How came 't, Camillo,
>   That he did stay?
> *Camillo*   At the good queen's entreaty.
> *Leontes* At the queen's be 't: 'good', should be pertinent,
>   But so it is, it is not.

$$\text{[i.2.219–22]}$$

The last sentence is the epitome of Leontes' style. The syntax is so awkward that the sentence is difficult to understand. One needs a second reading to work out that the first *it* is the so-called 'impersonal' *it* and that the second refers back to the word *good*. The effect of the difficulty one experiences in tracing the referents of the two pronouns is to isolate the sentence from its context. It is, in fact, easier to read the line out of its immediate context as a statement of the paradox upon which Leontes' illusion is based.

From this point on all the stylistic features that have hitherto characterised Leontes' soliloquies begin to appear in his speeches to Camillo, the only character to whom the private Leontes speaks, the only character to whom he can reveal what is going on in his mind, the man he trusts 'With all the nearest things to my heart.' One notices again the tendency to turn sentences into lists:

> To bide upon 't: thou art not honest: or,
> If thou inclin 'st that way, thou art a coward,
> Which hoxes honesty behind, restraining
> From course required: or else thou must be counted
> A servant, grafted in my serious trust,
> And therein negligent; or else a fool,
> That seest a game played home, the rich stake drawn,
> And tak 'st it all for jest.

$$\text{[i.2.242–9]}$$

and

> Ha' not you seen, Camillo
> (But that's past doubt: you have, or your eye-glass
> Is thicker than a cuckold's horn), or heard
> (For to a vision so apparent rumour
> Cannot be mute) or thought (for cogitation
> Resides not in that man that does not think)
> My wife is slippery?

$$\text{[i.2.267–73]}$$

It is as if Leontes is trying to convince himself of his objectivity, his ability to consider all possible points of view, to search out all possible explanations – as long as they fit in with his delusion. The last speech continues:

> If thou wilt confess,
> Or else be impudently negative,
> To have nor eyes, nor ears, nor thought, then say
> My wife's a hobby horse. . . .

The intense excitement and confusion of Leontes' state of mind is vividly conveyed through the compression and confusion of Leontes' style of speech. Indeed, so pronounced is this in the last few lines that it is easy enough at first reading to take them in exactly the opposite sense from that which Leontes seems to intend. (The most likely explanation is that Leontes has omitted a repetition of the verb *confess* at the end of line 273. *Cf* the omission of a repetition of *thee* as an object for *restraining* in line 244 above.)

The ungrammaticality of the following sentence in an earlier speech to Camillo has a similar effect:

> . . . but we have been
> Deceived in thy integrity, deceived
> In that which seems so.
>
> [I.2.239–41]

For such a sentence to be well-formed it would be necessary for sentences like *Thy integrity seems so or *My optimism seems so, also to be well-formed; which clearly is not the case. After verbs like *seem* and *appear* the adverb *so* takes the place in surface structure of a sentence, not just a noun phrase. Hence *He is clever or at least seems so* derives from deep structures roughly equivalent to *He is clever or at least it seems that he is clever*. The result of Leontes' mistake is to reduce the connection between the two parts of the sentence. Again the effect is to isolate the sentence from its context so that the reading of the second part, 'deceived in that which seems so,' as an ironical statement of Leontes' predicament becomes almost inescapable.

Subsequently Leontes lapses into two more syntactical errors. The first comes in the lines:

> I say thou liest, Camillo, and I hate thee,
> Pronounce thee a gross lout, a mindless slave,
> Or else a hovering temporiser, that
> Canst with thine eyes at once see good and evil,
> Inclining to them both.
>
> [I.2.300–4]

The syntactically correct version would be 'I . . . pronounce thee . . . a hovering temporiser, that *can* with *his* eyes at once see good and evil'. Leontes, characteristically, substitutes for the third person, the more immediate direct address forms of the second person.

The second mistake occurs in the passage:

> *Camillo*   Who does infect her?
> *Leontes* Why, he that wears her like her medal, hanging
>   About his neck – Bohemia! who, if I
>   Had servants true about me, that bare eyes
>   To see alike mine honour, as their profits
>   (Their own particular thrifts) they would do that
>   Which should undo more doing.
>
> [1.2.306–12]

Here the syntactically correct version would be 'to *whom* . . . they would do that'. Leontes begins a complex sentence in which *Bohemia* is the subject of both the matrix and constituent sentences, but, in his agitation, he loses control of the grammatical structure and switches to making *servants* the subject of the constituent sentence.

But these errors occur in speeches coming after that speech which, from the point of view of syntactic incoherence, marks the climax (perhaps nadir would be a better description) of Leontes' expression of his jealousy.

> Is whispering nothing?
> Is leaning cheek to cheek? is meeting noses?
> Kissing with inside lip? stopping the career
> Of laughter with a sigh (a note infallible
> Of breaking honesty)? horsing foot on foot?
> Skulking in corners? wishing clocks more swift?
> Hours, minutes? noon, midnight? and all eyes
> Blind with the pin and web but theirs; theirs only,
> That would unseen be wicked? Is this nothing?
> Why then the world, and all that's in 't, is nothing,
> The covering sky is nothing, Bohemia nothing,
> My wife is nothing, nor nothing have these nothings
> If this be nothing.
>
> [1.2.284–96]

The increasing compression in the questions at the beginning of this speech is such that by the seventh line (290) they are virtually devoid of structure altogether – 'Hours, minutes? noon, midnight?' They can only be interpreted by reference to the sentences in their context. But notice how much has to be supplied from these sentences – 'Is wishing that hours were minutes nothing?'

But the most interesting feature in this speech is Leontes' use of the negative indefinite pronoun *nothing*. In their analysis of the indefinite pronoun *something* (alternatively *someone* and *somebody* with the negative forms *nothing, no one* and *nobody*) Katz and Postal[8] treat it as a noun phrase consisting of the indefinite determiner *some* and a 'pro-form', the product of re-writing the noun symbol, not as a full noun, but as a dummy noun, or variable, which appears in the surface structure as *thing, one* or *body*. A late transformational rule then combines the two elements to produce the surface structure forms *something*, etc. A noticeable characteristic of indefinite pronouns is that they do not have plurals. But, as Katz and Postal point out, the element *thing* is not restricted in its occurrence to sentences with proforms in their deep structure. It can also be the product of a direct re-writing of the noun symbol. This accounts for the difference between the sentences *I saw something in the room* and *I saw some things in the room*. In the second case the determiner does not have to be *some*, nor does a transformation combining the surface structure forms of the determiner and the noun apply (a fact reflected in the orthography). Also, as the example shows, plural forms of noun phrases containing *thing* (as opposed to indefinite pronouns containing the proform *thing*) are well formed. The mistake, therefore, that Leontes makes in his use of the word *nothing* in this speech is to confuse the pronoun with the noun ('nor nothing have these nothings'). But, as the analysis of his earlier speeches has shown, this is a mistake Leontes has been making all along. The most obvious symptom of Leontes' disturbance, the basis from which his whole jealous delusion is projected, is to be found in his use of these forms – the mistake that makes him believe that to talk about *something* is to talk about *some thing*.

The peculiarities of syntax that distinguish Leontes' soliloquies and his speeches to Camillo in Act I, Scene 2 of *The Winter's Tale* are not to be found in any of his speeches in later scenes. The dramatic significance of this is clear. By the end of Act I, Scene 2 Leontes' construction of his fantasy is complete. From now on he proceeds to act upon it. The public Leontes takes over entirely; and the public Leontes talks to the other characters in the play in their own idiom. Of course, they are shocked by his speeches and his actions, because they, unlike the audience and Camillo, have not witnessed the development of Leontes' delusion. Incidentally, Camillo is obviously intended by Shakespeare to be the representative of the audience in the play – his main function in it is to listen. The sense of shock which the older critics registered with regard to Leontes' jealousy may in part have arisen from a tendency to identify with Hermione or Paulina, rather than Camillo.

Their criticism of Shakespeare's dramatisation of Leontes' jealousy is also connected with another and more general criticism, one originally made by Dr Johnson[9] when he declared that 'The style of Shakespeare was in itself ungrammatical, perplexed, and obscure.' (Cf Dover Wilson[10] who also finds 'logical breakdown or syntactical incoherence' to be a general feature of Shakespeare's writing, particularly in his later plays.) There are two points to be made regarding this criticism. The first – and it has been made often enough – is that it seems that in his later plays Shakespeare was making an increasingly successful attempt to reproduce in his dialogue the effect of actual speech, with all its hesitations, repetitions, and syntactic irregularities. This accounts for most of the 'tangles' in these plays. The second point – and this is what this paper tries to show – is that it does not account for them all. It is important that one should not try to judge the writing in Shakespeare's later plays in terms of a single criterion, but attempt, as far as possible, to relate the (in fact) extreme diversity in the writing of these plays to the wide range of dramatic effects they achieve.

Notes

1 R. Trienens, 'The Inception of Leontes' Jealousy', *Shakespeare Quarterly*, 4, 1953, 321–7, provides a convenient summary of the controversy.
2 F. Tinkler, 'The Winter's Tale', *Scrutiny*, 1937, 358.
3 W. Shakespeare, *The Winter's Tale*, Sir Arthur Quiller-Couch and J. D. Wilson (eds), Cambridge, 1950, *pp* xvi–xvii.
4 The text used is the one mentioned in the note above.
5 The OED gives as the definition of *neb* 'The beak or bill of a bird' and of *to round* in this sense 'To whisper.'
6 For an account of the grammatical model that is assumed here and in particular of the terms deep and surface structure see N. Chomsky, *Aspects of the Theory of Syntax*, Cambridge, Mass, 1965. For accounts of pronominalisation see R. Lees and E. Klima, 'Rules for English Pronominalisation', *Language*, 1963, and J. Ross, 'On the Cyclic Nature of English Pronominalisation', *For Roman Jacobson*, The Hague, 1968.
7 Shakespeare uses this device to indicate disturbance in a character on at least one other occasion. See Othello's speech just before the murder of Desdemona: 'It is the cause, it is the cause, my soul / Let me not name it to you, you chaste stars: / It is the cause . . .' (v.2.1–3).

8 J. Katz and P. Postal, *An Integrated Theory of Linguistic Descriptions*, Cambridge, Mass, 1964, *p* 91.
9 S. Johnson, 'Preface to Shakespeare', in A. Murray (ed), *Works*, Vol ɪɪ, London, 1810, *p* 171.
10 W. Shakespeare, *Richard* ɪɪɪ, J. D. Wilson (ed), Cambridge, 1954, *p* xxxv.

Modern English

John Anderson
Lecturer in English Language, University of Edinburgh

Some proposals concerning the modal verb in English

1 A subcategorisation of the modals

The intention of this paper is a modest one.* In it I would like to consider some of the set of phenomena that we could reasonably require a subcategorisation of the modal verb in English to provide an explanation for. These phenomena are often well documented in grammars purporting to give an account of the modals, both with respect to the set of interpretations to be associated with each modal,[1] and with respect to the superficial syntactic facts that serve to characterise 'the modal', and, sometimes, various subsets of modals.[2] But there has generally been little attempt to provide any more than a list of modals each with a list of 'functions' in dealing with their respective interpretations; and even less interest has been shown in trying to relate a systematic treatment of their interpretations to the variously observed facts of their syntax.[3]

I would like to suggest here some tentative groupings and subgroupings of the modals that appear to me to accord well with the range of interpretation and the syntactic possibilities associated with each modal. These depend on the assumption that it is possible to decompose each interpretation for a modal into a set of 'meaning components' (or 'features'), such that there may be an overlap in the sets of

* I am grateful to F. R. Palmer and D. J. Tittensor for their comments on a previous version of this paper, and to Angus McIntosh in respect both of this and of the benefit I have derived from a number of discussions on the topics dealt with here.

6—E.S.E.S.

components assigned to different modals, or to different interpretations of the same modal. Thus, a particular interpretation of a particular modal can be regarded as belonging simultaneously to several classes (of interpretations), membership of a particular class being characterised by the presence of a particular component in the sets assigned to the modal interpretations concerned. Each component is one term in a binary opposition, either 'marked' or 'unmarked' ('X' or 'non-X'). The marked alternative is (semantically, and usually syntactically) more restricted. Certain oppositions may be subordinate to others, in that a particular opposition may be relevant ('may be operative') only in cases where a particular term in another opposition is (has been) chosen.[4] The groupings are intended to correlate with the syntactic phenomena that have been noted – mostly to do with restrictions vis-à-vis 'adverbial' elements of the clause – together with such further phenomena as can be proposed as being relevant. That is, the subcategorisation should provide not only a systematisation of the semantics of the modal, but also an explanation (deriving from the nature of the systematisation) for restrictions on the co-occurrence of certain (groupings of) modals (or rather modal interpretations) with other elements.

I do not want to insist here on the particular label applied to each meaning component (and thus to the class defined by this component). I shall choose names which appear to me to be appropriate, but they are not to be regarded as having any systematic status – particularly in view of the present state of our knowledge. Nor shall I present a formalisation of the subclassification, except as an appendix.[5] The formalisation should be easily derivable, I hope, from the discussion, and would add little to it. Moreover, there is a further reason for diffidence with regard to those two areas (of appropriacy of labels, and formalisation); and this derives from one of the conclusions of the subsequent discussion, namely, that a simple subcategorisation of the modals, which regards them as directly realising underlying categories (along, perhaps, the lines suggested in note 5 and followed in the apdix to Part 1), does not provide the optimal account of their semantics or their syntax. Some tentative suggestions concerning an alternative derivation preferable to such a subcategorisation form the concluding section of the present paper.

I intend, in particular (initially, at least), to study the 'hard-core' modals, those which satisfy the simple distributional requirements that are usually suggested as defining the class of modals.[6] These are *will*, *shall, can, may, would, should, could, might* and perhaps *ought* (*to*). One of the problems of setting out to give a systematic account of the modals has always been the existence of certain 'quasi-modals', which satisfy some but not all of the criteria (and usually are obviously semantically similar). Such are *need* and *dare*,[7] *used* (*to*), and even, perhaps, *have* (*to*) and *am* (*to*). I shall, for the most part, ignore this problem as much as possible in the initial discussion of the 'hard-core' group; and shall bring in these others only where absolutely necessary. This is because I think that they are genuinely an awkward phenomenon for a simple subcategorisation to deal with. How most of them might be included in our account can, I think, only really be considered within a wider and more abstract framework, perhaps like that I shall propose to substitute for the simple subcategorisation.

In Part 1, however, I shall try to establish as appropriate a subcategorisation as I find possible. We shall be looking later at what components of meaning serve to differentiate between the different modals. But firstly I would like to look at a distinction that is not marked by having a 'different' modal, but with respect to which I suggest that each of the modals is ambiguous. Consider:

i(*a*) You may go now, Smith
 (*b*) He may be in Spain at the moment

(i*b*) is more simply predictive (if we allow for future and non-future 'prediction'),[8] it states a possibility; (*a*) adds an element of 'permission'[9] relevant to the occurrence of the event referred to. Compare with the preceding:

ii(*a*) He can swim
 (*b*) It can happen even today

Once more we have a prediction-like example contrasting with something in which another factor (Palmer's 'ability'[10]) is present, in this case with a minimisation of any 'predictive' element. There is the complicating feature that in many varieties of English as well as (i*a*) we can have:

iii　You can go now, Smith

One way of accommodating this is to regard this particular bundle of semantic features as being manifested either as *can* or *may*.[11] However this is handled, it does not substantially interfere with the distinction I have been trying to draw.

Consider now the following pairs:

iv1(*a*) OK, I'll do it if you like
   (*b*) No doubt it'll rain all day tomorrow

2(*a*) You must go to the dentist
   (*b*) You must be thirty-five, at least

3(*a*) You ought to be more respectful
   (*b*) It ought to be around here somewhere

4(*a*) You should leave me alone
   (*b*) It shouldn't arrive about six

5(*a*) You might visit your mother tomorrow
   (*b*) He might come back at any moment

6(*a*) I could walk fifty miles tomorrow
   (*b*) He could be lying

7(*a*) I would do it if necessary
   (*b*) That wouldn't happen here

In each case,[12] the (*b*) example is intended to illustrate an interpretation for the modal that is simply predictive or conjectural (with more or less assurance – *cf* Diver's 'scale of likelihood'[13]). In the (*a*) examples something else is present, usually characterised by terms like the following: 'volition', 'obligation' ('imaginative' or otherwise), 'permission', 'conditional ability', 'conditional volition' (or 'imaginative volition'), etc.[14] Each of these labels seems to be trying to indicate some factor inherent in or operative upon the subject[15] which is connected with a (possible) prediction. It is difficult at this stage to specify the semantic component relevant to the (*a*) examples any more precisely, in view of the rather diverse nature of the 'factor' involved (as reflected in the labels cited above). How this might be accounted for will, I hope, emerge later in the discussion. For the moment, I propose that we characterise the (*a*) examples as 'complex' (in involving factors other than those directly to do with prediction) and the (*b*) examples, correspondingly, as 'non-complex'.

As a distributional confirmation of this distinction, we can note that, for *may, can, must* and *will*, a complex interpretation becomes (at the least) much less likely when an 'auxiliary *have*' is also present as a constituent of the verb phrase (VP), unless an interpretation involving 'future reference' is possible. That is, if a sequence of one of these modals and 'auxiliary *have*' is interpreted as having 'non-future reference', then a complex interpretation for the modal is very unlikely.

Consider the following instances:

v(a) He may have arrived at six
  (b) He can have gone by then[16]
  (c) He'll have been to South America
  (d) He must have left

This is the case with the modals *may, can, will* and *must.* We shall see below that the division into these modals on the one hand, and *might, could, would, ought* and *should,* on the other, corresponds to the grouping prescribed by a further semantic distinction.

Before looking at this, I want to consider another distinction with respect to which most of the modals are ambiguous. Let us take the complex modals.

vi(a) I can come$\begin{cases}\text{tomorrow}\\\text{if I'm needed}\end{cases}$
  (b) I can swim

The VP in (a) has 'future reference', while that in (b) is 'inclusive of the present' and 'extensive' (this is Palmer's 'ability' use).[17] (a) could be interpreted in the 'permissive' sense that *can* shares with *may* (as, indeed, could (b)) – and we shall come back to this below – but there is a possible non-permissive, future, complex interpretation for *can.* It means something like 'I am in a position to', and is made unambiguous in some dialects of Scots and Northern English as *I'll can come* (vs *I can swim*).

There is a similar possibility with the 'permissive' modal realised alternatively as *can* or *may.* However, in my English, *may* seems to be restricted to the 'future' interpretation, *eg:*

vii(a) You$\left\{\begin{matrix}\text{can}\\\text{may}\end{matrix}\right\}$leave now
  (b) I can go out whenever I please

Thus, complex *may* is not ambiguous in this respect (in my speech). Similarly, *must* has the 'future' possibility only, and for a realisation of the 'present-inclusive' interpretation we must go outside the 'strict modals' to, perhaps, *have to,* which like ('permissive' or 'non-permissive') *can,* is ambiguous with regard to this distinction.[18] So:

viii(a) I$\left\{\begin{matrix}\text{have to}\\\text{must}\end{matrix}\right\}$go now
  (b) I have to visit my sister every month

Not all, then, of the complex modals are ambiguous in this respect. But *will* appears to be like *can* in permitting the ambiguity. Compare:

x(*a*) He'll come tomorrow (if you like)
  (*b*) He'll always help a friend

All the modals *can, may, must* and *will*, in their non-complex inter-pretations, appear to be ambiguous in this respect. So:

x1(*a*) The train $\begin{Bmatrix} can \\ may \end{Bmatrix}$ arrive at any time

  (*b*) The train $\begin{Bmatrix} will \\ must \end{Bmatrix}$ arrive before six

2(*a*) It $\begin{Bmatrix} can \\ may \end{Bmatrix}$ happen, even today

  (*b*) They $\begin{Bmatrix} will \\ must \end{Bmatrix}$ tie it differently in France

And this further difference from the situation with the complex modals provides another motivation for drawing the complex/non-complex distinction as we have done. We can, perhaps, label this new distinc-tion future/non-future.

There is perhaps a further distinction here, concerning the non-complex, non-future modals. It is easiest to see in the case of *will* and *must*. Compare with the examples in (x2*b*) the following:

xi(*a*) Sugar will dissolve in water
  (*b*) Capitalism must lead to war

The examples in (x2*b*) represent predictions/suppositions based on perhaps scanty evidence; those in (xi) are general statements of what is universally the case (*cf* Palmer's 'induction'[19] use). However, this is perhaps an instance where it is more plausible to ascribe the distinc-tion to other elements in the clauses rather than to suggest further polysemy for the modals concerned. The noun phrases in (xi) and like examples seem to be restricted to the generic mass or generic indefinite count varieties (*sugar, man, pigs, any/a particle* (not *some/a particle*), *some kinds of X*, etc).[20] It would seem to be the nature of the NP that is decisive with respect to this particular distinction.

A further possible distinction in these cases is illustrated by the pair:

xii(*a*) That'll be father
  (*b*) They'll not have such problems there

both non-future (or, at least, non-future in one of their interpretations), but the first more 'instantaneous'. But once again I think we can attribute the distinction to elements other than the modal. In this case, the presence of *be* is decisive — in particular 'continuous'/'locative' *be* and its variant *have*[21] rather than 'passive'/'copular' *be*. *Cf*:

xiii1(*a*) She'll be in the kitchen ⎫
   (*b*) They'll be passing through Bolton ⎬ at the moment

2(*a*) She'll be beautiful ⎫
  (*b*) It'll be highly polished ⎬ I expect

It is factors associated with the *be* construction used in the (xiii1) examples with which we can associate the 'instantaneous' element.

Palmer[22] notes another 'use' of *will*, which he labels 'characteristic', and he applies the same label to a 'use' of *can*.[23] This refers to instances like:

xiv(*a*) He'll sit there for hours
  (*b*) He can sit there for hours

Further, it would appear that *must* and *may* also appear with such an interpretation. *Cf*:

xv(*a*) He must sit there for hours ⎫
  (*b*) He may sit there for hours ⎬ without catching anything

This is not merely a special case of the complex interpretation ('habitual volition', etc), since clauses with subjects that would not normally permit a complex interpretation (otherwise) (*cf* note 8) can be found with a 'characteristic' interpretation.

xvi   It ⎧(*a*) will ⎫
         ⎨(*b*) can ⎬ rain for hours in Stockport
         ⎪(*c*) must ⎪
         ⎩(*d*) may ⎭

Such examples are also non-future rather than future.[24] Compare:

xvii1(*a*) It'll rain next Sunday
   (*b*) It'll rain for hours
  2   It'll rain for hours next Sunday

Of the (1) examples only (*b*) permits a 'characteristic' interpretation; and if it is interpreted as having future reference only (as made explicit in (2)), then it ceases to be 'characteristic'. However, once again, rather than propose a further ambiguity for the modals, we can perhaps in this case relate the distinction in meaning between the examples in (xiv), (xv), (xvi) and (xvii1b), and those in, say (x2), to the conjunction of a particular type of adverbial element and a 'non-continuous' verbal form – together requiring an 'iterative' interpretation. *He'll be sitting there for hours* has no strong 'characteristic' suggestion, though this possibility is not ruled out. Consider too the following examples:

xviii(*a*) He may stay there for hours
 (*b*) He stays there for hours
 (*c*) He may be staying there for hours
 (*d*) He is staying there for hours

It seems to me that the (*c*) and (*d*) examples are not necessarily iterative, the (*a*) example may be (it is ambiguous between a 'characteristic' non-future and a future interpretation), and (*b*) would normally be interpreted as 'iterative'.[25] The distinction in question, then, would seem to have nothing essentially to do with modals.

Thus, certain possible cases of modal polysemy are perhaps to be accounted for otherwise. There may be a case for reconsidering the other ambiguities suggested for the modals (particularly the future/non-future one, with respect to which it is probably more just to say that the modals are 'indifferent' – rather than ambiguous), but, for the moment, let us consider the individual modals to be ambiguous with respect to the complex/non-complex and (in most cases) the future/non-future interpretations. Having suggested this, I want now to turn to the (non-ambiguous) distinction hinted at above, in the course of the discussion of the complex/non-complex distinction.

A superficial distinction can be drawn between those modals which can be grouped into 'simple'/'modified' pairs, like *can* and *could* (assuming this grouping is valid), and those which do not, on the surface, enter into such groupings, namely *must* and *ought* (*to*) (and *used* (*to*)). In the case of *can/could*, *may/might* and *will/would*, it is possible to suggest that these pairings are also semantically appropriate. That is, it seems plausible to regard the 'modified' member of each of these pairs as differing from the 'simple' member by the presence of a particular component but otherwise sharing the same set of components. This is slightly complicated by the fact that the difference in shape in the case of, *eg*, *can* and *could*, relates not to a single distinction, but to two possible differences in componence. Consider:

xix He could run five miles $\begin{cases} (a) \text{ tomorrow (if necessary)} \\ (b) \text{ in those days} \end{cases}$

He could run five miles is ambiguous between a 'past-time' interpretation and what Palmer[26] calls a 'tentative use' and Jespersen[27] 'imaginative'. To account for this, we can assign to *could* two distinct but
overlapping sets of components, one containing a 'past' component
(contrasting with the 'non-past' of *can*), the other a 'conditional' component (contrasting with the 'non-conditional' of *can*).[28]

   This would seem to provide a reasonable account of the relationship
between *can* and *could*, *will* and *would*, and *may* and *might* – except
that, in my speech at least, there is no 'past' interpretation possible in
the case of *might* – I shall return to this below. A greater difficulty,
however, is presented by the similar-looking pair of *shall* and *should*.
Should, like *might*, has no 'past' interpretation. But, further, it is even
difficult to construe as the 'conditional form' of *shall*.[29] Indeed, *should*
seems to be interpretable as the conditional equivalent of *shall* only in
those cases where *shall* represents a 'stylistic variant'[30] of (an interpretation represented in other circumstances by) *will*. This is where *shall*
and *will* represent what Jespersen[31] calls 'a pure future', without factors of 'volition', etc. Consider:

xx(*a*) I shall be in London on Tuesday
   (*b*) He will be in London on Tuesday

In my own spoken English, *shall* and *will* are interchangeable in such
sentences. In other varieties (including my written one) there may be
found the situation described in many grammars,[32] whereby, in positive declaratives, *shall* appears with the 'first person', *will* otherwise,
and there are further rules governing their distribution in interrogative
and negative clauses. These are largely referable to a principle by
which the one form is used (for the 'future') where the other one might
be (or might have been) ambiguous between its non-complex ('pure
future') and (actual or former) complex interpretations.[33] Whatever
the rules determining distribution, the two forms (as 'pure futures')
are not to be assigned different sets of semantic components. In some
accents, at least, *should* appears as the conditional variant of *shall* in
this interpretation. *Cf*:

xxi(*a*) I should go mad $\left.\begin{matrix} \\ \end{matrix}\right\}$ if that happened
   (*b*) He would go mad

But, as noted above, *should* does not appear with a 'past' interpretation, even as a 'stylistic' variant of *would*. Thus:

xxii(*a*) I
   (*b*) He } would often visit her (in the old days)

We can represent this situation as follows (omitting 'past' forms):

xxiii

	NON-CONDITIONAL	CONDITIONAL
COMPLEX	will	would
NON-COMPLEX	shall/will	should/would

We must now look at other instances of *should* and *shall*, with a view to extending (and perhaps otherwise modifying) this table.

However, with respect to my own speech, it was perhaps misleading to say that *should* is the conditional equivalent of *shall* only in such cases as we have just been looking at. Such a statement implies that *shall* appears with other interpretations. In my English, and varieties described by Ehrman,[34] this is not the case: *shall* appears only with a simple predictive interpretation, and only as a variant of *will*. Thus, in this case, *shall* is defective not *should*. There is an interpretation for *should* that is not a simple conditional prediction (*ie*, that is complex), which is not matched by a corresponding (non-conditional) interpretation for *shall*. There is also a simple predictive (non-complex) interpretation for *should* distinct from the interpretation with respect to which it alternates with *would*. We have already exemplified (and differentiated between) these interpretations in (iv4). The former (complex) interpretation is what Jespersen[35] calls the 'obligational' use of *should*. More particularly, he terms this use 'imaginative obligation'; the parallel use of *would* is called 'imaginative volition'. This parallelism seems semantically just. Just as *would* is the 'conditional' (or 'imaginative') equivalent of *will* (in both a complex and a non-complex interpretation), I would suggest that *should* (complex, and also non-complex) is most satisfactorily interpretable as a 'conditional'. Palmer[36] recognises it as a 'tentative' form (along with *could*, *would* and *might*), but notes the problem presented by pairing it with *shall*. We seem, then, to have the following situation. Certain instances of *should* represent a variant (either free or conditioned) of non-complex *would*, on a par with the relationship between *shall* and *will*. But there are other instances of *should* where it is clearly not just an alternative for *would*, and where *shall*, having in its non-complex interpretation 'fallen together' with *will* and (in some accents at least) having been eliminated in its complex function, no longer represents the non-conditional equivalent of this 'independent' *should*.[37] The questions now arise: is this *should* to be interpreted as a conditional, and, if so, what is the corresponding non-conditional form? A look at two further pairs of modals might suggest some answers.

Firstly, *may* and *might*. *Might* has no 'past' interpretation, but (as suggested above) it seems possible to interpret it as the conditional equivalent of (complex or non-complex) *may*. Consider:

xxiv1(*a*) It may arrive tomorrow
    (*b*) It might arrive tomorrow
  2(*a*) You may go home now
    (*b*) You might go home now

The (*b*) instance in each pair is more 'tentative'. (Indeed, examples like (2*b*) are often to be interpreted as tendering a suggestion rather than giving permission – particularly if we substitute something like *a bit more often* for *now* in this example.) Compare these now with similar examples involving *must* and *ought* (*to*) (neither of which once again has a 'past' interpretation[38]):

xxv1(*a*) It must be in the study
    (*b*) It ought to be in the study
  2(*a*) He must behave more sensibly
    (*b*) He ought to behave more sensibly

Once more, the (*b*) instances are more 'tentative'. In (2) *ought to* 'leaves open the possibility of non-action'[39] as compared with *must*. It is tempting, in view of the semantic parallel here, to interpret *ought* (*to*) as the conditional equivalent of *must*.

However, I would further suggest that *ought* (*to*) is merely *one* conditional equivalent of *must*. By Zandvoort,[40] for example, *must*, *ought* and *should* are grouped together, and, within that grouping, *ought* and *should* are distinguished from *must*, as expressing 'moral obligation or desirability' or 'strong probability' as opposed to 'necessity' or 'an assumption or conclusion'. 'Independent' *should*, as we have seen, lacks a 'past' interpretation, and seemed to lack a non-conditional equivalent. In view of this, and of the fairly general agreement on the semantic equivalence of *should* and *ought* (*to*) (in this respect), it seems plausible to regard *must* as being complemented by two conditional forms.

Note too that, if such an analysis is accepted, the conditional/nonconditional distinction now divides *may, will, can* and *must* from the others – which division coincides with one we found relevant in discussing interpretations compatible with co-occurrence with 'auxiliary *have*' (see above (v)). VP's containing complex conditionals and 'auxiliary *have*' may have 'past reference' (unlike those with complex nonconditionals and *have*). Consider:

$$
\text{xxvi} \quad \text{He} \begin{cases} (a) \text{ would} \\ (b) \text{ could} \\ (c) \text{ ought to} \\ (d) \text{ might} \end{cases} \text{have come more often}
$$

We can now perhaps extend the table suggested in (xxiii), so:

xxvii

	CON-DITIONAL	NON-CONDITIONAL		CON-DITIONAL
COMPLEX	would	will	must (have to)	should/ought
NON-COMPLEX	should/would	shall/will	must	should/ought
	non-'X'		'X'	

(where 'X' represents a component or components the nature of which we shall have to investigate below). There are certain varieties of English in which some sort of 'independent' (complex) *shall* is retained (*cf* note 37). In such accents, *shall* may be said to share the role of non-conditional equivalent of complex *should/ought* (*to*) with *must* (/*have to*). The distinction between *shall* and *must* would seem to have to do with whether or not dependence on the speaker's (or addressee's, in a question) will is being emphasised (*shall*) or not (*must*).[41] As we shall see immediately below, this is quite a different distinction from that which separates *will* from both *must* and *shall* (the latter, of course only in the accents we have been looking at) – *ie*, 'X'/non-'X' – ; and the distinction between *shall* and *must* is subordinate to 'X'/non-'X'.

Let us, then, look at what separates *will*, etc, from *must*, etc. In discussing 'independent *shall*' (his 'promise' use), Palmer[42] distinguishes it from *will* as indicating 'that the initiation of the activity is always *external* to the subject'. This accounts for, among other things, the possible complex interpretation (in accents with 'independent *shall*') of *shall I* . . .? questions, since the activity is to be initiated by the person addressed, not the subject (the speaker in this case). However, the above observation of Palmer's also seems to hold for *must* as opposed to *will*, and *may* (and 'permissive' *can*) as opposed to ('non-permissive') *can*. Compare the complex interpretations for the following clauses:

xxviii 1(*a*) He will
    (*b*) He can
                 }leave tomorrow
   2(*a*) He must
    (*b*) He may/can

In the (2) instances the initiation of the action comes from outside the subject: an 'external' agent (supplying 'permission' or imposing 'obligation') is suggested (*cf* note 8). – I shall pursue this aspect further below. For the moment, compare further the following (in a complex interpretation):

xxix 1(*a*) I could do that
    (*b*) I would do that   {if I had to
   2(*a*) *I might do that   {if I was allowed to
    (*b*) *I ought to do that

In particular, then, in those accents with 'independent *shall*', both *must* and *shall* differ from *will* in suggesting initiation for the action external to the subject. *Shall* differs from *must* in making it explicit that the initiation is dependent on the speaker (or addressee); with *must*, it may or may not be. If we want a label for this subordinate distinction, it might be 'egocentric' vs 'non-egocentric' (though this is not appropriate in questions). We have already noted that *might* and *ought (to)/ should* lack a past interpretation. This distinguishes them from *could* and *would*, which do permit such. – Consider the examples in (xix), in which *would* can be substituted for *could* in both instances. A grouping of *can/could* and *will/would* is thus desirable on these grounds as well.[43]

Let us, then, label *must*, etc, and *may*, etc, 'external', and *will*, etc, and *can*, etc 'non-external'.[44] We can substitute 'external' for 'X' in the table in (xxvii), and extend it to include the *can* and *may* distinctions:

XXX		CON-DITIONAL	NON-CONDITIONAL		CON-DITIONAL	
	COMPLEX	would	will	must (have to)/ shall	should/ ought to	non-'Y'
	NON-COMPLEX	should/ would	shall/ will	must	should/ ought to	
		could	can	may	might	'Y'
	COMPLEX	could	can	can/ may	could/ might	
		NON-EXTERNAL		EXTERNAL		

(where 'Y' represents a component or components the nature of which we have still to determine). I want to return below to some further points concerning the external/non-external distinction (particularly with regard to the non-complex modals, which we have not considered above). But before doing so, we should perhaps attempt to identify 'Y', and, indeed, determine whether the table is correct in (without discussion) grouping together *can* and *may* as against *will* and *must*.

In suggesting that there was a parallel relationship between *can* and *may*, on the one hand, and *will* and *must* on the other, we have presumed groupings in accordance with the table in (xxx), in particular with respect to Y and non-Y. Most accounts of the modals[45] group together *can/could* and *may/might*. Their non-complex interpretations are semantically very close (and I shall be discussing this further below). With a complex interpretation, we have already noted that both *can* and *may* can represent the external 'Y' modal; that this has come to be the case suggests a closeness of relationship between the external and non-external interpretations labelled Y. The grouping in general seems to me intuitively sound, and underlies the acceptability or non-acceptibility of the following examples containing non-future complex modals:

xxxi 1(a) He can swim now ('non-external')
   (b) He can swim now ('external')   but perhaps he
   2(a) *He has to swim now   won't (today)
   (b) *He will swim now

Joos[46] describes *can* and *may* in terms of 'potentiality' (vs the 'assurance' of the others). I propose that we adopt his term and substitute 'potential' for 'Y' in the table in (xxx).

Let us now return to the external/non-external distinction. If we compare the non-complex interpretations of *can* and *may*, *could* and *might*, *will* and *must*, and *would* and *should/ought* (*to*), respectively, it becomes clear that the external/non-external distinction is in general considerably attenuated as compared with the corresponding complex pairs we considered above. Compare the following non-complex pairs:

xxxii 1(a) It can happen tomorrow
   (b) It may happen tomorrow
   2(a) It could be Uncle Fred
   (b) It might be Uncle Fred
   3(a) That'll be Uncle Fred
   (b) That must be Uncle Fred
   4(a) He would be in his study at this time of day
   (b) He ought to be in his study at this time of day

This has been observed quite often with regard to *can* and *may*, and *could* and *might* – cf, for instance, the discussion by Lebrun[47] (who goes as far as to suggest the synonymity of *can* and *may* in all instances where they can both occur[48]), and the assignment by Palmer[49] of 'possibility' uses to all four of them. However, I would suggest that there is a similar tendency in the other group, the non-potentials. It is indeed likely that such a tendency underlies many of the 'shifts' that have occurred in the history of the English modals.[50]

I would like to move on now to consider in a little more detail modal forms with past reference. We noted above that only the non-external modals disposed of forms permitting past reference. *Would* and *could* can be interpreted as the past equivalents of *will* and *can* (as well as their conditional equivalents). Do they also share the same distinctions as the non-past forms? A future interpretation for *would* is, as Palmer[51] points out, mostly restricted to literary works. – Such an interpretation seems to pre-suppose an extended narrative context. Consider:

xxxiii   He would soon be sixty-four

as an instance of a non-complex future in the past. *Could* does not seem likely in such an example, unless it is an instance of 'reported speech' or 'narrated thought'. It is also only in such a situation that complex future in the past interpretations are possible with either *would* or *could*; and *must* and *might* are also possible then. So:

$$\text{xxxiv   (She said that) he} \begin{cases} (a) \text{ would} \\ (b) \text{ could} \\ (c) \text{ must} \end{cases} \text{show them who was boss}$$

However, complex non-future interpretations for both *could* and *would* seem possible. Consider:

$$\text{xxxv} \begin{matrix} (a) \text{ That shop would accept cheques} \\ (b) \text{ He could swim} \end{matrix} \Big\} \text{in those days}$$

Similarly with equivalent non-complex interpretations:

$$\text{xxvi   It} \begin{cases} (a) \text{ would} \\ (b) \text{ could} \end{cases} \text{rain during our holidays}$$

But it is not quite as simple as that.

I tried above to account for the 'characteristic' interpretation noted, for instance, by Palmer[52] and exemplified in (xiv), (xv) and (xvi) in terms of the occurrence of a certain type of adverbial with a 'non-continuous' verbal form. However, if we now look at the past forms, it would seem that all instances of (past) non-future *would* are to be interpreted as 'characteristic', in that they relate to habitually repeated events. Consider:

$$\text{xxxvii   He would live in that house} \begin{cases} (a) \text{ whenever he came} \\ (b) \text{ (in those days)} \end{cases}$$

In the (a) example the 'iterativeness' is marked in the subordinating conjunction. But (b) too is to be interpreted as iterative (otherwise, it is unacceptable). The 'non-characteristic' equivalent would appear to be *used (to)*:

xxxviii   He used to live in that house (in those days)

In this case there is no requirement for the interpretation to include 'repetition' (though this is not excluded).[53]

This seems to suggest that the characteristic/non-characteristic distinction is directly involved in the subcategorisation of the modals, in that this is what separates *would* from *used (to)*. However, I would suggest that a rather different account is preferable. – Namely, that in all such instances of *would*, there is an 'iterative' adverbial in the underlying structure. *Would* is thus interpreted as a variant of *used (to)* which can appear only in such a context. If the adverbial element that thus makes possible the selection of *would* is itself deleted (as in (xxvii*b*)), then the presence of *would* (as opposed to *used (to)*) may be the only *superficial* marker of 'iterativeness'.[54] This seems to me preferable to suggesting that the difference in modal shape reflects directly such a deep structure distinction, which would add a number of anomalies to the modal subcategorisation. (However, compare the discussion in Part 2.)

Would and *could* are ambiguous between conditional and past interpretations. We should also consider whether there is another possibility, an interpretation that is *both* conditional and past. Once more, I find it difficult to substantiate such an interpretation outside of 'indirect speech'. In general, a conditional interpretation is limited to the non-past modals. The gap seems to be filled by one interpretation of the sequences *would have, could have, might have, should have*. And this presents us with the sort of problem that I want now to consider in more detail, as a prelude to a suggested alternative account of the modals (which nevertheless will have to take account of the distinctions we have drawn so far). A more formal presentation (in the terms suggested in note 5) of the subcategorisation discussed so far is proposed in the appendix to Part 1. This is intended to provide a more explicit formulation of the relationships holding between the distinctions I have suggested as relevant to the descriptions of the modals, whose relation to the different modal 'forms' is tabulated in (xxx) (with the exception of ± future). However, I want now to review various further phenomena suggesting a somewhat different derivation for the modals from the simple subcategorisation of VP attempted there and presupposed in the above discussion.

Appendix: some rules

The following rules are suggested as a possible characterisation of the subclassification of the modals proposed in the first part of this paper. They consist of a set of subcategorisation rules for VP and an associated set of constituency rules which introduce M as a constituent of VP and add to it (and to the tense marker) various terminal features. The nature of the different types of rules and of the various sets of primes has been discussed elsewhere;[55] and the interpretation of the present account is dependent on the discussion and the references presented there.

The first relevant subcategorisation rule would presumably be:

i   VP → ± modal

However, also relevant to our discussion has been the past/non-past distinction. This distinction is present whether + modal or − modal is selected; the two distinctions are 'simultaneous'. So:

ii $VP \rightarrow \begin{bmatrix} \pm\,\text{modal} \\ \pm\,\text{past} \end{bmatrix}$

If + modal is selected, then various other of the distinctions we have been discussing become relevant. Thus:

ii $+\,\text{modal} \rightarrow \begin{bmatrix} \pm\,\text{potential} \\ \pm\,\text{complex} \end{bmatrix}$

That is, if the VP is + modal, it is further either + potential or − potential, and either + complex or − complex. These particular further oppositions are independent of the ± past distinction, since a + potential modal may be either + past or − past (*could*/*can*); and so can a − potential modal (*would*/*will*). Similarly with ± complex.

However, there are certain modal forms that have no + past equivalent; and this is accounted for by the following rule:

iv $\begin{bmatrix} +\,\text{modal} \\ -\,\text{past} \end{bmatrix} \rightarrow \pm\,\text{external}$

This accounts for the absence of a + past equivalent for *may* (which is + potential but + external) and *must* (which is − potential but + external). If + past is chosen there is no opposition between + external and − external, and only the unmarked possibility occurs (*could* and *would*). (Considerations like these help to motivate the choice of 'marked' and 'unmarked' in an opposition; the unmarked alternative is (semantically and syntactically) equivalent to non-operation of the rule, except that certain further oppositions may depend on the selection of an unmarked alternative (as in (iv)).

We also found it difficult to substantiate a 'past conditional' interpretation for a simple modal form, rather than a modal + *have* sequence, say. We can, then, perhaps extend the rule in (iv):

$$\text{v} \quad \begin{bmatrix} +\text{modal} \\ -\text{past} \end{bmatrix} \rightarrow \begin{bmatrix} \pm\text{external} \\ \pm\text{conditional} \end{bmatrix}$$

We can amalgamate rules (iii) and (v) as the composite:

$$\text{vi} \quad +\text{modal} \rightarrow \begin{bmatrix} \begin{bmatrix} \pm\text{external} \\ \pm\text{conditional} \end{bmatrix} / \begin{bmatrix} \text{---} \\ -\text{past} \end{bmatrix} \\ \pm\text{potential} \\ \pm\text{complex} \end{bmatrix}$$

All of these further distinctions are dependent on +modal, but some are possible only in a particular environment, −past (*ie*, the complex symbol containing +modal must also contain −past).

Other distinctions seemed more appropriately construed as relevant to some element other than M. These could be relevant to selectional rules for M (as in the case of *used* (*to*) and *would*). But I do not intend to try and incorporate these here. There remains, however, the future/non-future distinction, if we consider this to be a modal distinction – the discussion in Part 2 makes this seem unlikely. This *could* be included perhaps on a par with ±potential and ±complex. Past futures for the modals seem somewhat marginal, however; and we could exclude them by grouping ±future with ±external. In either case, we should need to determine the relative ordering of ±future and ±conditional. The most plausible solution would seem to be to regard ±conditional as simultaneous with ±future, since conditionals may have either future or non-future reference:

$$\text{vii} \quad +\text{modal} \rightarrow \begin{bmatrix} \pm\text{external} \\ \pm\text{future} \\ \pm\text{conditional} \end{bmatrix} / \begin{bmatrix} \text{---} \\ -\text{past} \end{bmatrix}$$

(But a consideration of examples with conditionals merely confirms that the future/non-future distinction is essentially non-modal.)

We might have the following constituency rules:

viii1 $VP \rightarrow Tns + V$

2(a) $+modal \rightarrow M // Tns\underline{\quad}$

(b) $\left\{ \begin{matrix} +past \\ +conditional \end{matrix} \right\} \rightarrow pret // \left[\begin{matrix} Tns \\ \underline{\quad} \end{matrix} \right]$

The other constituency rules (for +complex, +external and +potential (and +future)) will add terminal features to M. Thus, for each modal interpretation there will be a unique complex symbol consisting of M, as category, and features like external, potential, etc. Polysemy occurs when a single modal form represents more than one complex symbol, and synonymity when one complex symbol has alternative representations. So:

ix

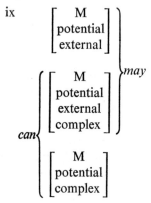

The subcategorisation rules could alternatively be presented as a 'system network':[56]

x

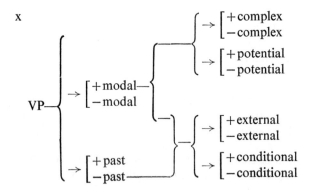

2 On the superficial status of the modals

One set of phenomena which will interest us here is connected with negation. Palmer,[57] for instance, points out there are two semantically distinct possibilities with *can*: *can't* (or *cannot*) and *can not* (with greater prominence given to the second word). As he puts it: '*can't* negates (semantically) the ability (or permission to act), while *can not* positively states ability (or permission) not to act'. We appear here to have two independent systems of negation, one applying to 'the meaning of the modal', the other to 'the meaning of the main verb'. So:

xxxix(*a*) It can't be true
    (*b*) It can not be true/It can be untrue[58]

or (with a complex interpretation):

xl(*a*) I can't leave tomorrow
   (*b*) I can not leave tomorrow

There is no parallel distinction with the equivalent non-complex external modal, *may*. Here, the phonetic distinction merely marks a difference in emphasis:

xli(*a*) It may not happen
   (*b*) It may *not* happen

(Note too the lack in my English of a contracted form: no non-complex *mayn't*.) However, we would seem to have to allow for the possibility with the complex equivalent:

xlii(*a*) He mayn't/may not/can't come
    (*b*) He may *not*/can not come

But the alternative with *may* in instance (*b*) I think somewhat unlikely for my speech.[59] Palmer, too, does not allow for them in his discussion of negation. However, he does cite along with the *can* forms a parallel series involving *must* and *need*: *You must go, You needn't go, You mustn't go*, parallel to *You can go, You can not go, You can't go*.[60] This applies to both complex and non-complex instances. So:

xliii1(*a*) You mustn't come today
     (*b*) You needn't come today
   2(*a*) He mustn't be in his study
    (*b*) He needn't be in his study

This suggests, among other things, that *need* is to be explained as, in this 'use', a variant of *must*, realising one of the two interpretations possible 'under negation'. An account of this in terms of the simple subclassificatory derivation suggested in Part 1 and developed in the appendix, would be rather cumbersome and unrevealing.

Palmer[61] also notes that in the case of VP's containing modals 'reference to past time is made with *have*'. Indeed, a form like *may have* is ambiguous between 'past' and 'perfect' interpretations. Compare:

xliv1(*a*) They may have done that in 200 BC
     (*b*) They may have arrived already

    2(*a*) *They have done that in 200 BC
     (*b*) They have arrived already

When the modal is present there is an additional possibility; from the occurrence of *have* elsewhere we would expect only (*b*) of the examples in (xliv1). Consider the ambiguity of *They may have been imprisoned:*

xlv   They may have been imprisoned $\begin{cases} (a) \text{ for that in those days} \\ (b) \text{ since we last heard} \end{cases}$

Again, only the (*b*) example is predictable from the 'behaviour' of *have* in the absence of a modal. The sequence *must have* (containing the other external modal) is similarly ambiguous:

xlvi   They must have been imprisoned $\begin{cases} (a) \text{ for that in those days} \\ (b) \text{ since we last heard} \end{cases}$

Examples with the other (*ie*, non-external) modals are also possible, but instance of *can* with *have* are in general rather marginal (unless negatived).[62] We also noted above that there was a past interpretation possible for a sequence of conditional modal + 'auxiliary *have*'. Phenomena like these can only with difficulty be added to the account of the modals given above; and once again the result would be rather unrevealing.

Such are phenomena not provided for in the above account. But even where the subcategorisation seemed appropriate and fairly natural, there are inadequacies. We have failed to explain why these particular ambiguities occur. Most of the labels have been perforce vague ('complex', 'external'), because the subcategorisation does not provide us with a framework for explaining the groupings and the contectual restrictions that have helped us to identify them. The subcategorisation seems to me to provide for the most part intuitively satisfying groupings that can be related to these restrictions, but does not provide in a systematic way a deeper insight into the semantic relations underlying the groupings and the contextual elements they select or reject. I think this will only be possible if we relate the modal subcategorisation to a wider range of (semantically, and, I think it can be shown, syntactically) related phenomena (where often, for instance, a modal ambiguity is resolved as two distinct forms).

Kruisinga[63] points out that 'in some uses *can* and *could* are alternatives of the group *to be able*'. More specifically, *to be able* can be related to complex *can* (expressing 'ability or capability, power or fitness'):[64]

xlvii He
$$
\begin{cases}
1(a) \text{ can} \\
\quad (b) \text{ could} \\
\quad (c) \text{ could} \\
2(a) \text{ is able to} \\
\quad (b) \text{ was able to} \\
\quad (c) \text{ would be able to}
\end{cases}
\text{tell fortunes}
$$

However, as Kruisinga goes on to indicate, the correspondence is only partial, in that complex non-external *can/could* matches only part of the paradigm of *be able to*.[65] Consider:

xlviii 1(a) I am able to
   (b) I can } swim

2(a) I am able to
  (b) I can } come tomorrow

3(a) I was able to
  (b) I could } swim in those days

4(a) I was able to catch the bus (this morning)[66]
  (b)

5(a) I shall be able to run for 5 miles when I grow up[67]
  (b)

6(a) I (shall) have been able to swim for years
  (b)

Kruisinga[68] also notes that certain uses of *may* are paralleled by 'forms of' *be allowed* (and also, I would suggest, *be permitted*). He further points out that *be* + V + *ed/en* is ambiguous between two interpretations, as indicating either (what he calls) 'state' or 'occurrence'.[69] It is the 'state' interpretation that *may* is to be matched with, and once again, with only part of the paradigm. We have already noted the absence of a 'past tense' interpretation for *might* (in my English, at least). Compare the following examples with those with for *can/be able to:*

xlix1(*a*) I am allowed/permitted to⎫
    (*b*) I can   ⎬swim

  2(*a*) I am allowed/permitted to⎫
    (*b*) I can/may   ⎬come tomorrow

  3(*a*) I was allowed/permitted to⎫
    (*b*) I could (?)[70]   ⎬swim

  4(*a*) I was allowed/permitted to get up early this morning
    (*b*)

  5(*a*) I shall be allowed/permitted to swim
    (*b*)

  6(*a*) I (shall) have been allowed/permitted to swim for years
    (*b*)

'State' vs 'occurrence' may be said to characterise the difference in the interpretations of *was allowed/permitted* in (3) and (4), respectively. But this distinction is clearly paralleled by (3) and (4) in (xlviii) (with *be able*). Thus, the distinction is not limited to obviously 'deverbative' adjectives;[71] it is the 'state' alternative with which the modal is associated in both cases.

I would also suggest that there is a *be* + adjective analogue for *will*, *viz*: *be willing to*, and that *must* is paralleled by (forms of) *be obliged to*, *be required to*, *be compelled to*, once again with a 'state' interpretation. Thus:

lA1(*a*) He is willing to⎫
    (*b*) He will   ⎬put up with a lot

  2(*a*) He is willing to⎫
    (*b*) He will   ⎬come tomorrow

  3(*a*) He was willing to⎫
    (*b*) He would   ⎬accept that in those days

  4(*a*) He was willing to come at the time[72]
    (*b*)

  5(*a*) He will be willing to live there
    (*b*)

  6(*a*) He (will) have been willing to come for years
    (*b*)

ʙ1(a) I am obliged to ⎱
  (b) I have to   ⎰ visit her every day (at the moment)

2(a) I am obliged to ⎱
  (b) I must/have to   ⎰ leave tomorrow

3(a) I was obliged to ⎱
  (b) I had to   ⎰ live there

4(a) I was obliged to ⎱
  (b) I had to   ⎰ leave that morning

5(a) I shall be obliged to ⎱
  (b) I shall have to   ⎰ revise my opinions

6(a) I (shall) have been obliged to ⎱
  (b) I (shall) have had to   ⎰ live here for years

We have already noted the absence of a non-future interpretation and of a past one for *must* (and *may*), and these are added, in this case, to the instances in which *can* did not parallel the *be able to* form. *Have (to)*, however, has a full range of possibilities (with even 'non-state' instances). An intermediate state is represented by *have got (to)*, which has a range like that for *can*. I shall return to this below.

Each of the complex modals, then, can be related to a sequence of *be* + adjective, the external modals differing from the non-external in being paralleled by a 'passive' adjective (*be permitted, be obliged*) compared with a 'non-passive' (*be able, be willing*).[73] So far I have been talking rather imprecisely about parallels, analogues, matches. This further correspondence (between type of adjective and subcategory of modal) suggests a rather more systematic relation. What I want to propose is that the sequence of *be* + adjective and the corresponding complex modal are derived from the same underlying (two-clause) structure (with the modal representing the greater deformation). This would seem to me semantically satisfying. It also enables us to relate the modals systematically to parts of the *be* + adjective paradigms (and thus to formulate more precisely their range of meanings), and provides insight into, for instance, the external/non-external distinction. I hope to suggest some further benefits of such an analysis below.[74]

One thing, however, that is immediately suggested is that the future/non-future distinction was incorrectly suggested to be directly relevant to the subcategorisation of the modals. The futurity or non-futurity is to be associated with the subordinate (non-modal) clause. The modals are always in relation with non-future *be* + adjective forms: the true futures (for the main clause underlying the *be* + adjective or modal part of the sentence) are forms like *I shall be able to*, forms for which there are no modal equivalents. In the case of the modals, the willingness, obligation, ability or permission are tied to the present, though the act denoted by the main verb may be future (and, in the case of *must* and *may*, must be future).

However, what about the non-complex modals? These do not appear to be easily associable with the *be* + adjective forms related to their complex equivalents, nor do they even seem to be paralleled by instances with a similar structure. Thus, non-complex *can* and *may* are paralleled by *it is possible that/for . . . , . . . possibly . . .* ; *must/need* by *I'm sure/certain/convinced that . . . , . . . bound to . . . , . . . surely . . . , . . . necessarily . . . .* So:

liA1(*a*) It's possible for it to ⎱ happen (even today)
   (*b*) It can ⎰

  2(*a*) It's possible that he'll ⎫
   (*b*) He'll possibly ⎬ arrive late
   (*c*) He may ⎭

  3(*a*) It was possible for it to ⎱ break down (in those days)
   (*b*) It could ⎰

B1(*a*) I'm sure that's ⎫
  (*b*) That's surely ⎪
  (*c*) That's {bound / sure} to be ⎬ father now
  (*d*) That must be ⎭

2(*a*) I'm sure it'll ⎫
  (*b*) It'll surely ⎪
  (*c*) It's {bound / sure} to ⎬ arrive before six
  (*d*) It must ⎭

3(*a*) I'm not sure that he'll ⎫
  (*b*) He won't necessarily ⎬ be in his study
  (*c*) He needn't ⎭

(I would like to postpone for the moment a discussion of the problems associated with non-complex *will*.) Once again I would suggest a common source for these variants, including the modal possibility. That is, *it's possible that . . . , . . . possibly . . . , . . . may . . .* are all to be derived from the same underlying (two-clause) structure (in those cases where all are possible – once more the modal matches only part of the paradigm of the fuller forms). In this case also we seem to have an intermediate stage between the full form (*cf* complex *must/have to*) and the modal, *viz* an alternant containing a 'sentence adverb'.[75] Similarly related are *I'm sure/convinced that* . . . ,[76] . . . *bound/sure to* . . . , . . . *surely* . . . and . . . *must* . . . , and *I'm not sure that* . . . , . . . *not necessarily* . . . , and *needn't* . . . .[77] In this case, we have two types of 'intermediate' variant, one of them again a 'sentence adverb'.[78]

In (li A) *can* as well as *may* was matched with forms containing *be possible*. Are they then to be derived from the same underlying structure (in cases where both are possible)? If so, how are we to reconcile this with the fact that, although the distinction may be so slight that Lebrun[79] can describe them as being 'in free variation', generally we (as native speakers) are reluctant to admit synonymity (despite our difficulties in 'pinning down' the distinction we feel to be there)? Compare:

lii   It$\left\{\begin{array}{l}(a)\ \text{can}\\(b)\ \text{may}\end{array}\right\}$fall down tomorrow

Here (*a*) suggests that the circumstances favouring (or at least not preventing) the 'falling down' exist; the *tomorrow* may be almost incidental, exemplificatory. Whereas (*b*) asserts the possibility or an event taking place tomorrow.[80] Moreover, we seem to find a similar distinction with two structures both containing *possible*. *Cf:*

liii (*a*) It's possible for it to happen tomorrow
     (*b*) It's possible that it will happen tomorrow

But perhaps these merely increase the scope of the problem, since are not (liii *a*) and (liii *b*) to be related to the same underlying structure? A consideration of this problem must await discussion of related phenomena, and I shall return to it below.

Immediately, however, I would like to extend our appraisal of the future/non-future distinction to the non-complex modals. We can associate with the future and non-future interpretations of the modal a full variant with and without *will* (respectively) in the subordinate clause. Thus:

liv A1(*a*) It's possible that he'll leave tomorrow
     (*b*) He'll possibly leave tomorrow
     (*c*) He may leave tomorrow

2(*a*) It's possible that he's telling the truth
   (*b*) He's possibly telling the truth
   (*c*) He may be telling the truth

B1(*a*) I'm sure they'll arrive soon
   (*b*) They're bound to arrive soon
   (*c*) They'll surely arrive soon
   (*d*) They must arrive soon

2(*a*) I'm sure he's on his way
   (*b*) He's bound to be on his way
   (*c*) He's surely on his way
   (*d*) He must be on his way

Again we can suggest that the ambiguity arises from the fact that (non-complex) *may* (and *can*) and *must* are derived from alternative underlying structures, one containing a 'predictive' category (in the underlying subordinate clause) written out in the 'full versions' as *will*, the other lacking this category.

However, did we not note in Part 1 that non-complex *will* itself was ambiguous in what looked like a parallel fashion? Consider:

lv (*a*) It'll $\left\{\begin{array}{l}\text{probably}\\\text{possibly}\\\text{certainly}\\\text{surely}\end{array}\right\}$ fall down tomorrow

   (*b*) He'll $\left\{\begin{array}{l}\text{probably}\\\text{possibly}\\\text{certainly}\\\text{surely}\end{array}\right\}$ be in his study at the moment

Perhaps, then, non-complex *may*, etc, are ambiguous in this further way, in that the interpretation associated with the derivation from a structure containing a predictive category (otherwise appearing as *will*) is in itself ambiguous between present and future reference. Compare:

lvi 1(*a*) It is possible that that is true
    (*b*) That is possibly true
    (*c*) That may be true

2(*a*) It is possible that it will fall down
   (*b*) It will possibly fall down
   (*c*) It may fall down

3(*a*) It is possible that that will be Uncle George
  (*b*) That'll possibly be Uncle George
  (*c*) That may be Uncle George

It seems to me that there is a real difference between:

lvii (*a*) It is possible that that is true
  (*b*) It is possible that that'll be true

even though both are matched by the same form with *may*. However that may be, it is clear that the ambiguity of non-complex *will* presents us with a rather different problem from that we found with *may* and *must*, at least. And I shall consider this problem further below, also.

However, let us turn now to the difficulties posed by the presence of two negative possibilities with certain modals. A possible solution to this is suggested (once more) by the fact that the modals concerned are derived from an underlying structure consisting of two clauses. Either or both of these clauses can be negated. One of the negative possibilities with the modal is derived from the negation of the subordinate clause; the other from that of the main clause. Thus, for example, with non-complex *can*:

lviii A1(*a*) It's possible for it to fall before six
  (*b*) It can fall before six
  2(*a*) It's possible for it not to fall before six
  (*b*) It can not fall before six
  3(*a*) It's not possible for it to fall before six
  (*b*) It can't fall before six

  B1(*a*) It's possible for it to be true
  (*b*) It can be true
  2(*a*) It's possible for it not to be true
  (*b*) It can not be true
  3(*a*) It's not possible for it to be true
  (*b*) It can't be true[81]

Similarly, with complex *can*:

lix A1(*a*) I am able to leave tomorrow
  (*b*) I can leave tomorrow
  2(*a*) I am able not to leave tomorrow
  (*b*) I can not leave tomorrow
  3(*a*) I am not able (unable) to leave tomorrow
  (*b*) I can't leave tomorrow

ʙ1(*a*) I am able to visit her
   (*b*) I can visit her

2(*a*) I am able not to visit her
   (*b*) I can not visit her

3(*a*) I am not able (unable) to visit her
   (*b*) I can't visit her

and with complex *must/need/have* (*to*):

lxᴀ 1(*a*) I am obliged to leave
   (*b*) I must/have to leave

2(*a*) I am obliged not to leave
   (*b*) I mustn't leave

3(*a*) I am not obliged to leave
   (*b*) I needn't/don't have to leave

ʙ1(*a*) I am obliged to visit her every day
   (*b*) I have to visit her every day

2(*a*) I am obliged not to visit her every day
   (*b*) I mustn't visit her every day

3(*a*) I am not obliged to visit her every day
   (*b*) I needn't/don't have to visit her every day

However, there appear to be some 'gaps' with non-complex *must/ need*:

lxiᴀ 1(*a*) I'm sure he'll arrive before six
   (*b*) He must arrive before six

2(*a*) I'm sure he'll not arrive before six
   (*b*)

3(*a*) I'm not sure he'll arrive before six
   (*b*) He needn't arrive before six

ʙ1(*a*) I'm sure it's true
   (*b*) It must be true

2(*a*) I'm sure it's not true
   (*b*)

3(*a*) I'm not sure it's true
   (*b*) It needn't be true

In (lxi ᴀ2*b*) the form we might expect with *must* is very unlikely, while
in (lxi ʙ2*b*) it has a much more restricted range of meaning than the

corresponding full form. (Corresponding forms with *bound to* also seem to be doubtful in my English.) In both these cases, an example with *can* seems more appropriate:

lxii(*a*) He can't arrive before six
    (*b*) It can't be true[82]

In the second case, the narrower range of meaning with *must* is apparent from:

lxiii(*a*) It can't be true   ⎫
    (*b*) It mustn't be true ⎬(after all)

By adding *after all* to the (*a*) example we give it an interpretation like that for the (*b*) example even when the *after all* is lacking. In this latter example it is redundant.

    I shall come back to this below. However, at this point we should also note that forms with *may* appear to be appropriate as alternatives in other parts of the paradigm in (lxi). Thus:

lxiv 1(*a*) I'm not sure he'll arrive before six
    (*b*) He needn't arrive before six
    (*c*) He may not arrive before six
  2(*a*) I'm not sure it's true
    (*b*) It needn't be true
    (*c*) It may not be true

Further, we can extend the paradigm by using forms with *may* where forms with *must/need* would be rather 'ungainly':

lxv 1(*a*) I'm not sure he'll not arrive soon
    (*b*) He needn't not arrive soon
    (*c*) He may arrive soon
  2(*a*) I'm not sure it's not true
    (*b*) It needn't not be true/be untrue
    (*c*) It may be true

It is obviously also possible to substitute forms with *it's possible that* and *possibly* where the forms with *may* were appropriate, and, indeed, the reader can demonstrate for himself that it is possible to substitute a form with *it's possible* throughout the entire paradigm in (lxi). Likewise we can substitute forms with *I'm sure . . .* , *must/need/have to*, etc for the example in (A) and (B) (1) and (2) in (lviii), where *may* alternatives were possible.[83]

This is all possible because of equations like:

lxvi   I'm not sure that . . . not . . . = . . . needn't not . . . = . . . may
       . . . = it is possible that . . .

The underlying equivalences can be tabulated as follows:

lxvii 1 I'm sure that . . . ⎫ ⎧ It's not possible for . . . not . . .
        must   ⎭ ⎩   can't not

      2 I'm sure that . . . not . . . ⎫ ⎧ It's not possible for . . .
        (mustn't)   ⎭ ⎩   can't

      3 I'm not sure that . . . ⎫ ⎧ It's possible that/for . . .
                                ⎬ ⎨   not . . .
        needn't   ⎭ ⎩   may/can . . . not

      4 I'm not sure that . . . ⎫ ⎧ It's possible that/for
                    not . . .   ⎬ ⎨
        needn't not   ⎭ ⎩   may/can

(We shall, however, have reason to revise our view of *can* below.) We
seem to have here, then, a complex sort of 'antonymy' holding between sentences containing *may*, etc and sentences containing *must*,
etc: *ie*, such sentences are apparently to be derived from very similar
underlying (two-clause) structures, containing, in particular, a 'first
person dative' in the main clause (appearing as the subject in *I'm sure
that* . . . , but otherwise normally deleted),[84] and related in terms of
this particular sort of 'antonymy'. I do not intend to develop an analysis here of this type of relationship, particularly since a much wider
range of phenomena than we have considered so far is clearly involved.[85] It will suffice for the present to indicate that such a relationship holds in these particular cases. A further confirmation of this
suggested relationship between *may*, etc and *must*, etc, would seem to
derive from the fact that those instances in the paradigm in (lxi) where
a form with *must* did not seem appropriate (*ie* (A2*b*) and (B2*b*), and
where forms with *can* were apparently preferable (as in lxii)) – these
instances correspond with the negative examples for *can* where we observed that a form with *may* was not possible (see note 80) – since
I'm sure that . . . *not* . . . = *It's not possible that* . . . .

   The interesting question arises at this point: is there a parallel underlying relationship in the case of the complex modals? Consider:

lxviii A1(*a*) I am obliged to leave
    (*b*) I must leave

  2(*a*) I am not permitted not to leave
    (*b*) I mayn't/can't not leave

  B1(*a*) I am obliged not to leave
    (*b*) I mustn't leave

  2(*a*) I am not permitted to leave
    (*b*) I mayn't/can't leave

  c1(*a*) I am not obliged to leave
    (*b*) I needn't leave

  2(*a*) I am permitted not to leave
    (*b*) I may/can not leave[86]

  D1(*a*) I am not obliged not to leave
    (*b*) I needn't not leave

  2(*a*) I am permitted to leave
    (*b*) I may/can leave

In both the complex and the non-complex cases, then, this same relationship holds between the (external) potential and non-potential modals.[87]

Before following up some of the problems to do with *will* and *can*, I would like to look at the other major set of phenomena which we found it difficult to reconcile with a simple subcategorisation. This has to do with the 'past'/'perfect' ambiguity associated with a sequence of non-complex modal + 'auxiliary *have*'. Once more, the suggested two-clause derivation for the modals may provide a possible solution. Compare the following:

lxix 1(*a*) That may have happened in 200 BC
    (*b*) It's possible that that happened in 200 BC

  2(*a*) They may have arrived already
    (*b*) It's possible that they've arrived already

Thus, the 'perfect' interpretation for *may have* is associated with a structure containing a 'perfect' in the subordinate clause; the 'past' interpretation with a structure containing a past tense element. In the first case we have an underlying sequence of 'present' + 'perfect', in the second 'present' + 'past'. They both result in a superficial 'perfect' when 'modalised'. Similarly, for *must*:

8—E.S.E.S.

lxx 1(*a*) They must have done that in 200 BC

   (*b*) I'm sure they did that in 200 BC

   2(*a*) They must have arrived already

   (*b*) I'm sure they've arrived already

and for *will* and *can* (though, as noted above, the sequence *can have* is somewhat marginal). The fact that *will have* is similarly ambiguous makes possible the following examples:

lxxi 1(*a*) It's possible that⎫
   (*b*) I'm sure   ⎬that will have happened in 200 BC
                            ⎭

   2(*a*) It's possible that⎫
   (*b*) I'm sure   ⎬that they'll have arrived already
                            ⎭

And we might suggest that *may have* and *must have* are perhaps ambiguous in this further respect, as in 'non-perfect' instances (*cf* (lv–lvii)) – although telling examples are difficult to find (in both cases).

We looked above at the 'future'/'non-future' ambiguity and how it might be accounted for in the case of both the complex and the non-complex cases. This further ambiguity is also possible with the 'perfect' interpretation for non-complex modal + *have:*

lxxii   They may have arrived⎰(*a*) already
                             ⎱(*b*) by the time you get back

and is presumably to be explained in the same way. Note, however, that the complex modals can have only the future interpretation, as is also the case with their non-modal equivalents. So:

lxxiii 1(*a*) I am willing to have left by Tuesday

   (*b*) I will have left by Tuesday

   2(*a*) I am obliged to have left by Tuesday

   (*b*) I must have left by Tuesday

   3(*a*) I am allowed to have left by Tuesday

   (*b*) I may/can have left by Tuesday

   4(*a*) I am able to have left by Tuesday

   (*b*) I can have left by Tuesday

And even with a future interpretation, some of these are rather unlikely.

Let us consider now the past interpretations for *could* and *would*, since this could enable us to carry further our analysis of the non-externals, with respect to which (in particular) there are a number of outstanding problems. The interpretation of the complex variety seems fairly straightforward. Compare:

lxxiv   1(*a*) He was always willing to ⎱
        (*b*) He would always   ⎰ help a friend

       2(*a*) He was able to ⎱
        (*b*) He could   ⎰ swim (in those days)

We have already noted the absence of modal equivalents for 'non-state' interpretations and various other restrictions (in the last section of Part 1). But consider a non-complex instance of *could* like:

lxxv   It could happen in those days

It seems reasonable to associate this with:

lxxvi   It was possible for it to happen in those days

but not with a form of *I am/was not sure that . . . not. . . . I'm not sure that it didn't happen in those days* is paralleled by *It may have happened in those days*; and *I wasn't sure that it didn't happen in those days* has no modal equivalent. That is, the form of *be possible* in cases like that in (lxxvi) and an associated *can* form like that in (lxxv) are apparently not to be associated with *I am/was not sure that . . . not . . .*, but are to be derived from an underlying structure somewhat different from any underlying an *I am sure* form. In particular, an underlying structure containing a reference to the 'first person' seems unnecessary and, indeed, undesirable. *Could* and *it was possible* can, perhaps, be associated in this instance with *It was not certain not. . . .* It is also likely that a non-complex conditional like:

lxxvii   They could arrive before six (if they left early this morning)

is to be associated with a form like:

lxxviii   It would be possible for them to arrive before six (if they left early this morning)

Once again, there is no obvious *I'm not sure that . . . not . . .* parallel, and the examples in (lxxvii) and (lxxviii) are rather to be associated with:

lxxix   They wouldn't be certain not to arrive before six (if they left early this morning)

(We shall return to the other conditional forms below.)
    This suggests that we reconsider the derivation implied for *can* in

other cases. Can they too be interpreted as (differing from *may* and *must* in) lacking a reference to the 'first person' in their underlying structure? In so far as *can* seems to emphasise the existence of the circumstances favourable to the actualisation of a (type of) event rather than the speaker's judgment of the likelihood of occurrence for a particular event or events, this would be plausible. Note, for instance, that *can/could* is derived from underlying structures varying in the tense, etc, of the *main* clause. This is not the case with *may/might* and *must/should* (they have, for example, no past tense interpretation[88]), since they are always to be related to forms of *I'm sure that* . . . (representing the speaker's present judgment). *Can/could* is rather to be related to various members of the paradigm of *be certain to*. I suggest, then, that as forms with *it's possible that* . . . , . . . *possibly* . . . and *may* are to be related in a particular way to *I'm not sure that* . . . *not* . . . with respect to their underlying structures, so forms with *it's possible for* . . . and *can* are related to . . . *isn't certain not*. . . . As we have seen, *could* can be related to two alternative further members of this paradigm: . . . *wasn't certain not* . . . and . . . *wouldn't be certain not*. . . . We can set up the following composite paradigm:

lxxx 1(*a*) It can happen
 (*b*) It's possible for it to happen
 (*c*) It isn't certain not to happen
 2(*a*) It can't happen
 (*b*) It isn't possible for it to happen
 (*c*) It is certain not to happen
 3(*a*) It can not happen
 (*b*) It is possible for it not to happen
 (*c*) It isn't certain to happen
 4(*a*) It can't not happen
 (*b*) It's not possible for it not to happen
 (*c*) It's certain to happen

All of these can have either a future or a non-future interpretation.[89]

A further consideration is this: if *be certain to* and *it's possible for* . . . are related in approximately the same way as *I'm sure that* . . . and *it's possible that* . . . , is there also a modal form corresponding to *be certain to*, as there is in the case of the other three, namely *can, must* (etc) and *may*, respectively? The only real contender is *will*. How plausible would be the suggested relationship with *be certain to*? Compare:[90]

lxxxi 1(a) It isn't certain not to happen
    (b) It won't not happen

  2(a) It's certain not to happen
    (b) It won't happen

  3(a) It isn't certain to happen
    (b) It won't happen

  4(a) It's certain to happen
    (b) It will happen

Only in the case of (2) and (4) is the relationship plausible. (1) and (3) are matched rather by *needn't not* and *needn't*, respectively.[91] Now, this is not a unique situation. Remember that at certain places in the *I'm sure that/It's possible that* paradigm, *can't* seemed more appropriate than a form of *must*. This was as a match to *I'm sure that . . . not . . .* and *it's not possible that. . . .* In the present case, we find *needn't* rather than a form of *will* as a match for *It isn't certain (not) to . . . | It's possible for X (not) to. . . .* That is, when with the *sure/certain* forms, a negative appears in the main clause, we find *needn't* in both paradigms; whereas when there is a negative only in the subordinate clause, we find *can't* in both paradigms. The presence of a negative seems to 'neutralise' the distinction between the two paradigms. *Can't* and *needn't* belong to both. The plausibility of pairings like *He would (always) live in that hotel (when he came here)/He was certain to live in that hotel (when he came here)* tends to confirm the suggested relationship, and indeed goes some way towards explaining the 'iterative' character of such instances with *would*.

    What conclusions about the derivation of (non-complex) *will* can we draw from the immediately above and previous discussions? *Will* represents the 'predictive' category present in the subordinate clause in certain of the full forms corresponding to *must* and *may* (*I'm sure it'll turn out OK*, *It's possible that it'll turn out OK*, etc). It is perhaps also the modal equivalent of *be certain to. . . .* In both cases it is ambiguous between future and non-future interpretations. Perhaps, then, 'ambiguous' is the wrong word, and we should say rather that the category represented by *will* is *indifferent* with respect to this distinction, which resides in quite other (*eg* 'adverbial') elements and which none of the variants of *will*-forms disambiguate. The category, then, would be purely predictive, with future and non-future reference marked in other ways. It seems plausible to suggest that the complex modals (which even lack the presence of the predictive category in their underlying structure) are also 'indifferent' in this respect: compare *I can swim* and *I can swim tomorrow*.

According to our present account only certain instances of *may* and *must*, for instance, derive from a structure containing this predictive category. The *may* corresponding to the full forms *it is possible that it is true* and *it is possible that they completed that by* AD *10* contains no predictive category in its underlying structure. However, I have found difficulty in producing examples to demonstrate a distinction between a modal form with present reference and no underlying predictive category, and a modal form differing only in deriving from an underlying structure containing such a category. It is possible to show such a distinction with the full forms (*cf* (lvii) for example). It may be, then, that all non-complex modal instances are to be derived from underlying structures containing a predictive category (neutral between future and non-future). Thus, we could distinguish between 'modalised' *will* (which, like *may*, *must* and *can*, is associated with an underlying structure containing the predictive category) and *will* as the direct realisation of the predictive category (in full forms).

This also suggests then that sentences containing *can*, *will*, *be possible for* and *be certain to* should perhaps be related to sentences like:

lxxxii (*a*) It's certain that he'll be in his study
     (*b*) He'll certainly be in his study

which presumably have a derivation like that for a parallel *I'm sure that*... form but for the absence in the underlying structure for (lxxxii) of the 'dative' NP that appears as the subject in the *I'm sure that* case. Compare the following with the examples in (lxxxii):

lxxxiii 1(*a*) He's certain to be in his study
     (*b*) It's not possible for him not to be in his study
    2(*a*) He'll be in his study
     (*b*) He can't not be in his study

If this sort of connection proved acceptable, then we could characterise the difference between the external non-complex modals (*must* and *may*) and the non-external ones (*will* and *can*) as residing in the presence vs the absence of the underlying 'first-person dative'. However, there are a number of difficulties associated with this interpretation of non-complex *will* and *can*, particularly with regard to the plausibility of certain of the pairings of variants that result. The derivations of non-complex *will* and *can*, in particular, remain in many respects obscure to me.

Before concluding, I would like to glance briefly at the conditional modals, which I have almost entirely neglected in the preceding discussion. In particular, I want to determine whether some of the tentative suggestions I have been making concerning underlying relationships for the modals are borne out in this area. We have already seen that it seems plausible to associate conditional non-complex *could* with *it would be possible* forms. Similarly complex *could* can be related to *would be able to*, and complex *would* to *would be willing to*. So:

lxxxiv 1(*a*) I would be willing to come at once
    (*b*) I would willingly come at once
    (*c*) I would come at once
    2(*a*) I would be able to come at once
    (*b*) I could come at once

ie, the complex conditionals are in these cases paralleled by sequences of non-complex conditional *would* + *be* + adjective, as we might expect.

However, the situation with the external conditionals is not so simple. Consider first the non-potential complex modal:

lxxxv(*a*) You should/ought to leave at once
    (*b*) That should/ought to be against the law

If these followed the pattern set immediately above, they ought to be matched by sentences of the form:

lxxxvi(*a*) You would be obliged to leave tomorrow
    (*b*) That would be required to be against the law[92]

However, the examples in (lxxxv) can be associated rather with sentences like:

lxxxvii(*a*) You would be obliged to leave tomorrow
    { if you had any conscience
    { if you took my advice
    { . . .

    (*b*) That would be required to be against the law
    { if things were organised properly
    { if I had my way
    { . . .

ie, sentences consisting of the clauses in (lxxxvi) *plus* one of a restricted set of conditional clauses. The interpretation of sentences containing this conditional form presupposes one of a particular set of conditional clauses (*could*, in comparison, is non-selective) – or rather not a particular one, but what all of the set have in common. We would seem to require in the derivation of such a conditional some sort of deleted conditional element, of a semantic specification equivalent to what the clauses in the fuller forms have in common.[93] The characterisation of this suggested derivation poses a number of problems whose solutions are unclear (to me). But, however this is to be characterised, it does at least seem clear that complex *should/ought to* is to be accounted for by some sort of extension of rules which otherwise overlap with those for the non-external forms already discussed.

Similarly, *might/could* seems to be matched by sentences containing a particular subset of conditional clauses:

lxxxviii(*a*) You might go now
     (*b*) You would be permitted to go now (if you wanted)

as also appears to be the case with the non-complex externals (except that the *would* appears in the subordinate clause in their case):

lxxxix 1(*a*) That ought to be the train now
     (*b*) I'm sure that that would be the train now
       (if I've calculated correctly)
   2(*a*) They might arrive before six
     (*b*) It's possible that they would arrive before six (if they
       started out early this morning)

Compare *could* and *might*:

xc1(*a*) It could finish tomorrow
   (*b*) It would be possible for it to finish tomorrow
  2(*a*) It might finish tomorrow
   (*b*) It's possible that it would finish tomorrow

$$\left\{\begin{array}{l}\text{if all went well}\\\text{if it went as planned}\\\cdots\end{array}\right.$$

Once again, despite the problems involved, the derivation suggested would be consistent with the account of the modals suggested so far.

I have noted that with non-complex *might* and *should/ought to*, the corresponding full forms have conditional *would* in the subordinate clause, whereas with the other non-complex modals and all the complex modals, it is the main clause which contains the conditional.

Moreover, in the full forms corresponding to non-complex *may* and *must*, *will* appears as the realisation of the predictive category. This confirms that, in these cases, we should regard the conditional as a 'modification' of the predictive category (*cf* the derivation of the conditional forms as modal + pret in the appendix to Part 1). However, with the other modals, the conditional appears in the main clause of the corresponding full forms. And this poses a problem, since there is no corresponding full form with *will* in the main clause (or at least not one that is related to the modal forms – see *eg* (xlviii5)). Is there a predictive element 'inherent in' the category underlying *can*, *able*, etc, and if so how are we to characterise this?[94] Moreover, what underlies the derivation of non-complex *would*? Perhaps dependent on an account of this is a resolution of the further problem presented by the ambiguity of such sentences as *We could be in Greenland* (*if we hadn't cancelled our flight/to judge by the scenery*), where the corresponding *would be possible* form is similarly ambiguous. The former interpretation appears to be equivalent to one interpretation of *We could have been in Greenland*; perhaps the solution resides in this.

These are some of many problems whose solutions are uncertain. This is a reflection of the fact that the present account constitutes no more than a programme for research. I have merely tried to suggest that the range of phenomena relevant to the grammar of the modal is wider than is usually proposed, and that greater illumination is thrown on these phenomena if we consider the modal forms not as directly realising a simple subcategorisation (with respect to a category M(odal)) but rather as variants of an underlying two-clause structure.[95] I have tried also to suggest relationships between the structures underlying different modals, with a view to reducing the number of 'primes'.

The tentative nature of the present account has precluded any serious attempt at formalisation.[96] Apart from this (but perhaps dependent on it) there remains the problem of characterising (semantically) *can* and *able*, for instance, and relating this characterisation to those for the other modals. Only some of the underlying relationships have been formulated here. In particular, and most strikingly, the complex and non-complex modals have had to be treated separately in many instances, despite the fact that there is evidence of an underlying relationship between the relevant pairs.[97] I have also not considered here the derivation of 'optative' *may* (as in *May your cabbages wither away*), sentences containing which seem to pre-suppose a deleted superordinate clause (otherwise written out as *I wish that . . .*). The permutation of *may* and the subject is the superficial reflex of this underlying structure.[98] In this case, the presence of *may* here is a feature of the syntax of certain embedded sentences – which again has been outside the scope of my discussion. There are also further structures that should be related to those I have been discussing. Some of these are illustrated by the following:

xci(*a*) He has the$\left\{\begin{array}{l}\text{power}\\\text{ability}\\\text{capability}\end{array}\right\}$to do it

    (*b*) He has my$\left\{\begin{array}{l}\text{permission}\\\text{authority}\end{array}\right\}$to do it

    (*c*) He has an obligation to do it[99]

I have also neglected related phenomena connected with imperatives and the problems relating to 'prediction' recently discussed by McIntosh.[100] Note too that the phenomena surveyed here form a sub-part of a wider set including forms like *it is probable/likely that . . . , probably, likely to . . .* , etc. But perhaps the first requirement is for a formal treatment and more extensive testing of my tentative suggestions, which have been made in the hope of facilitating the future task of providing a systematic account of the grammar of the modals.

Appendix: some structures

The complex modals appear to be derived from an underlying structure that can be abbreviated as:[101]

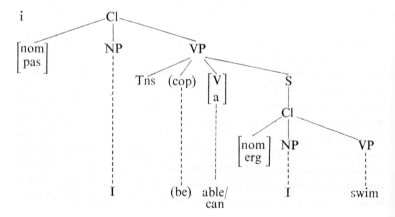

in the case of 'intransitive' main verbs (in which the matrix
NP(/$\begin{bmatrix} nom \\ pas \end{bmatrix}$ ——) is identical with the embedded NP(/$\begin{bmatrix} nom \\ erg \end{bmatrix}$ ——); and
'a' represents a set of features including those characterising the class
of V's that can be modalised): *I am able to swim, I can swim.* In the
case of 'transitive' main verbs we have rather:

ii

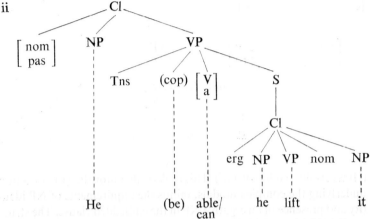

in which the matrix NP is identical with the NP in the embedded clause
which follows erg. We can generalise over both cases by requiring the
identity to hold between the matrix NP and the embedded NP which is
preceded by erg (either as category or feature). (This abbreviated structure represents the situation after the operation of the rules permuting
erg and nom and introducing the NP's after such case categories.)[102]

The presence of an ergative in the embedded clause is not required in
the case of non-complex instances, which also differ in showing nomi-
nal rather than verbal complementation,[103] though this may be a
rather more superficial phenomenon than Rosenbaum, for instance,
suggests. Consider:

iii

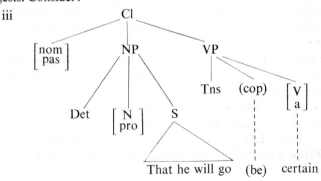

('That he will go is certain'). There are none of the restrictions on the development of S (in this case) that there were with the complex modals. However, the structure abbreviated in (iii) would seem to be transformed into something like that in (iv) before modalisation:

iv

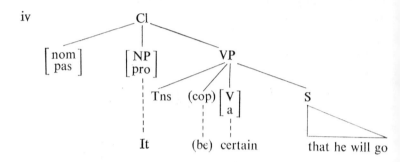

('It is certain that he will go'). This looks rather more like the structure underlying the complex modals, minus the requirements of NP identity and presence of an ergative NP in the embedded clause. The structure index for modalisation can thus be the same in both instances, except for these particular requirements.

The difference between the external and non-external non-complex modals (*must* and *may* vs *will* and *can*) would seem to reside in the presence in the underlying structure for the former of a human egocentric 'dative' (underlying the subject in the *I am sure* . . . forms, but in most cases deleted – but cf: *I was convinced by him that* . . . , *He convinced me that* . . . , as 'non-state' instances). There is one further requirement for the structures underlying non-complex modal forms in general, and that is the presence of the predictive category in the embedded clause. Members of the paradigm lacking this are excluded from the modalisation possibility. When modalisation does not occur but the predictive category is present in the underlying structure, then it is 'written out' as *will* or the *to* infinitive: *It's certain that he'll go, He's certain to go*. The derivation of this category itself is a further unresolved problem, and I have omitted any characterisation of it from diagrams (iii) and (iv).

It is possible that we should regard modalisation as finally being 'triggered off' by the presence of the feature 'modal' in the complex symbol with category V in the main clause. The differences in 'emphasis' between modal and non-modal forms could then be associated with the presence vs the absence of this feature in the underlying structure (*cf* the role of pas(sive)). I should like to conclude by noting that attempts to characterise 'a' in structures (i)–(iv) above suggest that the structures proposed here are still somewhat superficial and that the complex and non-complex variants can be shown to be much more intimately related. But this is a further paper.[104]

Notes

1 See *eg* O. Jespersen, *A Modern English Grammar*, IV, London, 1931, *pp* 235–352; E. Kruisinga, *English Accidence and Syntax*, I, Groningen, 1931, *pp* 430–502; R. W. Zandvoort, *A Handbook of English Grammar*, Groningen, 1957, Chap 5; F. R. Palmer, *A Linguistic Study of the English Verb*, London, 1965, Chaps 6 and 7. But sometimes, as I shall try to suggest, distinctions that we find (or look as if they are to be) associated with the modals are probably more appropriately assigned to other elements in the relevant utterances. (*Cf* the discussion of tense and 'time relationships' in D. Crystal, 'Specification and English tenses', *JL*, 2, 1966, 1–34.)

2 See *eg* C. C. Fries, *The Structure of English*, London, 1957, *pp* 90–1; B. M. H. Strang, *Modern English Structure*, London, 1962, *pp* 136–40; N. Chomsky, 'A transformational approach to syntax', *Third Texas Conference on Problems of Linguistic Analysis in English*, Austin, 1962, 131, 139; Palmer, *op cit*, *loc cit*.

3 Two recent attempts at a systematic account of the modals, M. Joos, *The English Verb*, Madison & Milwaukee, 1965, Chap 6, and W. Diver 'The modal system of the English verb', *Word*, 20, 1964, 322–52, among other things, are reviewed by Palmer, 'The semantics of the English verb', *Lingua*, 18, 1967, 179–95, and also briefly in M. Ehrman, *The Meaning of the Modals in Present-day American English*, The Hague, 1966, *p* 105. Palmer finds Joos's analysis of the modals 'utterly implausible', and points out that Joos fails to relate his semantic 'cube' to the superficial distributional behaviour ('formal pattern') of the modals (*op cit*, 187). He finds greatest difficulty in motivating the particular 'relational statements' implied by Joos's cube (*eg*, 'WILL is to SHALL, as CAN is to MAY, as MUST is to OUGHT TO, as DARE is to NEED'); and I must admit to sharing his difficulty, and also to an inability to understand Joos's explanations of *his* motivations. These difficulties are compounded by the opacity of the labels which Joos chooses to characterise his classes of modals. With respect to these, I must agree with Palmer and Ehrman in finding them vague and general – as, no doubt, they have to be to obscure the polysemy of the individual modal forms. But I think that this charge can be levelled at Ehrman's own account, also (since its stated intention is to confirm one of the weakest possible hypotheses – see Ehrman, *op cit*, *p* 9). The criticisms that Palmer makes of Diver's account are likewise for the most part quite just.

Palmer's own presentation (*A Linguistic Study of the English Verb*, *pp* 105–39) takes fairly full account of the 'polysemic nature' of the modals (perhaps too full, at times), and he is careful to relate the distinctions made to associated facts of distribution. (My indebtedness to his clear presentation of many of the modal distinctions will be apparent from the frequency with which his work is cited.) But his approach seems to me rather unsystematic and lacking in explanatory power. – It is perhaps already clear that I cannot share Ehrman's (*op cit, p* 9) pessimism with respect to the possibility of giving a more systematic account of the modals than she found possible – even if restricted to the framework of a simple subclassification (*cf p* 70).

I should like to note here, too, that many of the distinctions I shall be making are well illustrated in the discussion in R. B. Long, *The Sentence and its Parts*, Chicago, 1961, *pp* 138–51.

4 Just as, for instance, in the subcategorisation of the noun phrase, the human/ non-human opposition is presumably subordinate to the animate/non-animate. More formal presentations of similar frameworks can be found in M. A. K. Halliday, 'Syntax and the consumer', *Report of the Fifteenth Annual Round-table Meeting on Linguistics and Language Studies* (*Monograph Series on Languages and Linguistics*, 17), Washington, 1964, 11–24, and 'Some notes on "deep" grammar', *JL*, 2, 1966, 57–67, and N. Chomsky, *Aspects of the Theory of Syntax*, Cambridge, Mass, 1965, particularly *pp* 75–83; see too J. M. Anderson, 'A note on "rank" and "delicacy"', *JL*, 5, 1969 (although Halliday allows for non-binary 'systems'). I do not intend here to discuss at length the motivations for favouring a 'componential' analysis, and in particular a binary one. This represents a hypothesis concerning the nature of language. However, grave difficulties with respect to logical structure and empirical validation attend on the proposal of ternary, etc, oppositions for natural language. See further the discussion in R. Jakobson, 'Boas' view of grammatical meaning', *American Anthropologist*, suppl. 89, 1959 (*The Anthropology of Franz Boas*, ed W. Goldschmidt), 139–45.

5 Moreover, the appendices are not self-contained, and depend for their interpretation on the references cited therein. The presentation there comprises a set of subcategorisation and constituency rules for VP (*cf* J. M. Anderson, 'Ergative and nominative in English', *JL*, 4, 1968, 1–8), the first of which introduces a category M(odal) as a constituent of VP, with subsequent rules adding subclassificatory features.

6 As presented in, for instance, Strang, *op cit, pp* 137–40, and M. Ehrman, 'The Meaning of the Modals in Present-day American English', *Linguistics*, 28, 1966, 46–58.

7 *Cf* Strang, *op cit, p* 137.

8 See A. McIntosh, 'Predictive statements', in *In Memory of J. R. Firth*, London, 1966, *p* 317.

9 *Cf eg* Palmer, *op cit, p* 118.

10 *Ibid, p* 116.

11 Alternatively, we could regard (iii) as manifesting the same bundle of components as (ii*a*), and allow for a semantic overlap between *can* and *may*. Since *can* represents the unmarked member of the opposition separating *can* and *may* (see below), the particular direction of the overlap would not be unnatural.

12 The reason for the absence of *shall* from this list should be clear from what follows.

13 W. Diver, *op cit*.

14 Jespersen, *op cit, pp* 8, 304, 325; Palmer, *op cit, p* 130.

15 In terms of the account suggested in Anderson, *op cit*, if the factor is 'inherent in' the subject, then the subject is derived from an underlying ergative phrase. *Cf: He can climb very well* and *He can die tomorrow*, the second of which can only be 'simply predictive' and has a non-ergative subject. Notice that it is the presence of an ergative that is important here, and the ergative phrase may not be identical with the subject, as in the passive form *It can be lifted by three men*, where *by three men* represents the ergative phrase. The

'simply predictive' and the other instance thus differ in these cases in that the 'non-simply-predictive' requires the presence of an ergative, as category or feature. As we shall see, the cases where the factor is 'operative upon' the subject require that the subject be not derived from an underlying ergative, but rather, perhaps, from an underlying 'dative', in Fillmore's terms (see C. J. Fillmore, 'The case for case', in E. Bach and R. Harms, *Universals in Linguistic Theory*, New York, 1968, § 3). It is obviously not as simple as this; these phenomena are not explicable in a natural way in terms of simple subcategorisational account of the modals. See further notes 69, 71 and 73, which modify the suggestions made here considerably.

16 Example from Palmer, *op cit, p* 138. His other example for *can + have* illustrates a complex instance with 'future reference'.

17 Palmer, *op cit, p* 116. This distinction is not merely a function of the difference in the main verb, since we could substitute *swim* for *come* in (*a*).

18 But *must* appears with a complex 'present-inclusive' interpretation with a negative: *I mustn't leave the house at any time. May* is similar in some varieties of English.

19 Palmer, *op cit, p* 111.

20 It is, of course, rather more complicated than this, in that, for example, we must allow for anaphoric reference to a generic NP (*If sugar is placed in water, it will dissolve*), but in principle, the distinction would seem to be extramodal.

21 See Anderson, *op cit*; J. Lyons, 'A note on possessive, existential and locative sentences', *FL*, 3, 1967, 390–6.

22 Palmer, *op cit, pp* 111, 112, 116.

23 *Cf* too Kruisinga, *op cit* (see note 1), §§ 655, 722.

24 *Cf* Palmer, *op cit, pp* 111, 116.

25 Similarly, examples like *He can be rather nasty (sometimes/at times)* (*cf* Palmer, *op cit*, 116) can be regarded as having an underlying adverbial (optionally deleted), which marks the distinction between such an instance and a simple present-inclusive one like (x2a). Notice too the restriction to *be + non-stative adjective. However, an interesting problem is posed by examples like *They can be beautiful*, which has a stative adjective and is paraphrasable by *Some of them are beautiful* or *They're sometimes beautiful*. See further note 85.

26 Palmer, *op cit, pp* 129–32.

27 Jespersen, *op cit*.

28 We could, in terms of the sort of formalisation suggested in note 5, derive *could* (as opposed to *can*) via two different subcategorisation rules (± past, ± conditional), but the constituency rules for + past and + conditional could add the same feature, say, pret(erite), to the tense marker. See further the appendix to Part 1.

29 *Cf eg* Kruisinga, *op cit, p* 463.

30 See Ehrman, *op cit* (see note 6), 57; Diver, *op cit* (see note 3), 340, fn. 15.

31 Jespersen, *op cit*.

32 *Ibid, pp* 290–300.

33 *Ibid, p* 297.

34 Ehrman, *op cit* (see note 6), 56–7.

35 Jespersen, *op cit, p* 325.

36 Palmer, *op cit, p* 130.

37 For examples illustrating an earlier stage at which it was, see Jespersen, *op cit, pp* 266–75. In varieties in which *He shall go* is normally interpreted as implying the exertion of some sort of compulsion on the subject, guaranteed by the

speaker (if the sentence is non-interrogative) or inquired of the hearer (if interrogative), there would seem to be a partial retention of the *shall/should* relationship. See further below.

38 But we do find *had to*. *Cf* subsequent examples, particularly (lʙ) (*p* 93).
39 Palmer, *op cit, p* 120.
40 Zandvoort, *op cit* (see note 1), *pp* 90–2.
41 *Cf* Jespersen, *op cit, pp* 272–3.
42 Palmer, *op cit, pp* 113–14.
43 *May* and *must* were also 'defective' (in my English) in their non-conditional forms, in that they occur themselves only with future reference, while *can* and *have* (*to*) supplied the non-futures. But see note 18.
44 Which alternative to designate as 'marked' is not obvious here. But see note 11.
45 See, for instance, Zandvoort, *op cit, pp* 85–90.
46 M. Joos, *op cit* (see note 3), *p* 150.
47 Y. Lebrun, *Can and May in Present-day English*, Bruxelles, 1965.
48 The incorrectness of this general conclusion seems to me beyond dispute.
49 Palmer, *op cit, pp* 116–19, 123.
50 There is a continuous history linking most of the Modern English modal 'forms' with their Old English 'ancestors', and, to a large extent, similar distinctions are made at both periods (but note *cann/mæʒ* – and see *eg* B. Mitchell, *A Guide to Old English*, Oxford, 1964, *pp* 112–15); but the historically related forms no longer (for the most part) have the same interpretations associated with them. – And many of the 'shifts' have occurred over the external/non-external 'boundary'. On the history of the modal verbs (and their cognates in other Germanic languages) see A. Tellier, *Les verbes perfecto-présents et les auxiliaires de mode en anglais ancien*, Paris, 1962. We have already noted that *may* and *can* are interchangeable as manifestations of a complex, external, potential interpretation: *You can/may leave now*. In this respect, too, the external/non-external boundary is not 'well-defined'. The situation with *shall* and *should* would also appear to be partly the result of a 'break-down' in the external/non-external boundary, such that we have had to recognise the partial dislocation of *should* from *shall*, despite the apparent parallelism with other pairs.
51 Palmer, *op cit, p* 124.
52 *Op cit, pp* 111, 116.
53 *Cf* Kruisinga, *op cit*, §§ 745, 746.
54 Compare the treatment of *He can be nasty*, etc, suggested in note 25.
55 Anderson, *op cit*, 1–9.
56 M. A. K. Halliday, 'Some notes on "deep" grammar', and 'Syntax and the consumer'. On this equivalence, see further J. M. Anderson, 'A note on "rank" and "delicacy".'
57 Palmer, *op cit, p* 139.
58 Or *It may not be true* (*It may be untrue*). See the subsequent discussion.
59 This would tend to support the suggestion made in note 11, since we could then restrict the dual negative to the bundle of components underlying *can* (and the bundle underlying *must/need*), and exclude instances of *may*. This situation is problematic if *can* realises two different bundles, one of which also underlies *may*.
60 See too J. Lyons, 'Review of Katz and Postal, *An Integrated Theory of Linguistic Descriptions*, Cambridge, Mass, 1964', *JL*, 2, 1966, 120–21, and Joos, *op cit*, 197–201.
61 Palmer, *op cit, p* 131.

62 The 'perfect' interpretation also shows the ambiguity we found in 'non-perfect' forms (cf (vi–x)) with respect to the future/non-future opposition:

$$\text{The train}\left\{\begin{array}{l}\text{may}\\ \text{must}\\ \text{can}\\ \text{will}\end{array}\right\}\text{have arrived}\left\{\begin{array}{l}\text{already}\\ \text{by six tomorrow}\end{array}\right.$$

63 Kruisinga, *op cit, p* 447.
64 *Ibid, p* 442.
65 See too Palmer, *op cit, p* 116.
66 Compare Palmer's (*op cit, p* 124): **I ran fast and so could catch the bus.* Cf: I *ran fast and so managed to catch the bus.* See too note 72.
67 Compare here Palmer's (*op cit, p* 116): **When he's older he can lift a hundred-weight.*
68 Kruisinga, *op cit, pp* 454–5.
69 *Ibid, pp* 38–40. *Cf* here the discussion in Anderson, 'Ergative and nominative in English', 19–24, 30, where it is suggested that the 'occurrence' interpretation can be related to examples with an underlying ergative phrase (perhaps deleted), as in *It was finished (by John)*, whereas the ergative is lacking with the 'state' interpretation, as in *It was (quite) finished*.
70 *Cf* notes 11 and 59.
71 Regarding 'adjectives' as 'copular non-ergative verbs' (see Anderson, *op cit*, 14–18). Once again I would think the 'occurrence'/'state' distinction is to be related to the presence vs. the absence of an ergative. However, this time it would appear that the ergative (or active) is a feature attached to the nominative category rather than a category forming part of a (deleted) phrase.
72 *Cf: He agreed to come at the time.* Cf: *could/managed* in note 66. Note that the negative equivalent seems to be possible: *He wouldn't come (when I asked him).* This is pointed out by Palmer (*op cit, p* 124), who also cites *I ran fast but still couldn't catch the bus* to illustrate the same point with respect to the other non-external modal. It would appear that the 'state'/'occurrence' distinction is 'neutralised' in such cases in the presence of a negative.
73 *Be permitted* is the 'state' equivalent of a form with an underlying ergative phrase external to the subject. *Be able* is not such. See notes 69 and 71.
74 Lamb ('The sememic approach to structural semantics', in A. K. Romney and R. G. D'Andrade (eds) *Transcultural Studies in Cognition (American Anthropologist*, 66, 1964, 3, 2), also suggests a common source (sememic identity) for *can* and *be able*, and describes *He will be able* as the 'future' of *He can* (*cf* note 67). In some languages, *eg* Tibetan, only the 'adjectival' variant appears to be possible. Consider Tibetan (C. A. Bell, *Grammar of Colloquial Tibetan*, Calcutta, 1919, *p* 69): *khö di che thup-kyi-re* ('He (*ergative*) this to do able is'). Historically too in English, there is evidence of a two-clause origin for the modal VP's, in that the 'to-less infinitive' following the modals would seem to have its source in the accusative singular of a verbal noun (see A. Meillet, *L'étude comparative des langues indo-européennes*, Paris, 1926, *pp* 136–7, J. Kuryłowicz, *The Inflexional Categories of Indo-European*, Heidelberg, 1964, *p* 162) – *ie*, it represents a nominalisation of an embedded clause. One can also find examples of OE 'modals' with non-infinitival objects.
75 *Cf* Fillmore, *op cit* (see note 15), *p* 23, fn. 29: 'Many sentence adverbs are introduced from superordinate sentences (by transformations of a type we may wish to call 'infrajection'). This possibility has long been clear for unmistakable sentence adverbs like *unfortunately*, but there are equally convincing reasons for extending the infrajection interpretation to adverbs like

willingly, easily and *carefully*, etc.' I would like to add *possibly*, etc to this list, together with the modal verbs themselves (though the details of their derivation are obviously slightly different). See too the discussion in H. Poutsma, *A Grammar of Late Modern English*, Groningen, 1926, Part II, Section II, *p* 163.

76 The fact that non-complex *must* is derived from a structure containing the 'first person' as subject accounts for the distinction made by Palmer ('The semantics of the English verb', 182): '*Must* indicates either obligation on the part of the subject or certainty on the part of the speaker.'

77 The set of variants associated with *needn't* (as against *must*) will be looked at in more detail on *p* 98 *f*, when we come to consider the problems connected with modal negation.

78 As a distributional confirmation of such pairings, consider:

$$(a)\ \text{It may} \left\{ \begin{array}{l} \text{possibly} \\ \text{*probably} \\ \text{*surely} \end{array} \right\} \text{happen}$$

$$(b)\ \text{It must} \left\{ \begin{array}{l} \text{*possibly} \\ \text{*probably} \\ \text{surely} \end{array} \right\} \text{happen}$$

79 Lebrun, *op cit* (see note 47).

80 *Cf* the distinctions drawn by Ehrman, *op cit* (see note 3), *p* 76, and Diver, *op cit* (see note 3), 330–1.

81 Note that *may* is only possible in instances parallel to the (1) and (2) examples, but where the underlying negative occurs in the main clause *may* is excluded (and even the *it is possible that* . . . variant associated with *may* seems to me unlikely in a (3) example). See further *p* 106.

82 *Can't* has frequently been described as 'the negative of' *must*.

83 Note too that we can find similar examples with the 'adverbial' forms that represent an intermediate stage between the full 'adjectival' forms and the modals. *Cf:*

(a) He's not necessarily the man
(b) He's possibly not the man

84 Kruisinga (*op cit* (see note 1), *p* 448) notes that '*may* can also express the speaker's uncertainty with regard to an action, state or occurrence' (*cf* note 76). Of course, the possibility of 'non-first-person' judgments is introduced when the forms we have been looking at are subordinated to 'reporting clauses' like *I'm told that* . . . , *They say that* . . . or *He assured me that*. . . . But we can regard these as all reporting 'first person' judgments.

85 Householder (in Chap 6 of an as yet unpublished book), following Aristotle, points out that (non-complex) *may* is 'analogous' to *some* and *must* to *all*. It is clear from the 'equivalence' of, for instance, *Not all of the men came* and *Some of the men (didn't) come*, and the ambiguity of *I don't like all of the chocolates* as compared with *I (don't) like some of the chocolates* vs *I don't like any of the chocolates/I like none of the chocolates*, that similar sorts of relationships (to the modal ones) hold here, again involving differences in the placement of the negative element. It is also clear from the examples cited at the end of note 25 and those provided by Householder that these two sets of phenomena are themselves related in some way. On this, see the discussion in Jespersen, *The Philosophy of Grammar*, London, 1924, *pp* 324–9. Consider too the causative tripartition *I made him go/I allowed him to go* (*I didn't make him not go)/I prevented him from going* (*I didn't allow him to go*).

86 The *may not* instance is extremely unlikely in my English, and such a sequence would normally be associated with a non-complex interpretation. Conversely, *may* in a question is usually complex (*cf* Palmer, *A Linguistic Study of the English Verb, p* 117). See too Jespersen's (*The Philosophy of Grammar, p* 325; *A Modern English Grammar,* v, London, 1940, *pp* 464–6) discussions of the relationship between *may* and *must.*

87 Thus, to paraphrase loosely, just as 'possibility' could be related to the lack of an assurance to the contrary, so 'permission' relates to the lack of a contrary obligation.

88 The derivation of the external conditionals is discussed on *p* 107 *f.* The unusualness of non-complex *may* in questions may also perhaps be accounted for in terms of its derivation from a structure related to one that is represented more fully by *I'm not sure that . . . not. . . .* Note that there is no suitable 'second person' interrogative form of this variant to be matched by a *may* form: *cf Aren't you sure that it won't happen?,* with quite a different interpretation.

89 The nature of the structure underlying these variants is discussed further on *p* 106 *f.*

90 And see McIntosh, *op cit, pp* 314, 317.

91 The corresponding 'adverbial' forms are perhaps:
(*a*) It won't necessarily not happen
(*b*) It necessarily won't happen
(*c*) It won't necessarily happen
(*d*) It will necessarily/necessarily will happen
We have already noted the relationship between *not necessarily* and *needn't.*

92 *Obliged* seems to permit only animate subjects: hence the substitution of *required* in this example.

93 Compare the discussion by Katz and Postal (J. J. Katz and P. M. Postal, *An Integrated Theory of Linguistic Descriptions,* Cambridge, Mass, 1964, *p* 149, notes 6 and 9) of the derivation and semantic characterisation of their I(mperative) element.

94 It may be that in all cases of conditional modals there is an underlying conditional element (like that suggested in the case of the external modals, but not, in other cases, so restricted) which requires the presence of *would* (or under modalisation, other conditional modal forms) in the VP, even where there is no corresponding *will.* Only some such consideration will allow for the derivation of non-complex (modalised) *would* (as in *It would fall*).

95 Thus, the rules introducing most instances (at least) of modals are further candidates for 'demotion' from the rules of the base (*cf* J. Lyons, 'Towards a "notional" theory of the "parts of speech"', *JL,* 2, 1966, 209–36).

96 Some aspects of a more formal presentation are discussed in the appendix to Part 2.

97 *eg: possible* (in some instances, at least) seems to represent a 'neutralisation' of (complex) *can* and *may* (*be able* and *be permitted*), with respect to whether or not the action depends on the subject. Consider *It's possible for him to come tomorrow,* which may be complex or non-complex, and, in a complex interpretation, is ambiguous between external and non-external.

98 *Cf* the derivation for questions proposed in Katz and Postal, *op cit, p* 149, note 9.

99 *Cf* the Basque 'modal' forms corresponding to complex *can: ahal du* ('he has the power to'); and *must: behar du* ('he has an obligation/need to'). See P. Lafitte, *Grammaire basque,* Bayonne, 1962, *pp* 348–9. A similar structure presumably underlies *He has (got) to visit her*; just as *be to* is to be related to forms like *be obliged to, be expected to* (the meaning of *be to* being what such

verbs have in common). In both cases we have to do with a deleted pro-element (*cf* note 93).

100 McIntosh, *op cit* (see note 8).
101 See again Anderson, 'Ergative and nominative in English', 1–9.
102 Rules II.iii.1 and II.iii.2 in Anderson, *op cit* (liii).
103 P. S. Rosenbaum, 'Phrase structure principles of English complex sentence formation', *JL*, 3, 1967, 103–18.
104 However, see O. Jespersen, *The Philosophy of Grammar*, p 325.

Norman Macleod
Lecturer in English Language, University of Edinburgh

This familiar regressive series
Aspects of style in the novels of Kingsley Amis

There is no branch of criticism in which learning as well as good sense is more required than to forming an accurate judgment of style, though there is none, I believe, in which every trifling reader is more ready to give his decision.[1]

Of all kinds of writing, there is none on which this variety of opinions is so common as in those of humour, as perhaps there is no word in our language of which men have in general so vague and indeterminate an idea.[2]

1

It is perhaps not inappropriate to preface this study of style in the work of Kingsley Amis with these two quotations from Henry Fielding. Not just because Fielding is a master in the field of comic fiction where Amis is perhaps our most distinguished contemporary practitioner; nor because of similarities that can occur to us in their practice of – and their ideas about – the art of fiction. Rather, these epigraphs are useful in focusing attention on the two major topics of this paper and in giving us timely caution as to how tentative and personal our conclusions must be at this moment. Perhaps by the end of this essay the epigraphs may themselves be taken as a useful starting-point for a study of one stylistic aspect of Henry Fielding's critical pronouncements. Some might even want to say that the opinions and critical *dicta* of Fielding hold out more interesting and rewarding areas of study than any aspect of Kingsley Amis's fiction. Despite, or perhaps because of (to use an Amisism), any such view this paper will consider some features of language in the work of Amis and, following the focus of our epigraphs, attempt to define (*a*) some aspects of his style and (*b*) some of the sources and functions of comedy in his novels. The undertaking will be seen to be revealing and interesting.

Perhaps the best way to approach the fiction of Kingsley Amis is to read the whole group of his novels together in the sequence of their publication.[3] From such a reading will emerge a sense that these novels are held together by more than just being the work of one author. For instance, the minor character L. S. Caton, who purloins Jim Dixon's first attempt at academic publication and brings it out in a foreign language and under his own name, turns up in all the other novels, briefly impingeing on the hero's life, as a signature on 'a sheet hastily torn from a pad bearing a few ill-written lines in green ink', a sheet which informs the reader that Caton will be available 'in due course' and that he will be writing again 'before very long'. These same phrases are always repeated from novel to novel, as Caton, after his involvement with Dixon, moves off to the Argentine, then returns, and then turns up in the USA with the claim that he has written a book on his experiences in South America. This curious, zany trick is very like that used by Waugh in his treatment of Tangent in *Decline and Fall*. Indeed, a dentist's mistress, almost as ubiquitous in Amis's fiction as Caton, may have some relation to the one who appears in *Decline and Fall*. She turns up in the thoughts of Garnet Bowen, the hero of *I Like it Here*, among other types most of whom are found as characters in other Amis novels:

> You never knew the sort of people you might meet in connection with horses: auctioneers' wives, solicitors' daughters, dentists' mistresses, on a bad day even – he supposed dimly – aristocrats with titles, all talking horribly about horses and not about horses.

Other instances of this link by repetition and cross-reference between the novels can be found. 'Oh, I never count them. It's a bad habit, counting them', says Julian Ormerod in *Take a Girl Like You* when talking about women, using almost exactly the words Jim Dixon used when telling Christine about how much he had had to drink the night he stayed at the Welch household.

John Lewis, in *That Uncertain Feeling*, observes:

> I couldn't remember ever, since getting married, going to make a cup of tea without encountering, at the very outset, a heavy teapot.

When Lewis later re-appears in a short story (*Moral Fibre*)[4] he is still bedevilled by the uncooperativeness of the objects of everyday living:

I could hardly remember ever having made up the fire without encountering, at the very outset, a light coal scuttle.

Other examples could be cited. What they add up to is a sense that these novels of Amis's are linked and inter-related with each other in a deliberate manner by means of devices of comic writing which add to the amusement or entertainment that each of the novels offers to the reader capable of spotting them, *ie* the reader familiar with the novels – and treating them – as a body of work, and not as separate fictional efforts.

That is the first point. But these devices are also, more importantly and with others, means towards the creation of that much-recognised (if somewhat unjustly maligned) type, the Amis hero. They point to the fact that the Amis hero's experiences are those of everyday, that his thoughts, feelings and expressions are not unusual, that they are far from being extraordinary. In fact, to the contrary. The devices compel our willing involvement, our necessary (and perhaps relieved) identification with the Amis hero by the fact that what happens to him is what may have happened to us, what he says is what we, in our casual public utterances, might say. Garnet Bowen spent his schooldays making a book on how often during the course of a lesson the French master would say 'of course' and 'and so on'. When he returns his books to the public library he automatically pays fines.[5] Jim Dixon, impatient and hurrying to catch a train, endures a slow, halting bus-journey. And John Lewis mournfully contemplates uncooperative teapots and coal scuttles, not coffee percolators and off-peak heaters. In their everyday experiences, in their ordinary settings, the Amis heroes are related to each other and we are involved with them. In their everyday, muddling-along, phatic expressions, their expressions are common, currently shared clichés, applicable to many situations.

The Amis hero, the central character of each of the novels, is most frequently a male whose everyday troubles at work and in love are presented to us in detail: Jim Dixon, John Lewis, Garnet Bowen, Patrick Standish, Roger H. St John W. Micheldene (the latter is more than any of the others an 'odd man out' and not only because of his name: a lapsed Catholic, a divorcé, anti-semitic, ignorant of jazz and science fiction, a *bon viveur* and expert on snuff and cigars, he is a puzzling mutation of the earlier Amis hero and in some ways their reverse image. But he does exhibit, more emphatically, a more ferocious expression of their anguishes and difficulties with God, death, marriage, language – human relations in general). There are recurrent minor types in the novels like Bertrand Welch, Harry Bannion, Julian Ormerod, and lately, in *The Anti-Death League*, a female character related to these, particularly by her social dialect, Lady Hazell. And, of course, Jenny Bunn, the most centrally important female character of any Amis novel, has many affinities with the usual male hero. But the line of central characters, from Dixon to Micheldene, is the group with most obvious recurrent similarities: the group of typical Amis heroes.

The Amis hero is obsessively interested in women, preoccupied with that area of human relationships involving the opposite sex. He is literate, well read, with definite 'no-nonsense' tastes of his own: his passion for science fiction is based upon a long-standing and well-informed interest. His other major hobby is jazz, as listener rather than performer. He is usually a university graduate, though not possessing the highest qualifications: only Garnet Bowen appears to have graduated, or to admit to graduating, with a first-class degree (in English: the Amis figure is resolutely an Arts man, and his profession is tenuously related to that training: teaching, librarianship, literary journalism, publishing). He is not entirely happy, though the misgivings are minor, about the process of education he has undergone. The Amis hero cannot avoid difficulties and nagging troubles in his everyday life. But there is something else, over and above these details of habits, interests and outlook, that holds together these five male Amis heroes. And it is an aspect of their language, particularly the language of their thoughts and private reactions, as it is presented to the reader in a mode akin to 'free indirect speech'. It is here perhaps that Emmon Bach's characterisation of style as 'a set of characteristics of linguistic usage'[6] can be seen to apply most helpfully. The Amis heroes are related by a style, by a shared set of characteristics of linguistic usage that recur in the private language of each of them. Buffon said that the style is the man: 'le style, c'est l'homme même'. Perhaps it is better to think of style as the man speaking or the man using language. Certainly the Amis hero's style can be seen usefully in this light. This, of course, is not to exclude the possibility of the Amis hero having a style in the strict interpretation of Buffon's phrase: shared views, feelings, reactions, beliefs. Rather, by emphasising the linguistic nature of this style, we are admitting that this style will have a philosophic or thematic dimension as well. We should not be content to define style merely by listing various utterances typically found in the language of a text, an author, or a character, or, as in the case of Amis's novels, a type who is easily identifiable on other grounds in addition to linguistic ones; and then exhibiting the relatedness of these utterances by analytic techniques. Bach's characterisation can be usefully seen as ambiguous. When we speak of 'characteristics of *linguistic usage*' we should be understood as meaning not only the language used but also the purpose of this usage and the effect gained by this usage. To the examination of *what* language is used we should add considerations of *how* and *why* this language is used before we make any claim to having examined *style* in the work of a writer, or in the expression of a character. *Formal* aspects of a style are of importance but this importance should not be stressed to the total exclusion of matters of a *contextual* nature, relating not to an utterance's *shape* or structure but to its *sense*, its effect, its purpose. We shall now look at some linguistic usages characteristic of the Amis hero.

We can observe how, for much of *Lucky Jim*, Jim Dixon is content to keep his views of the world and situation in which he finds himself to himself. Though Dixon pretends otherwise, by devices of cliché and phatic communion in his conversations with most of the other characters in the book – particularly those like Professor Welch who might have a bearing on his future retention of his appointment – the reader is left in no doubt that Dixon finds himself at odds with this world, with its pretences. This is shown to us very clearly by Dixon's habit of privately exposing the clichés of others. In his own mind Dixon takes their clichés literally and exposes their hollowness and carelessness. Here are some examples:

(*a*) '. . . I must say one or two pastels seemed to fetch him, . . .'
Fetch him a vomiting basin, Dixon thought   (LJ/113)

(*b*) 'He's such a queer mixture, you see'
Naming to himself the two substances of which he personally thought Bertrand a mixture, Dixon said: 'In what way?' (LJ/142)

(*c*) '. . . and the resulting confusion . . . my word . . .'
Quickly deciding on his own word Dixon said it to himself   (LJ/8)

(*d*) 'I've not seen her for a week or two'
Or three, Dixon added uneasily to himself   (LJ/9)

This next example shows how this destruction of clichés is not confined to those noticed in the usage of others. Dixon is capable of catching himself:

(*e*) Yes, hang on at all costs.
   One of the costs was immediately presented in the form of a well-remembered voice baying directly into his ear.   (LJ/99)

Dixon is quick to spot clichés and to expose them by taking some word as being used neutrally and pointing to its normal lexical relations in any such ordinary usage. The Amis hero is quick to notice ways in which language can mislead, in which language can fail to be acute as it should be, in which language can be played around with. This playing around with language leads to amusement and is a source of comedy in Amis. It is funny, yes: but it is funny as a way of being serious. This in fact could provide an excellent characterisation of Amis's work: as he himself has remarked in print 'laughter [is] to be taken seriously'.[7] Here are some examples of one way in which this effect is achieved.

(*a*) the fake, or possibly genuine, eighteenth-century sideboard
                                                                        (LJ/59)

(*b*) . . . a smart lad from whom great things, or at any rate things, might be expected . . .   (TUF/217)

(*c*) It was queer, or possibly not so queer, that this crowd . . .
                                                                        (TUF/36)

(*d*) – just as hard as it was to remember that anything in trousers, or rather divested of its trousers, would have suited her equally well
                                                                        (TAG/145)

(*e*) . . . why I shouldn't let my thoughts wander, or rather sprint, in that direction   (TUF/11)

(*f*) . . . a . . . painting from the brush, or perhaps the trowel, of a fashionable Czech artist . . .   (TUF/43)

   In these examples we find clichés or idioms, conventional much-used expressions, being undercut by the insertion of the alternative clause introduced by 'or possibly', 'or at any rate', 'or rather', 'or perhaps' and followed by an antonym of the original term so that in the end what is really said is the very opposite of what was going to be said originally: so that the language reveals the character's mind and attitude more precisely and revealingly than his original cliché might have done. There are times when the Amis hero employs this device, again amusingly, and again against his own original word, but on these occasions it is done to gain imprecision rather than precision. There are occasions when the Amis hero does not have available enough situational information to be clear as to what he should say. But this imprecision is again as precise and truthful for this type of situation as the earlier examples were for their contexts. Once more the Amis hero avoids what would be, for him, a lie.

(a) Interlocked, they slid along the smooth white door of the man-high refrigerator and came to rest against the dishwasher, or perhaps the spindrier. (OFE/58)

(b) A man wearing a bright ginger-coloured cap was planting something, or digging it up, in a garden opposite. (TUF/92)

John Lewis is sharpest of all Amis figures in catching imprecisions and clichés, not only like Dixon in the speech of others but also in his own narration; here we see examples of the devices noted above:

(a) 'You know, John, that I'm in fairly close touch with the Council?'
    'Yes.' This fairly close touch, publicised by Jenkins almost daily, was a hyperbole, or perhaps a euphemism, for his relations with a chicaning and tattling old alderman ... (TUF/122)

(b) '... it wouldn't surprise me in the least if he decided to throw his influence behind you in the matter of the forthcoming election.'
    While Jenkins paused, perhaps to review the propriety of an *influence* being said to be *thrown behind* a person, I exulted for a moment. (TUF/122)

Language is shown to be a convention which can mislead, and which can be used misleadingly by the character: but also a convention that allows the character to be honest, that can be made to state this perception clearly, and not misleadingly. The Amis hero is here, as almost always in his private thoughts, using language to exhibit its trickiness and its conventionality, playing around with it to get it to say exactly what he wants it to say. The 'playing around' leads to amusement, to linguistically based comedy: the achievement of exact statement – the purpose and effect of the utterance – marks a serious aspect of the Amis hero and his mind. The same effect is attained as was attained by privately treating the clichés of others literally. Now the clichés of oneself are warily taken apart.

It might be said of an Amis novel that we can never be sure who is doing the talking – author or character. In fact, we can, or rather it does not matter. The thoughts of characters being carefully presented to us by an author are shown directly to us – by a mode of 'free indirect speech'. Significantly, on the points discussed, there is no difference between the first person narration of *That Uncertain Feeling* and the other novels. But whoever is speaking to us – and it does not matter – in the following examples we find another characteristic of the Amis hero in the similes – exaggerated, far-fetched, highly contemporary similes – which occur when the Amis hero is troubled, mildly or seriously.

Again, language is an object of play and a source of comedy but in these instances the point of the amusement of the reader (and, perhaps the character) is to play down some difficulty he has encountered or some serious implication of his behaviour.

(*a*) As I got nearer I felt more and more like a man going into bat in his first Test Match with the score at 19 for 3.   (TUF/173)

(*b*) A burst of neurotic frustration rocked Bowen in his seat: it was like putting a new ribbon in his typewriter to the accompaniment of a ringing telephone, a waiting taxi, and a full bladder.   (LIH/174)

(*c*) Within quite a short time he was contriving to sound like an unusually fanatical Nazi trooper in charge of a book-burning reading out to the crowd excerpts from a pamphlet written by a pacifist, Jewish, literate communist.   (LJ/226)

(*d*) If my character was, as it appeared to be, not so much bad or weak as unworkable, farcically unfitted for its task, like an asbestos firefighter, then that was more than merely bad luck on Jean.
                                                              (TUF/142)

Next, some examples of another type of linguistic play in the Amis hero's consciousness. This usage is a device which relies on the extension of a reporting or stating clause by a progression of verbs of 'stating' *eg: feel, think, say*, etc.

(*a*) 'Very good indeed', I said, though I really thought, or thought I thought . . .   (TUF/39)

(*b*) He now felt convinced, or felt he thought he felt convinced, . . .
                                                              (LIH/124)

Here the character makes fun of his own apparently serious perceptions or thoughts. But again a serious point is made. What emerges is that the hero is chary of being definite about his own thoughts and statement, of thinking or feeling something absolutely and without some qualification.

These latter examples can be tied up with all previous examples:

language is played around with to expose the character's perception and thoughts as precisely as possible. 'He now felt convinced, or felt he thought he felt convinced . . .' is again a truthful statement where merely 'He now felt convinced' would not be. The character perceives how language may fail to express perfectly, may be an imprecision, a protective cover, and takes appropriate steps to attain the clarity he desires. Language is played about with to prevent the user being led down the semantic garden path, so that he can be clear, perceptive and serious in his statement.

But there are other expressions in the Amis hero's private language which exhibit him playing with language, not just to attain a more clear statement of his perceptions but also – and primarily – to avoid, to escape from, the serious implications of this realisation. There are things which occur to the Amis hero which he prefers to hide from, to run away from. Here he plays about with language to escape from one thought, which he prefers not to know about, and often the purpose of this play is to enable him to move to another, less frightening view which he is quite prepared to tolerate mentally – and express clearly. But when this idea is expressed he has moved from the original, more pressing, revealing and often self-critical thought.

Here is John Lewis coming home after an evening's entanglement with Elizabeth Gruffydd-Williams, the upperclass woman with whom he is becoming involved, and using a 'characteristic Amis locution':[8]

Feeling a tremendous rakehell, and not liking myself much for it, and feeling rather a good chap for not liking myself much for it, and not liking myself at all for feeling rather a good chap, I got indoors, vigorously rubbing lipstick off my mouth with my handkerchief.

(TUF/81)

Lewis's language has the following characteristics : a recursive clause structure; an unusual degree (in one sentence) of repetition of lexical items; reflexive pronouns; balancing of negative and positive statements; pronominal 'it' as a frequent anaphoric referent. The whole sentence enables Lewis to go indoors not liking himself, yes, but for a much less worrying reason than originally. And in letting himself off the hook, Lewis manages to prevent, for any length of time, his being worried about his conduct. The reader, too, is affected by the zany tortuousness of the sentence. It puzzles, it amuses: but like the Amis simile, it leads us into forgetting the original point of moral and self-perceptive seriousness that fails to develop as it shifts amusingly to express some other point.

Jim Dixon exhibits this same trait. One of his students, the unfriendly Michie, approaches him and says:

> 'Ah, Mr Dixon, I hope you're not busy.'
> Dixon knew exactly how well Michie knew exactly how and why he, Dixon, couldn't be busy.   (LJ/97)

What Dixon 'knows' is not a simple admission that he is not busy. Nor is it merely an awareness that Michie knows *that* he is not busy – it is the extent to which Michie knows *how* and *why*. The admissible fact of Dixon's idleness is buried deep in his realisation, with Michie being apparently more guilty than Dixon.

Perhaps Patrick Standish, worrying about his behaviour, particularly towards Jenny Bunn, is the one who most clearly exhibits this characteristic trick with language – and perhaps betrays its contemporary philosophical origins.[9] Again his expressions have many of the linguistic features noted in the language of John Lewis. Patrick can lose his thread, though, as well as change it.

(a) He hoped that if he ever saw himself as a bastard, instead of just seeing himself as seeing himself as a bastard, he would be drunk or in bed with a woman at the time.   (TAG/232)

(b) All that type of stuff, dying and so on, was a long way off, not such a long way off as it had once been admitted, and no doubt the time when it wouldn't be such a long way off as all that wasn't such a long way off as all that, but still. Still what?   (TAG/274)

(c) After that he thought about Jenny for a bit, and then about how odd it was that what you did when people were not there turned out afterwards to be as important as what you did when they were there. 'Never again,' he said. 'I know now.' He walked a few yards into the darkness. 'I'm sorry, I know I'm a bastard, but I'm trying not to be. But you know all that. That's your job, isn't it? You may not be much good at anything else but you're scholarship standard on that one. But I'm not trying to get credit with you by saying I know I'm a bastard. Nor by saying I'm not trying to get credit. Nor by saying I'm not trying to by saying . . . trying . . . you know what I mean. Nor by saying that. Nor by saying that.'
He broke off this familiar regressive series . . .   (TAG/245)

This latter makes most clear how the language works to evade, how it is made amusing to be less serious. By describing his statements (obviously addressed to the somewhat inefficient being who fulfils the Amis hero's idea of God) as a 'regressive series' – a 'familiar' one not only to him but to the devoted reader of Amis – Patrick is obviously thinking in a logical terminology. Interestingly enough, his statements form a recursive linguistic structure. Other linguistic features, already indicated, are also present. But this particular recursion (or progression) is based on one important fact about Patrick's statements to his deity: the use of the verb *say* as a prefatory verb to most of his later sentences. 'I'm sorry, I know I'm a bastard, but I'm trying not to be,' says Patrick in the early part of his monologue. But it is not on the basis of this self-knowledge that Patrick suspects that he is trying to get credit: it is on the basis of *saying* that very sentence 'I know I'm a bastard'. The reporting verb *say* becomes a part of his direct statement. Nor is he trying to get credit 'by not trying to get credit' but rather by '*saying* I'm not trying to get credit with you'. And the series is allowed to go on, each time prefaced by a use of *say* within the direct statement, until Patrick loses his thread and finishes up lamely: 'Nor by saying that. Nor by saying that', where the first of the pair refers to the sentence that has gone before, and the second refers to the first instance of 'Nor by saying that'. It could go on forever, always moving away from the forgotten, original point 'I know I'm a bastard, but I'm trying not to be'.

The prefatory *say* in Patrick's utterances significantly alters their point. 'I say I know' is much less an admission of fault than 'I know'. It is ambivalent: it is more at risk of denial: its effect is to render less useful and valid his perception about himself by showing that his perception always is in his own statement. Patrick's admission of fault is merely a linguistic act like 'I promise' where 'I promise' is to make the promise. 'I say I know' reduces knowledge to an act of language. It is this very action by statement – the fact that an admission of weakness is primarily and necessarily a saying – that Patrick perceives: and it is what he tries to avoid by his denials. But these denials are themselves linguistic acts and entail further denials. In all this we see again Amis's play with the trickiness of language to expose that very trickiness. And, through this, for Patrick, as for Dixon in his exchange with Michie, blame is attached in a quarter other than the hero. It is blame for a fault that is not the hero's and is different from the one originally brought to light. But in Patrick's case the new point is at least an admission of how he and the other Amis heroes can – and indeed must – avoid their own primary perceptions about themselves. The important point that Patrick comes to is that his moral perceptions about himself are his own moral perceptions. As such they are as likely to be wrong as they are to be right, as likely to be dishonest as to be honest, as likely to be funny and evasive as serious and frank. It is in the end a serious point, to precisely identify why one cannot and must not be serious: and to admit it.

Here we can recall a poem of Amis's, *The Voice of Authority: A Language Game*. Many important and effective sections of Amis's fiction are echoed in his poems.[10] Here is no exception: the poem can be seen as encouraging 'precise statement rather than the cloudy concepts of metaphysics'.[11]

Do this. Don't move. O'Grady says do this,
You get a move on, see, do what I say.
Look lively when I say O'Grady says.

Say this. Shut up. O'Grady says say this,
You talk fast without thinking what to say.
What goes is what I say O'Grady says.

Or rather let me put the point like this:
O'Grady says what goes is what I say
O'Grady says; that's what O'Grady says.

By substituting you can shorten this,
Since any god you like will do to say
The things you like, that's what O'Grady says.

The harm lies not in that, but in that this
Progression's first and last terms are I say
O'Grady says, not just O'Grady says.

Yet it's O'Grady must be out of this
Before what we say goes, not what we say
O'Grady says. Or so O'Grady says.

As a note by Amis makes clear the poem refers to an army training game where instructions prefaced by 'O'Grady says' are to be followed, those not so prefaced to be ignored.

The instruction 'Do this' in fact means its negative opposite 'Don't move': 'Say this' demands silence: 'shut up'. But 'O'Grady says do this' or 'O'Grady says say this' bring forth appropriate reactions of movement or talk, they in fact mean *Do this* and *say this*. The language game allows language to be played around with so that a statement can mean its opposite. In this language game the only really meaningful utterances are those prefaced by the performative-like 'O'Grady says':

What goes is what I say O'Grady says.[12]

But already lurking in here is the fact that such a statement itself is not permissible without the prefatory 'O'Grady says' and, putting the point another way, the above line acquires a synonymous expression just as *Do this* and *Say this* did:

O'Grady says what goes is what I say
O'Grady says.

The progression can be continued

: that's what O'Grady says.

And the progression can continue, as it does in the poem, but sometime the fact must be faced

that this
Progression's first and last terms are I say
O'Grady says, not just O'Grady says.

As is said in *Against Romanticism:*

But complexities crowd the simplest thing
And flaw the surface that they cannot break.

In relation to language the point of both poems would be appreciated by Patrick Standish and the other Amis figures and it is a point that they would welcome and regret at the same time. But at least they know about it and appreciate its implications.

To conclude, some sentences which fall into the category Christopher Ricks characterised as 'tail-biting rotations'.[13] Often similarly structured to those previously discussed (in their complicated and balanced syntax and lexical repetition) these are expressions where a perception of a wry and bitter sort is made, not about the character or conduct of oneself, but of others, or of some apparently inevitable fact of life, applicable to the Amis hero, but not restricted to him. It is a perception of general validity in his mind and he himself is within its scope.

10—E.S.E.S.

It is a facet of life where by observing the point one is merely noting an irritating concomitant of human activities, one of the many minor hindrances to the perfect running of human affairs and relationships. Once it has been said, moreover, it is so obviously true as to make one wonder why it has not been perceived before. Like the objects – and some of the people – in its population, the organisation of the world of the Amis hero is not completely to his liking.

(a) . . . even if it had been mildly annoying to have on hand at the same time somebody who wanted him but whom he did not want and somebody whom he wanted but who did not want him.
                                                                              (TAG/85)
(b) This was a bit of the old cleft stick method, where they asked you to commit yourself without committing themselves to asking you to commit yourself.   (TAG/57)
(c) A man's sexual aim, he had often said to himself, is to convert a creature who is cool, dry, calm, articulate, independent, purposeful into a creature that is the opposite of these; to demonstrate to an animal which is pretending not to be an animal that it is an animal.
                                                                              (OFE/122)
(d) Not caring what one drank unfortunately did not guarantee not caring what one had drunk.   (OFE/73)
(e) . . . how odd it was that what you did when people were not there turned out afterwards to be as important as what you did when they were there.   (TAG/245)
(f) On the other hand, being one of the landlord's sort [homosexual] undoubtedly gave you an edge over my sort when it came to dealing with Elizabeth's sort.   (TUF/127)

And the feature, as Ricks noted in his review, turns up in Amis's sixth novel, *The Anti-Death League*:

(g) Only by having been to bed with somebody was it possible to attain the pitch of conversational intimacy that was needed as a prelude to getting them into bed.   (p 161)

Always these views are expressed in such a way that we are amused more than we are instructed by what they perceive. The Amis hero fights shy – and helps us to fight shy – of the irritating facts of life: the Amis hero stylises his view in his own particular way to sugar another pill.

But these also exhibit the Amis hero's ever-present search for precise statement, clarity and exactness, in their definitions by modification of imprecise, 'empty' general lexical items as *somebody, animal,
do, sort*. The definition of this last item, *sort*, by its modifiers *the landlord's, my, Elizabeth's* gives an exactitude to the statement that we do
not expect from a repetition of an 'empty' lexical item like *sort*. John
Lewis's sentence is no less clear or truthful than would be 'Being a
homosexual male undoubtedly gave you an edge over a heterosexual
male when it came to dealing with a heterosexual female'. But in the
characteristic demotic of the Amis character it is more appreciable,
more penetratingly funny. And, not only in the context where it
occurs, it has a particularity of reference that the reader can accept,
just as the character can, and that neither would realise if it were stated
as a generic and indefinite generalisation. By being so particular, so
concrete, the 'tail-biting rotation' achieves a more general relevance
than any abstraction.

There is one kind of sentence of this 'tail-biting' type, with general
and particular application, which perhaps constitutes the only serious
perception about life and conduct that the Amis hero allows himself.
His linguistic guard is still up in these expressions which encompass the
whole predicament of the Amis hero as he tackles the difficulties of his
everyday behaviour in his typical problem-inducing settings: love
affairs, travelling abroad, attempted seductions, working, trying to
be nice rather than nasty, trying to behave correctly rather than badly,
trying to behave as he thinks he ought to rather than as he actually does.
The point occurs to him as a kind of revelation that is obvious. His
character and conduct may, recalling John Lewis's words, be farcically
unsuited to their task, but the real lesson the Amis hero learns is that
his character and his conduct are unalterable. It is the world and the
task of living that must take the blame as being farcically unsuited to
the Amis character. He must go on behaving as he has always done,
being what he has always been. This is the only point the Amis hero
can really take to heart. But he himself is not solely involved: he sees
that he is no different from other people. Assuming that he was has
been his mistake before. He is no better and no worse than other
people. And in these expressions other people are ironically condemned as the Amis hero is justified, because they demand that he be
justified in this way. The 'tail-biting rotations' here are subtly different
from those that went before. The pronoun *you*, used impersonally in
the sense of *one*, has a particular application that covers, but goes be-

yond, the Amis figure himself. It is more general because it is not *I* or *he*: it is more particular because it is not simply *one* or *they*.

(*a*) Doing what you wanted to do was the only training, and the only preliminary, needed for doing more of what you wanted to do.

(LJ/146)

(*b*) It wasn't so much doing what you wanted to do that was important, I ruminated, as wanting to do what you did.   (TUF/82)

(*c*) . . . doing something you didn't want to do (like going abroad) was going to be just as hard as doing something you did want to do.

(LIH/120)

What you do and what you *want* to do are expected by the Amis hero to be, and to remain, two very different things, but in the end he sees, and shows us, that they are the same, linguistically equivalent, synonymous. Jenny Bunn and Roger Micheldene make the point of possible linguistic equivalence, though their sentences in their complex structure appear to hide their structural ambiguities:

(*a*) What was he doing that he ought not to do, or not doing that he ought to do?   (OFE/59)

(*b*) She was getting tired of being told authoritatively that she was a fool for doing or not doing what she intended to do or not to do.

(TAG/266)

In each sentence we are led to believe that the positive alternative of one clause is primarily related to the negative alternative of the following clause. But the construction of each sentence makes for ambiguity, so that the positive alternatives of each clause can be related, as can the negative alternatives.

Garnet Bowen, at the end of *I Like it Here*, sums up the dilemma that faces the Amis hero in many of his plights, in all his experience, in all his moral dilemmas, and afterwards too:

But he was going to write something else instead, about a man who was forced by circumstances to do the very thing he most disliked the thought of doing and found out afterwards that he was exactly the same man as he was before.   (LIH/223)

Reflexively, or if you like regressively, it would characterise, not only the hero-type he has created, but also the fictional purpose and achievement of Kingsley Amis.

2

I would want to follow David Lodge[14] in making a distinction between the *modern novel* and the *contemporary novel* and to base this distinction as Lodge does, but perhaps more firmly, and in a sense, in a different way, in language and use of language. What I mean is clearly summed up by Robert Oliphant.[15]

> One measure of the vitality of the contemporary novel might well be the extent to which the conventions of language are adapted and reshaped. With the exception of the French 'anti-novelists', there have been no recent bold innovations in the actual language of the novel. Joyce's verbal play, Faulkner's prose jungle, Dos Passos's camera eye, Virginia Woolf's hydra-headed speaker – these heresies of a previous generation are the commonplaces of the present. Innovations, where they exist today, are less striking.

In contemporary novels, as I would want to use the term, the rules of ordinary English grammar are not broken deliberately and obviously. There are no bold innovations within the grammatical and lexical structural possibilities of the language in the usage of contemporary novels that immediately strike us as interesting forms of language which we have quite definitely not encountered before in our experience of the language. If we accept a contemporary linguistic motto we could say that most of the sentences that we encounter in our language are new to us and our experience of the language.[16] But with a modern novelist like Joyce or Faulkner we are aware of the novelty of the experience of their sentences in quite a different way from the novelty of sentences (if we notice it at all) that we encounter in non-literary uses of language. And, in turn, we are much more likely to be struck by the novelty of an expression of Joyce's or Faulkner's than we are with expressions of novelists like Amis who appear content to write in something very closely akin to our intuition of what is ordinary everyday English, without breaking any formal rules.

It seems to me, however, that just because of this we cannot regard the contemporary novel as stylistically neutral but rather that we get at its style in a somewhat different way from the methods of stylistic analysis that we would bring to bear on a novel by Joyce. Perhaps we should seek to identify the style of a contemporary fiction, not in novel (and, except in parody, destined to be unique) forms of language, but in novel usages of acceptable forms, which are equally destined to be uniquely associated with a contemporary novelist. Our rallying-cry

should, perhaps, not be that indefinitely many of the sentences we encounter are, beyond question or doubt, new to our linguistic experience (and, by implication, new in form) but that many of the sentences
we encounter are new to our linguistic experience – or are striking to
us – because of their usage, their situational and contextual implications rather than their formal characteristics.

With a novel by Joyce the analysis of unusual, non-casual language
can precede the explication of the role of such utterances in terms of significance in the context of the understanding of the whole novel. But I
do not think we would get very far if we were to follow this method in
studying the style of a contemporary novel, whose interest and vitality,
linguistically speaking, lies, not in extensions of the existing grammatical and lexical structure of English, but rather in the adaptation and
reworking, with recurrence and repetition, of perfectly acceptable and
grammatical English expressions within a unique context – the context of theme, view and tone of a work of fiction that is built up through
the text of that work. It may be that with contemporary novels what is
stylistic must be perceived through a process where emphasis is placed
on comparative semantic considerations rather than on comparative
lexical and grammatical considerations.

In brief, what puzzles me is this question: is it true that we can make
much more telling comments of a linguistic nature about some expressions of Amis's if we see them in relation to a view of what his
novels are about, or are trying to say, rather than by comparing them
with other, casual and ordinary-looking English utterances? We can
see just why Joyce's language is interesting by referring to more normal
non-Joycean English. On the basis of such a consideration we would
not indicate everything about Joyce's expression. But we would still
indicate something useful. But just how helpful, or useful, or insight-
ful would be an analysis in isolation from other considerations of the
grammar and lexis of sentences from an Amis novel? I feel as I have
tried to show that much more relevant comments about linguistic
structures could be made if these considerations took place after, and
in the light of, a reasonable critical response to Amis's fiction. I am not
redefining, by suggestion, the methodology of all stylistic analysis of
literature; but assuming, in an *ad hoc* way, that stylistics is concerned
with language deliberately used in a way that interests us; and that
sometimes, as in the case of a contemporary novelist like Amis, the
stylistic effect of an expression is better treated contextually or semantically rather than formally – in terms of sense as much as of shape.

I have tried to indicate already, in looking at the experiences and reactions of the Amis hero, one aspect of what these novels are trying to say. This I would claim is relevant background to my later comments about language.

Kingsley Amis has often said in contradiction of critics who have attempted a serious view of his novels as serious documents, moral or sociological or whatever, that he is only trying to write comic novels. In this aim he has been very successful, although a disavowal of any other purpose may be slightly disingenuous. And very often the source of his comedy lies in the use of language – not only by Amis himself in the narrative, or in any aside, but also in how language is used by characters in the acting out of the novels, in their dialogue, in their own silent reflections. Dixon – and Lewis and Bowen – always make fun of clichés, Amis characters see the funny side of misunderstandings, conversations abound in situational ambiguities; characters are identifiable by their speech exhibiting aspects of a particular social dialect, often to the reader's amusement *eg* the 'RAF-and-Jaguar' dialect of Julian Ormerod – 'a man made out of words' – and Wendy in *Take a Girl Like You*. There is the fun poked at foreigners' pronunciation of author's names in *I Like it Here*. And in every novel we encounter at least one instance of linguistic puzzle, that may never become clear to us. For instance, in *Take a Girl Like You* Patrick and Julian motor up to London, have an alcoholic lunch, go on drinking and then go off to visit the lady friends of Julian's with whom they are going to stay and neither of whom Patrick has met before. Patrick, very drunk by now, enters the sitting room on his own to make the acquaintance of one of the ladies, Joan. When she looks up he says:

> 'Hullo, I parry stashed a nowhere hermes peck humour speech own,' he heard himself say. 'June I haggle unction when donned ring gone oh swear.'   (TAG/220)

Patrick, we must remember, is drunk and what he hears himself say is his alcoholic articulation of (more or less):

> 'Hallo, I'm Patrick Standish – don't know – where I am – expect you must be Joan. Julian and I had lunch and went on drinking, God knows where.'

The representation of his drunken speech as a series of English words is funny in itself but also the close contrived collocations of words are hilarious, *viz – peck humour speech, haggle unction.*

Such comedy of language is very much in the nature of Amis's fiction. As David Lodge has said:

> there is this kind of delight in strange locutions, odd pronunciations, verbal errors and unconscious puns. It is indeed a recurrent feature of Amis's work, and the one which brings him closest to the 'techniques' of 'modern' fiction.[17]

But it does not bring him all that close. These are features of Amis's work that can be discussed apart from contextual significance within the novel (if they have any), in terms of their form and substance – their shape – rather than their sense. To make any such aspects of language stylistically important would seem to be out of the question for Amis. Some comments in reviews written by him make this clear. Reviewing *Lolita*,[18] Amis had this to say:

> The long battle against style hangs in the balance, and a reverse over Lolita could be damaging. Style, a personal style, a distinguished style, usually turn out in practice to mean a high idiosyncratic noise-level in the writing, with plenty of rumble and wow from imagery, syntax, and diction: Donne, Pater, Virginia Woolf. There is, however, a good deal of nostalgia for style nowadays among people of oldster age group or literary training; it shows in snorting accusations of gracelessness levelled against some younger novelists and merges into the hankering for 'experiment' that still dies hard. Those interested will have noticed a connection here with that yearning for uplift, or rich man's Billy Graham, which masquerades as reasoned apathy to modern British philosophy.

Quoting an extract from *Lolita*, Amis adds:

> No extract, however, could do justice to the sustained din of pun, allusion, neologism, alliteration, *cynghanedd*, apostrophe, parenthesis, rhetorical question, French, Latin, *anent*, *perchance*, *would fain, for the nonce* – here is style and no mistake.

and concludes:

> The end product sadly invokes a Charles Atlas muscleman of language. . . .

A year earlier[19] Amis had made similar points, identifying as villains 'those who are reared on Joyce and Virginia Woolf' and who are 'also likely to suffer from a craving for uplift, manifested in bouts of transitory enthusiasm for digests of the Kierkegaard-Nietzsche-Shaw line-up and a hysterical aversion to contemporary British philosophy'.[20] He added, revealingly:

> 'Experiment' in this context, boils down pretty regularly to 'obtruded oddity', whether in construction – multiple viewpoints and such – or in style: it is not felt that adventurousness in subject matter or attitude or tone really counts.

Amis, clearly, is not one to tolerate – or follow – 'the naive concept of style as ornament'.[21]

It is not in comic linguistic oddity, obtrusive and obvious, that Amis's style resides but in a teasing, playing around with language where not only is there no obtrusive oddity but, in fact, where expressions emerge that must be admitted as lexically acceptable and grammatical forms of English. This other type of linguistic play is also a source of comedy but this is comedy not only for the sake of being funny but also in order to avoid seriousness, in fact to be serious 'without the aid of evangelical puffing and blowing'.[22] There is a kind of shift during the expression or perception of a serious or straightforward idea, a playing around with the expression so that the idea, a serious one and often a moral one, is itself played around with and rendered less serious, or unserious, though never merely funny. The funniness is that of 'funny peculiar' rather than simply that of 'funny ha-ha': it is the essential funniness of life.

3

The far-from-comprehensive examples I have dealt can be taken as some of the stylistic 'fingerprints' of Kingsley Amis. The following passage is representative, not only of these formal stylistic 'fingerprints' but also of the thematic 'fingerprints' of Amis, with which the formal features are so intimately bound up, both causally and effectually, in making his style:

> Feeling that he would never be sure now about almost any given problem was beginning to obsess Bowen to a degree comparable with the liquidation of Mrs Knowles. For instance, his uncertainty about whether ot not it was right to spy on old Buckmaster now felt more or less permanently jelled. (Jelly, while he was on imagery, was a pretty good equivalent for the properties of his mind, Bowen decided: it was soft, it set easily, and it shook whenever anyone

went near it.) Anyway, he now felt convinced, or felt he thought he felt convinced, that Buckmaster must be Strether. It was so unlikely that he wasn't. On the other hand – and why was there always another hand? and not just *an*other hand, but half a dozen? – *Briareus and Scaevola*: an examination of the predicament of modern man, by Garnet Bowen: Hiscock & Weinstein, 25s. ON THE OTHER HAND, that earthquake they had had along the road a couple of hundred years ago must have seemed almost inconceivably unlikely right up to the time when the first tiles started dropping. Mm. You never could tell.   (LIH/124)

The reader, looking at this extract, was enlightened, or perhaps baffled, like a man at a Post Office counter who has been told that he still hasn't followed the instructions on the form correctly and must try again. This was just one of the many ways in which a problem which troubled him a lot manifested itself. So far he had not come up with an adequate answer to this question, the question of whether, if somebody did something funny, in the full knowledge that it was something funny done to avoid something serious, it was still something funny or had become, in the process, something serious. At the moment the question was complicated, or perhaps simplified, by the possibility that your awareness of what he wanted to do and your awareness that he was doing it in some way justified what he was doing.

Notes

1 Henry Fielding, *Familiar Letters between the Principal Characters in David Simple and Some Others*, ed W. E. Henley, London, 1903, *p* 19.
2 Henry Fielding, *Covent Garden Journal*, ed G. E. Jensen, London and New Haven, 1915, Vol 1, *p* 249.
3 In this study, we shall be principally concerned with the first five of Amis's novels, which form a group into which it would be very difficult indeed to integrate the sixth, and most recent, *The Anti-Death League* (Gollancz, London, 1966). These novels are (with details of editions used and abbreviations by which they are identified): *Lucky Jim* (Penguin paperback, London, 1961: LJ); *That Uncertain Feeling* (Foursquare paperback, London, 1960: TUF); *I Like It Here* (Foursquare paperback, London, 1961: LIH); *Take a Girl Like You* (Gollancz, London, 1961: TAG); *One Fat Englishman* (Gollancz, London, 1963: OFE).
4 Included in Amis's collection of short stories, *My Enemy's Enemy* (Penguin paperback, London, 1963).
5 In my own case, the stylo-statistics of 'and so on' and 'of course' were first studied during geography lessons. And I can hardly remember ever, since becoming a member, going to return books to the library without paying, at the very outset, a light, or perhaps a heavy, fine.

6 *Cf* Emmon Bach, 'The Syntax of Hölderlin's Poems: I', *Texas Studies in Literature and Language*, 2, 1960–1, 383–97.

7 *Cf* Kingsley Amis, 'Laughter's to be Taken Seriously', *New York Times Book Review*, 7 July 1957.

8 *Cf* David Lodge, 'The Modern, The Contemporary, And the Importance of being Amis', in his excellent *The Language of Fiction*, London, 1961, *pp* 243–67. In discussing *Lucky Jim*, Lodge was the first to point out the distinct kinds of language that Dixon uses in public and private.

9 The influence of present-day British philosophy and other contemporary intellectual phenomena, not only on Amis but also on his contemporaries Philip Larkin, John Wain and others (and their mutual influences) might make an interesting study in contemporary literary history.

10 The poems referred to are to be found in Amis's collection, *A Case of Samples: Poems 1946–1956*, London, 1956.

11 The phrase is from Bernard Bergonzi's useful and interesting article, 'Reputations – IX: Kingsley Amis', *London Magazine*, Vol 3, no 10, January 1964, 50–65. The phrase I use later, 'a man made out of words' of Julian Ormerod, is also from Bergonzi.

12 Dr Macdonald Emslie points out to me that a structural ambiguity in this line is important to the poem's tactics.

13 Christopher Ricks, Review of '*The Anti-Death League*', *New Statesman*, 71, 1966, 387.

14 Lodge, *op. cit.*

15 *Cf* Robert Oliphant, 'Public Voices and Wise Guys', *Virginia Quarterly Review*, 37, 1961, 522–37.

16 The notion that indefinitely many of the sentences we hear or speak are new to us is principally associated in linguistics with the theories of Noam Chomsky; *cf* his *Syntactic Structures*, The Hague, 1957; *Current Issues in Linguistic Theory*, The Hague, 1963.

17 *Cf* Lodge, *op cit*, *p* 262.

18 Kingsley Amis, Review of '*Lolita*', *The Spectator*, 6 November 1959, 635–6.

19 Kingsley Amis, 'Fresh Winds from the West', *The Spectator*, 2 May 1958, 565.

20 Here Amis's comments particularly point to the importance, to an understanding of his work and stance, of recent British philosophy, and especially, perhaps, the work of J. L. Austin.

21 Kingsley Amis, 'Anglo-Saxon Platitudes', *The Spectator*, 7 April 1957, 445.

22 The phrase occurs in *I Like It Here* (*p* 201) while Garnet Bowen muses about the world of Fielding's novels, while on a visit to Fielding's grave.

Phonetics

David Abercrombie

Professor of Phonetics, University of Edinburgh

Some functions of silent stress

I am not sure that 'silent stress' is the best term for what I want to discuss here. For one thing, stress is often equated with loudness, so it might at first seem difficult to see how stress could be silent. I prefer, however, to regard stress in a way which has nothing to do with loudness, that is to say as a 'gesture of the respiratory muscles' to use Peter Ladefoged's apt phrase,[1] and a gesture of course can be quite silent. For another thing, there are various other terms in this area which might be thought preferable to 'stress' in the present context – 'accent', or 'ictus', for example. Still, the expression 'silent stress' is fairly well established in several quarters, and so I shall continue to use it here, even though I believe it may not be the happiest choice; I believe a careful examination and redefinition of the terminology of this whole area is badly needed. What I want to discuss here is a certain kind of *pause*, found in all kinds of spoken English, which is not, like pauses of other kinds, paralinguistic, but is (potentially, at any rate) phonological – it is part of the structure of an utterance. Let me make clear why I want to call a pause of this kind a 'silent stress'.

English, like most Germanic languages, is a language with (in Pike's terminology) a 'stress-timed' rhythm – in nearly all its forms, at least (some West Indian dialects may have a syllable-timed rhythm, and so may Krio of Sierra Leone). In utterances in a language with stress-timed rhythm, the stresses tend to recur at approximately equal intervals of time – they are isochronous, provided nothing extra-linguistic occurs to prevent this (such as forgetting what one is going to say next). A strong rhythmic beat is thus established, for both the speaker and those listening to him. (It may be observed that the timing of this beat is quite often preserved between participants in conversation, when one speaker takes over from another. This may be especially marked when the conversation is animated. And D. S. MacColl has pointed out that 'any one who studies stage-dialogue will become aware that much of the art of a finished actor depends on *keeping time*, taking up his cue on the right beat'.[2])

However, there is sometimes a pause where a beat, according to the timing already established, might be expected to come, a pause which fills a gap which otherwise would be filled by a stressed syllable. The 'respiratory gesture' of stress, though without accompanying articulatory movements, perhaps still takes place during the pause. I believe it often does do so, even if in an inhibited form. But whether it does so or not is of little importance for our present purposes; the point is that this sort of pause does not throw out the rhythmic beat of stress-timing. It is such a pause, coinciding with the beat, that I call a silent stress. A pause like this is different in kind from other speech pauses. A silent stress is not felt by the listener to be a discontinuity in the utterance; it does not interrupt it, but is part of it; no hesitation is involved.

Not everyone, by any means, believes or has believed in the theory (which goes back to Joshua Steele in the eighteenth century) that English is a language of stress-timed rhythm. A. J. Ellis, for instance, did not believe it, and neither did Henry Sweet. But those who do not believe the theory, it should be noted, do not take account of silent stresses. If one looks for isochronism between stressed *syllables* only, it is fairly certain that, in a stretch of speech of any length, one will not find it. It is the *silent* stresses that keep the isochronous stress-pulse going, in all but the shortest utterances.

The importance of silent stress in the analysis of verse structure has been pointed out by many writers (who have used a variety of names for it), but the existence of silent stresses in other kinds of spoken English has much less frequently been noticed. A few people have drawn attention to them (including Joshua Steele himself), but there has been little systematic attempt to explain why or when they occur, and what sort of functions they perform. An analogy with punctuation, in the written language, has sometimes been drawn, but this does not go very far in explaining their occurrence. I want here to take a preliminary look at some of the functions of silent stress. It seems clear that it has several functions, and that these functions are not equally common in the various modes of use of spoken English. It seems also that sometimes a speaker has a choice whether to insert a silent stress into an utterance or not, so that one may speak of an optional silent stress;

and that at other times he *has* to insert one – the silent stress is obligatory. In illustrations of these different functions, I shall use the caret-mark, ∧, to show where a silent stress occurs in an utterance.

One common function of silent stress might be called its *syntactic* function; syntactic silent stresses are closely related to, indeed are part of, the syntax of the utterance. They are found in all kinds of spoken English. Their function can best be demonstrated by comparing sentences which form minimal pairs, and which, in writing and without context, would be ambiguous. A good example is provided by J. P. Thorne in his 'English imperative sentences'.³ The words 'boys stop here', he points out, can have either an imperative or a declarative interpretation. There are two possible ways of saying the words:

boys stop here
boys ∧ stop here

In the second of these, Thorne says, the silent stress, coming immediately after the noun, 'removes the possibility of the sentence being taken as a declarative'; it must be an imperative. The ambiguity of the well-known notice 'Gentlemen lift the seat' could be resolved, if spoken, in the same way. Such ambiguities can also be resolved, as Thorne points out, in writing too: 'boys, stop here', with the comma, must be imperative; though perhaps it is sometimes more effective, as in the second example, to refrain in writing from resolving the ambiguity (the sentence is seldom likely to be spoken).

In Act II Scene ii of *Macbeth* we find, after the line 'The multitudinous seas incarnadine', the ambiguous (in writing) phrase 'Making the green one red'. What is the meaning of 'one' here? Is it what Jespersen has called the *prop-word*, so that 'the green one' means the sea? Or does it go with 'red', so that the meaning is 'a single uniform red'? But it is only in writing that the phrase is ambiguous; in speaking it cannot be. One of the interpretations – the second – requires a silent stress, while the other does not:

making the green one red
making the green ∧ one red

The different pronunciations are obligatory for the different interpretations. Garrick, it appears, originally used the first interpretation, but later on came to prefer the other one. (In this instance also it is, of course, possible to disambiguate the phrase, by means of a comma, in writing. Some editions have 'Making the green one, red', and others
11—E.S.E.S.

have 'Making the green, one red'. There is also another way of doing
it: 'Making the green-one red' and 'Making the green – one red' can
also be found.)

Some phrases and sentences may be ambiguous in spoken form as
well as in writing, but may still have the possibility of disambiguation
by silent stress if necessary. 'Players please' is a rather doubtful
example.

Players ∧ please

would seem to be the usual way of giving an order in a tobacconist's
shop; but even without the silent stress, the intonation would almost
certainly show that a somewhat gratuitous assertion was not being
made. But an ambiguous spoken phrase such as 'old men and women'
cannot be clarified by intonation only. The two pronunciations

old ∧ men and women

and

old men ∧ and women,

however, will always clear up the ambiguity when it is necessary to do
so. The silent stress, in either case, is optional.

Syntactic silent stresses can be heard very frequently in prose read
aloud, and they are often obligatory there. The syntax of Dr Johnson's
sentence 'Prudence, as it is always wanted, is without great difficulty
obtained', for example, demands, when spoken, silent stresses after
'Prudence' and after 'wanted', just as the commas are obligatory in
writing. There has been a close connection, at least since the eighteenth
century, between punctuation and silent stresses, and it can be observed that most people, when reading aloud, follow a rather rough-
and-ready rule that a comma should be given a spoken value of a
single silent stress, and the stronger stops two consecutive silent
stresses.[4]

Syntactic silent stresses, we have seen, are sometimes optional,
sometimes obligatory. J. P. Thorne says, rather cautiously, that 'boys
stop here', in its imperative interpretation, *may* be marked by a silent
stress. It seems to me, though, that it *must* be; I feel the silent stress to
be obligatory for the imperative. I am not sure, on the other hand, that
in all contexts this silent stress rules out taking the sentence as a declarative one, as Thorne claims it does. I believe there are occasions
when

boys ∧ stop here

could be declarative; but this leads us to recognise that there are other functions of silent stress beside the syntactic. One of these functions might be called *emphatic*: in this function, a silent stress 'points up', gives special prominence to, the word or phrase which follows it. Thus an 'emphatic' silent stress could occur in a declarative sentence in some such context as:

(girls do what they like but) boys ∧ stop here.

This emphatic function of silent stress is a favourite device of radio and television commentators and announcers, but it is common enough in conversation too, as careful listening will reveal. For instance:

The most ∧ awful thing has happened

Another function of silent stress to which I want to draw attention is a curious one. I have not found it in conversation, but it is nevertheless quite common in certain other uses of spoken English, particularly on radio or television. This function is not related to the syntax of the sentence, nor to any of the individual words in it. The silent stress always comes between the last two stressed syllables of the utterance, whatever they are, and usually immediately following the word containing the penultimate stress; and what it does is to signal an immediately impending transition, either from one speaker to another, or from one topic to another. Thus in the television announcement

The time is nine and a half minutes ∧ to nine

the silent stress is a sign that a continuity announcer has come to the end of what he has to say, and a news-reader is about to take over. We might call this the *terminal* function of silent stress. Such silent stresses are commonly heard in many routine announcements:

BBC Television ∧ from Scotland

but they are often heard in other circumstances as well, as for instance when the title of the record which brings a programme to a conclusion is given thus:

The Way You Look ∧ Tonight

Out of context, utterances containing silent stresses thus placed would seem bizarre and inexplicable. In context, they can often be a valuable guide to the listener, as, for example, in the reading of long lists of football results:

Hearts two Rangers ∧ three
Arsenal one Sheffield United ∧ one,

the optional syntactic silent stress after the score of the first team being avoided. This use of terminal silent stress is adopted by many sports commentators.

The terminal function of silent stress may be reinforced by putting more than one in the utterance. I have noticed two, and even three, silent stresses in this function, alternating with the concluding stressed syllables of the utterance. For example, the last sentence of a news item in a television bulletin:

An inquiry into the accident ∧ will open ∧ tomorrow.

The more silent stresses there are, the greater the degree of finality indicated. The following sentence from a television news bulletin was not only the end of the news item, but of the bulletin itself. The story was about a chaffeur and his wife who had just inherited a very large sum from their late employer, and the announcer said:

They wouldn't ∧ be doing anything ∧ extravagant ∧ with the money.

And a similar example from a continuity announcer who was then going off the air:

You'll hear all about it ∧ at ten fifty ∧ in ∧ Grandstand

(the word 'in' receiving a stress). The terminal function of silent stress is not however confined to television and radio. It can be heard, for instance, from many public speakers when they come to the end of what they have to say.

Genuine hesitations in conversation, and other modes of spoken language, are recognised as such by various symptoms, among them being the fact that they tend to throw off the regular beat of the stress-pulse. Hesitations which are not genuine, but feigned in order to give the impression that the speaker is speaking impromptu when he is not, and at that particular moment is seeking for the *mot juste*, are seldom convincing; even when accompanied, as they often are, by a fleeting expression of pain. One reason why they are not convincing is because the speaker usually turns his feigned hesitation into a silent stress and the regular beat is thus not disturbed. (It is indeed very difficult to avoid maintaining the regular beat, and surprisingly often even genuine hesitations are so managed by the speaker that the beat is taken up again at the expected moment. The genuineness of the hesitation must then be revealed by other symptoms.) This – scarcely phonological – function of silent stress could be called *tentative* (more properly, perhaps, *pseudo-tentative*).

The use of silent stresses can easily become, with people who speak a lot in public, an apparently pointless mannerism. Certain television personalities, for example, insert silent stresses into their utterances in quite unpredictable places. The sentence

He has to be all things to all men

would normally be said either without a silent stress, or it could be said with an optional syntactic silent stress after 'things':

He has to be all things ∧ to all men.

However, this sentence was recently spoken by a professional television broadcaster (with the same intonation as one would use in the preceding version) as follows:

He has to be all things to ∧ all men

where the silent stress seems quite unmotivated (it clearly was not a 'tentative' one, as could be seen from the speaker's air of confidence at that point. Nor was it emphatic, and nobody could be in doubt about what the next words were going to be.) Perhaps this is something comparable to what the Fowlers[5] called 'elegant variation', when talking of writers' choice of words: it is *rhythmic* elegant variation, and does not seem to fulfil any purpose except to be unexpected and different. Perhaps we could call this oddly idiosyncratic, but easily identifiable, use of silent stress its *rhetorical* function.

I have distinguished here, in a rather rough and ready way, five functions of silent stress: syntactic, emphatic, terminal, tentative and rhetorical. Clearly this classification could be refined in various ways, but it may do for a start. It will be of interest to examine, very briefly, how these functions occur in four typically different modes of use of spoken English: conversation, spoken prose, monologue and verse.

Conversation, as I have pointed out elsewhere,[6] is the least investigated mode of use of spoken English. My rather desultory observations seem to show that, although there is much personal variation, silent stresses in conversation are almost entirely syntactic and emphatic, and that there are relatively not very many of either. In spoken prose silent stresses are very much more common, and they are practically all syntactic.

What appears to be monologue – unscripted uninterrupted talking – is often not, of course: on television the speaker may in fact be reading what he is saying from the teleprompter without the viewer realising it; or someone who is making a speech may have learnt it by heart. But a great deal of genuine monologue exists, in the form of lectures, radio and television commentaries, sermons, and so on, and here one may find all the functions of silent stress, and certainly more of the rhetorical kind than are found elsewhere. (There are many differences, not only in silent stresses, between the way spoken language is used on television and the way it is used on the radio. In the latter, in fact, monologue is rather rare. The differences clearly arise in part from the fact that in the one you can see the speaker, in the other you can not.)

It is in verse that the existence of silent stresses has been most widely recognised, and they have been referred to by various names. For instance, a silent stress within a line is sometimes called a *caesura*, and at the end of a line *catalexis*, or more often *brachycatalexis*, terms which are not very fortunately chosen. *Pause*, *silent space* and *rest* have also been used, and they at least do not entail confusions with classical prosody. Whatever they may be called, they are almost always syntactic silent stresses, either obligatory or optional. They are, and probably always have been, an integral part of the structure of English verse, as many writers on prosody have admitted. Saintsbury, for example, after saying that a monosyllabic foot 'is always long, strong, stressed, accented, what-not', adds in a footnote 'Except, to speak paradoxically, when it is nothing at all', and he illustrates this (using the caret-mark in the same way as it is used here) by the line from *Macbeth* I.v:

Under my battlements. ᴧ Come you spirits.

T. S. Omond wrote 'Recognition of these silent spaces is essential to just prosody, and often revolutionises our ideas of a line's structure.' Coventry Patmore, in his 'Essay on Metrical Law', gave an example of how our ideas may be so revolutionised; he pointed out that the line

And some I see again sit still, and say but small

is very likely to be read wrong at first sight, without its context, though the rest of the poem makes it clear that an optional syntactic silent stress is required within the line:

And some I see again ∧ sit still, and say but small.[7]

Silent stresses at the end of the line have a special importance in verse. First of all they serve the purpose of ensuring an even number of beats in the line when the number of stressed syllables, or stressed syllables together with line-internal silent stresses, is uneven, in accordance with the theory that the unit of English verse is the *double foot*. (This, the 'dipode', theory was put forward by Patmore, who called it his 'great general law', and independently by Morris Croll, who did not appear to know Patmore had formulated it first.[8]) Silent stresses at the end of the line also serve as *line-end markers* – they are one of the means by which the line may be delimited as a metrical unit.[9]

Silent stresses may sometimes take a form which is not, strictly speaking, silent: the final sound of the preceding syllable may be prolonged over the space they occupy. This prolongation appears to be in free variation with silence, though it is more common with some people than others. It is, however, curious that emphatic and rhetorical silent stresses seem always to be really silent.

When written language, whether prose or verse, is to be read aloud, there is seldom only one right way of doing it. Obviously, there is almost always a choice in the matter of intonation. There is often also a choice, among other things, in the number and placing of silent stresses. This is of no very great consequence as far as prose is concerned. The choices made are a matter of the reader's taste and experience, and it is often difficult to say why one rendering is more effective than another. In verse, too, such choices must usually be left to taste. Nevertheless, poets must often wish it was not so, though there is not much they can do to ensure that a particular rendering is given to a poem by a reader. Gerard Manley Hopkins clearly felt this strongly, and he used various devices, such as differences in indentation of the lines, acute accents, and various other marks (not always preserved when his poems are printed) in an attempt to ensure the rendering he wanted. Few other poets have made such efforts. There is, however, an interesting problem here. What exactly are the rhythmic constraints introduced by printing words as verse – if any? It seems to be widely believed that the same words, with the same punctuation, are somehow not the same in their rhythmic effect when printed as continuous prose as when printed in lines of verse. Why are they not the same? What difference can the visual arrangement make? There are numbers of examples available. Yeats printed Walter Pater's prose arranged as verse in the *Oxford Book of Modern Verse*; D. S. MacColl printed various passages of prose arranged as verse in *Essays and Studies by Members of the English Association*, Vol 5; Saintsbury, in his *Historical Manual*, showed some of Henley's verse printed as prose side-by-side with the original; there is a long correspondence in the *Times Literary Supplement* in the early months of 1965 on the problem in general, and in particular on Hugh MacDiarmid's use of other people's prose in his own poems. It seems possible that the arrangement in lines influences the placing of silent stresses, thereby producing a certain rhythmic effect which is different from the effect produced by a prose arrangement. There are certainly interesting opportunities for speculation here.

Notes

1 *Three Areas of Experimental Phonetics*, London, 1967, *p* v.
2 'Rhythm in English verse, prose, and speech', *Essays and Studies by Members of the English Association*, Vol 5, Oxford, 1914, *p* 42 note.
3 *JL*, 2, 1966, 69–78.
4 This, in effect, is the advice given to young preachers in P. E. Sangster, *Speech in the Pulpit*, London, 1958, where caret-marks are used in the same way as here. An interesting account of the development of punctuation marks and their connection with what the author calls 'time-pauses' can be found in A. C. Partridge, *Orthography in Shakespeare and Elizabethan Drama*, London, 1964.
5 In *The King's English* and *A Dictionary of English Usage*.
6 *Studies in Phonetics and Linguistics*, London, 1965, Chap 1.
7 See G. Saintsbury, *Historical Manual of English Prosody*, London, 1910, *p* 23; T. S. Omond, *English Metrists*, Oxford, 1921, *p* 176; Coventry Patmore, *Poems*, second collective edn, Vol 2, London, 1886, *p* 241.
8 Patmore, *op cit, p* 242; 'The elementary measure, or integer, of English verse is double the measure of ordinary prose, – that is to say, it is the space which is bounded by *alternate* accents.' See also Morris W. Croll, *The Rhythm of English Verse*, Princeton, New Jersey, 1925 (mimeographed. This scarce and little-known work is now available in *Style, Rhetoric and Rhythm*, Essays by Morris W. Croll edited by J. Max Patrick *et al*, Princeton, New Jersey, 1966.)
9 See Thomas Taig, *Rhythm and Metre*, Cardiff, 1929, *p* 39. I owe to Angus McIntosh my knowledge of this remarkable book.

Scots

David Murison
Editor, The Scottish National Dictionary

The Dutch element in the vocabulary of Scots

1

The relations of Scotland with the Low Countries, or Netherlands in the broadest sense of that term, including Flanders and Brabant in the modern kingdom of Belgium, as well as 'the Lowlands of Holland' proper, have been frequently written up on general lines, by *eg* W. Cunningham, *Alien Immigrants to England*, London, 1897; J. F. Bense, *Anglo–Dutch Relations*, The Hague, 1925; J. A. Fleming, *Flemish Influence in Britain*, Glasgow, 1930 and more particularly by J. Yair, *The Scotch Trade in the Netherlands*, London, 1776, and J. Davidson and A. Gray, *The Scottish Staple at Veere*, London, 1909, for trade, and for military and political contacts *The Papers illustrating the History of the Scots Brigade in the Netherlands* and *The Journal of Thomas Cuningham of Campvere* published by the Scottish History Society, 1899–1901, 1927. The linguistic aspect of the subject has also been briefly treated by T. De Vries in *Holland's Influence on English Language and Literature*, Chicago, 1916, and in great detail by J. F. Bense in his *Dictionary of the Low-Dutch Element in the English Vocabulary*, Oxford, 1926–38, to which this article is chiefly indebted. Its chief purpose is to segregate Bense's Scottish material and discuss it for its historical relevance, to add to it where necessary from the new material provided by *A Dictionary of the Older Scottish Tongue* and *The Scottish National Dictionary* in so far as they are available to date, and to subtract where Bense's over-enthusiasm led him into making insupportable claims for the Dutch origin of some words or equivocating, like a practised lexicographer, in the admittedly and frequently difficult matter of distinguishing between Middle Dutch and Middle Low German. As it is, the lists below do not claim to be complete and of course those many words have been omitted which English, as well as Scots, has borrowed from Dutch, like *brandy, buoy, bulwark, cruise, deck, decoy, drill, frolic, freebooter, hobble, harpoon, loiter, luck, minx, rant, schooner, skipper, snuff, trick, uproar, waggon*, to mention but a few of the best known.

2 The Historical Background

Considering the relative paucity of records in early Scotland, references to the Netherlands and their people are reasonably frequent. We hear of Flemings first in 1138 in the army of David I. These may have been mercenaries, and certainly Flemings were given lands in Scotland for military services, Theobaldus Flamaticus in Douglasdale in 1147 and Beroaldus Flamaticus in Moray in 1161, but political factors may also have been involved and in that same 1138 a granddaughter of David married the Count of Holland, the basis of the claim of their great-grandson in the competition for the Scottish throne in 1291.[1]

Closer relations developed when Henry II of England expelled the Flemings for insurrection in 1155 and many refugees found their way to Scotland, among them one Baldwin who received a grant of land in Biggar and founded a lineage still in existence, which included one of the 'Queen's Maries'.[2] These brought with them their skill in various crafts and especially weaving, on the strength of which most of their future history in and with Scotland is firmly based. In the same reign (of William the Lion) we find royal writs addressed to 'Francis et Anglis et Flamingis et Scotis' and among the burgesses of Edinburgh, Perth and St Andrews there are already not a few at least denominated Fleming, if it is premature to use 'surnamed' in this connection.

But by the fourteenth century when family names have been more or less established, we can trace Flemish names like Crab in Aberdeen and Berwick, where John Crab, a refugee from the Count of Flanders, did yeoman service with his patent catapult against the English besiegers in 1319, not the last time that Flemish artillery was put to good use in the Scottish army. There is incidentally a Frisian, Rakstra, recorded in Perth in 1291, a spiritual ancestor perhaps of the gallant tar of the *Pinafore*. Later on when Brabant rose to prominence, Brabanders also found their way to Scotland and one Walter Brabounare turns up at Irvine in 1418 and another, with the significant christian name of Gerard, appears as a doctor in Glasgow in 1486.[3]

These immigrants seem to have come in groups, often on an industrial basis, and naturally formed themselves into communities wherever they settled. In Aberdeenshire for instance an enclave of Flemings in the Garioch was large enough to be allowed by a series of charters from David II and various barons in the fourteenth century to have its own laws and customs,[4] and the place-name Flinders in that district still attests the fact. There are, besides, Flemingtons in Berwick, Peebles, Lanark and Angus.

Throughout the next three centuries and even into the eighteenth, the process of encouraging Dutch artisans by means of various concessions to come to Scotland to ply their craft went on fairly steadily. James I imported weavers from the Netherlands and, if this can be spoken of in the same category, his son brought the daughter of the Duke of Gelderland home in 1449 to be his wife. Later on Dutchmen came to work the lead and silver mines in Lanarkshire, to make salt, to set up printing presses in Edinburgh and Aberdeen, to weave fine cloth and linen, to refine sugar and to make pottery.

They were by long tradition town-dwellers, whose ancestors had built the cities of Antwerp, Ghent and Bruges; in Scotland they take a prominent part in civic life as provosts, burgesses and merchants, and no doubt Scotland owes the long-standing solidity of her trade guilds and incorporations in large measure to the Dutch.[5] The Flemings had a guild of their own in Berwick in the late thirteenth century and later on also in Edinburgh, Perth and Inverkeithing. Flemish weavers indeed had their own incorporation in Edinburgh in 1475 and over a hundred years later an Act of James VI in 1587 gave Flemings further inducements to settle in any Scottish burgh of their choice, including the right to have their own church.[6] Conversely, the wrights and masons of Edinburgh had their seals of cause expressly formulated on those of Bruges.

In the finer arts too Flemings made their contribution to Scotland. Flemish portrait-painters were employed by the royal family and the work of Jan Van Eyck can still be seen in Holyroodhouse. Flemish architects were employed on the various royal castles and palaces in the middle of the sixteenth century, and the atmosphere of Dutch and Flemish towns can be felt again in the curved gables and ogee roofs of the seaports of Fife.

But Flemish contacts with Scotland were not all one-sided. Commercial relations must of necessity be reciprocal and as early as 1182 we have a glimpse of some monks from Melrose being given immunity from tolls on their passage through Flanders, presumably on a trade-mission to sell their wool. Even amid the confusions of the War of Independence and the efforts of the Plantagenets to put a stop to it, there was freedom of trade with the Netherlands, Holland and Zeeland as well as Flanders; from Scotland came coarse cloth, hides, skins, salmon and trout, and in return drugs, fine cloth, gold and silver work and wines from the Rhineland.

The Scots were given special privileges in Bruges in various charters; there was a Scotsen-straet in the town as early as 1291 and Bruges remained as their chief entrepôt, in effect a hanse, for a century. After 1488, when Bruges lost its supremacy, the Scottish staple was transferred to Middleburg where the accounts of a Scottish merchant and agent, Andrew Halyburton, have been preserved from 1492–1503, and finally to Veere in Zeeland in 1541 where it remained till its extinction in 1799.

This move northwards of Scottish interests from Flanders was accelerated when the Reformation came and the northern parts of the Netherlands became, like Scotland, Protestant and ultimately Calvinist. The subsequent series of wars of the United Provinces under the Prince of Orange against Spain and later France for over 120 years involved thousands of Scots troops as mercenaries and of course finally as regulars after 1688 when the Prince of Orange became King of Great Britain. The last of these indeed were naturalised as Dutch citizens and no doubt their descendants are to be found in Holland to this day, as in the case of the Mackays of Reay.

In the period 1666–88 Holland provided a refuge for the Presbyterians during the persecutions of the Covenanting times, and the Universities of Leyden, Utrecht and Groningen, and the Dutch Reformed Church gave men like Cameron, Livingston, Renwick and Shields not only their theology but their ordination. Probably the most famous of them all was Dalrymple of Stair, whose studies of Roman–Dutch law laid the foundations of his *Institutions* and of Scots law as we know it today. And there was the famous Edinburgh doctor, Archibald Pitcairne, who was professor of medicine at Leyden in 1691 and colleague of Boerhaave.

The Catholic Netherlands also continued to attract Scots of that faith who had no future in their own country and we have glimpses in the eighteenth century of priests and nuns of Scottish birth in the many religious houses of Antwerp, Bruges, Louvain and Liège from various sources, not least the delightful *Journal* of Mrs Calderwood of Polton, a great-granddaughter incidentally of Stair, who toured the Low Countries in 1756 and picked up some Dutch in her travels. A sentence or two from a letter of 1739 from a nun at Bergen-op-Zoom, a cousin of the Earl of Kilmarnock, illustrates the linguistic repercussions of all this – 'My Love is always the sem to you sa it was when I leved with you; my absence chal never mack mij vergiting of you. Lett me know if you cannot rid French or Vlames, for I heve forgot most all mij Scots'.[7]

There is incidentally some wry amusement to be got out of the semantic developments of the adjective *schotsch* from meaning in Middle Dutch 'rash, headstrong' (the *praefervidum ingenium* no doubt) through the senses of 'scornful, arrogant, obstinate', to 'queer, daft, uncouth, funny, droll'; a *schotschrift* signified a lampoon, a *schotsch kooper* a pedlar, a packman, a common meaning of *Scot* all over Northern Europe, a *schots*, a middleman of any kind, a shipping or business agent, as no doubt many of the Scots in the Netherlands were. Obviously the more the Dutch got to know the Scots, the better they saw through them. And Marin in his *Woordenboek* of 1717 gives as his illustrative sentence under *Schotsman*, with sad finality and a shake of his head over the vagaries of womankind, '*Zy is met een Schots man getrouwd* (she married a Scotsman)'.

It can be seen from all this that contacts between Scotland and the Netherlands have extended over a period of 800 years and more, with few breaks and the close intimacy that trade, camaraderie in war, and religious sympathy all produce, and that no country with the exception of England has had so long and continuous an influence on our own as the Dutch lands – Dutch in the sense of Dutch-speaking, for it is the language contacts which are our concern here.

The history of the Dutch language in no small measure reflects the political history of the country as a collection of smallish regions, each with its own marked character and dialect and rather conservative in speech as in other matters, but gradually fusing or federating as internal need or external pressure compelled them. The first important region, as we have seen, was Western Flanders with its commercial ports and manufacturing cities, and it was here in the later thirteenth century that Dutch literature began, with translations of French romances, not into the pure local speech but into a mixed literary language, 'Dietsch', which included elements from all the other Frankish dialects of the Netherlands. One of the pioneers in this, Jacob van Maerlant, speaks of borrowing from the dialects of Holland,

Brabant, Zeeland, as well as Flemish, not to mention French, Latin, Greek and Hebrew, in order to find rhymes and to represent adequately the thought of the original, and this is curiously similar to Gavin Douglas's problem more than two hundred years later when he set out to translate the *Aeneid* into Scots and 'quhair scant was Scottis . . . sum bastard Latyn, French or Inglys oyss' to eke out his vocabulary.

In the latter half of the fourteenth century, the centre of literary activity shifted from Flanders to Brabant, and the speech of Antwerp and Brussels and of the new University of Louvain took over as the bookish form of Dutch. The first Dutch dictionaries, of Plantijn and Kilian, deal essentially with this speech, though Kilian is careful to note words from other dialects with their appropriate location. In any case by this time the Middle Dutch, *ie* basically Flemish, period has passed and the language was, as it were, pausing before its next phase of development and change, under the influence first of the Renaissance which led to a heightened interest in literary and linguistic matters and hence to the grammarians, orthoepists and lexicographers, and then of the Reformation in the mid-sixteenth century which led to the division of the Netherlands on religious issues and to the rise of the Northern States and the House of Orange. The south capitulated to Spain and it was the north that kept the national spirit and speech going during the fight for their independence, and although there was no small linguistic influence from Protestant refugees from Brabant and Flanders, not to mention French itself from Calvinism and Geneva, it was in the end the dialect of Holland proper that was moulded into literary Dutch under the influence of poets of the early seventeenth century like Vondel and of the authorised translation of the Bible (1637). The Reformation which destroyed Scots as a full language had at the same time finally consolidated the many dialects of the Netherlands (outside Friesland) into one national tongue. It was at this same period, as we have seen, that those who made modern Scotland had their closest links with Holland.

It now remains to examine the influence of the language of the Netherlands, *ie* Middle and Modern Dutch, on the vocabulary of Scots from the earliest period from which it can be traced in the fourteenth century, to the latest in which it ceased, in the early eighteenth, when Scots broke down as an independent speech and was replaced by English as the formal and literary language of Scotland. Thereafter there are no direct borrowings except in Shetland, which will be discussed later.

3 Dutch words in Scots

It should be remembered that where Halyburton's Ledger is the source of the word, the entry, recording as it does an actual transaction of goods in Holland, may employ Dutch words which were used only in this commercial context and never actually passed into current Scots usage.

AGRICULTURE

Fifteenth century: bucht, a sheep-pen (Flem *bocht*, which in certain modern dialects of Zeeland also refers to a square-sided church pew, as it does in Scotland, though probably by an independent development); *ferrow cow*, a cow not in calf (Flem *verrekoe*, barren cow), *slipe*, a sledge (Flem *slijp*, a drag).

Sixteenth century: cavie, a chicken-coop (Flem *kevie*); *owse*, ox, is a difficult form to explain as a variant of *ox* and may have been influenced by Du *oss*; *roddiken*, the fourth stomach of a ruminant, a diminutive form of Flemish *roode*, idem; *spean*, to wean, may be Flem *spenen*, though a Low German origin is also possible, if not more probable.

Seventeenth century: clyre, a gland in meat (MDu *cliere*); *kesart*, a cheese-vat (Flem *kaeshorde*), not surprising in view of the traditional skill of the Dutch in cheese-making.

Obviously the influence of Dutch on Scottish agriculture is very small, sporadic and specialised, as might be expected in a sphere so inveterately native as farming. A much larger and more important quota of words comes from trade and commerce, especially in the fifteenth century when both countries were relatively peaceful and prosperous.

TRADE

Fourteenth century: cran, a crane for lifting (MFlem *craen*), is generally used in connection with harbours and shipping, though the first instance, from Barbour, refers, significantly enough, to the military engineering of John Crab in 1319; the modern pronunciation [krɑn], together with the secondary modern meaning of a tap or spigot [Du *kraan*], attests its Dutch origin; *knorhald*, oaken boards, shows in its earliest Scots form the MDu *knorhout*, a variant of *knarholt*, *knapholt*, *clapholt*, a word of LG origin from East

12—E.S.E.S.

Prussia. Probably the article itself came to Scotland first through Holland from its original source in the Baltic.

Fifteenth century: bait, an extra given to a customer by way of discount, 'boot' (MDu *baet*). Halyburton, and possibly never naturalised in Scots; *coft*, bought (MDu past tense *cofte*, past participle *ghecoft*, of *copen*), on the contrary established itself universally in Scots, one of the few Dutch inflexional forms to have done so. See *smout* below; *crame*, a merchant's booth (MDu *craeme*), very frequent in medieval burgh usage; *crangilt*, cranage (MDu *kraangelt*). *Cf: cran* above; *forpak*, to repack (MDu *verpakken*). Halyburton; *hope*, pile of goods (MDu *hoop*). Halyburton; *kip*, bundle (MDu *kip*, a bundle, especially of hides); *lacrissye*, liquorice (MDu *lacrisie*); *laykyn*, a drawer (MDu *laykijn*). Halyburton; *los*, to discharge a cargo (MDu *lossen*); *oncost*, overheads (MDu *oncosten*), has now been adopted from Scots into Standard English accountancy practice; *piner*, a labourer (MDu *pijner*, also in Antwerp, a kind of stevedore). In this latter sense the word was applied in Aberdeen at the end of the century to a guild or corporation of stevedores, still existing under the name of the Shore Porters, pretty certain evidence of a direct link; *wissel*, change of money (Flem *wissel*). Halyburton, though also found in English and as a verb = to exchange. The Scots phrase *to get the wissel of one's groat*, to be paid in one's own coin, suggests that the word is Flemish rather than Middle Low German, which is another possibility.

Sixteenth century: alacreische, liquorice, probably a variant of *lacrissye* above; *calland*, a customer (Flem *caland*, from French *chaland*). Halyburton. The word established itself early in colloquial use in the sense of fellow or chap (which developed semantically on parallel lines from *chapman*, a merchant) and is still common in the west of Scotland for boy, lad; *maisterstick*, a test-piece of his skill submitted by a craftsman for his admission to membership of a trade-guild (MDu or Flem *meesterstuck*). This was a practice on the Continent and in Scotland but not apparently in England which anglicised the word to *masterpiece*, with a somewhat different meaning;[8] *primegilt*, payment to a ship's crew for loading, is first recorded in connection with shipments to Flanders, and contains the earliest usage of *gelt*, in the sense of money; *rattlegold*, gold-leaf, tinsel (Du *ratelgoud*); *smout*, smelted, of iron (MDu *ghesmouten*, past participle of *smelten*), another verbal inflected form, like *coft*.

Seventeenth century: lastgilt, a toll on cargo, specifically in reference to the staple ports (MDu *lastgelt*).

CLOTH

The chief commodity of the Netherlands in the Middle Ages being cloth, it is not surprising to find names of materials and garments of Dutch origin both in England and Scotland from the earliest records, not a few actually indicating the town where they were made, as *cambric* from Kamerijk (Cambrai) and *dornick* from Doornik (Tournai), which became one of the commonest items in Scottish household linen and one which the Scots began to manufacture for themselves in the seventeenth century.

Fourteenth century: cortrik, a kind of black serge or velvet, made at *Cortrik* (Courtrai) in Flanders; *haik*, a woman's mantle (MDu *heyke*).

Fifteenth century: birges, a kind of satin thread or cloth, a metathetic variant of *Bruges* in Flanders; *copy*, another sort of cloth, also listed by Halyburton, is probably of Flemish origin, though untraced; *eik*, the grease of wool (MFlem *iecke*, corresponding etymologically to the English synonym *yolk*); *mutch*, a night-cap, a linen coif (MDu *muts(ch)e*), still known to old ladies, if seldom used. See also *mutchkin* below; *ryssil*, a woollen stuff, from *Ryssel*, the Flemish name of Lille. See also under *ley* below.

Sixteenth century: brabanar, a weaver (MDu *Brabander*, a native of Brabant), obsolete by the eighteenth century in this sense but surviving as the surname *Brebner* and in the Gaelic word for a weaver, *breabadair*; *hunscot*, a kind of cloth made in South Holland (Du *honskoten*); *lapkin*, a remnant of cloth, found only in reference to cambric and presumably MDu *lappekyn*, a piece of material; *lay*, the batten of a loom (Du *lade*, with early by-forms *laey*, *lay*, *la*, and with similar meaning); *ley*, some kind of cloth or canvas, is probably from the name of the river *Leie* in Flanders, according to DOST, a suggestion supported by the variant *lias*, from *Lys*, the French (Walloon) form of the name. The French name of *Ryssel*, incidentally, has given *lilles*, cloth of Lille, a kind of worsted.

Eighteenth century: fala, used by Ramsay to refer to a kind of kerchief worn by Dutch women (Du *falie*, from French *voile*), though probably never naturalised in Scotland, at least shows some familiarity with Dutch life in post-Union Edinburgh; *toy*, a woman's linen cap with flaps, also in Ramsay, is very probably Du *tooi*, attire. OED is somewhat dubious of associating Shakespeare's *toy* of the *Winter's Tale* and *toy* in the ordinary English sense with this.

WEIGHTS AND MEASURES

Trade involves the measurement of commodities and any country has an interest and a tendency to assimilate its measures to those of its best customers. In the fifteenth century a system of weights in common use in Northern France and the Netherlands was adopted in Scotland for meal, meat, iron, hemp, and for goods which passed in or out in foreign trade, and was called variously Scots Troyes, Paris, French, and commonly, later, Amsterdam or Dutch weight. This was in regular use till abolished by statute in 1826.

> *Fourteenth century: maise*, a measure of herring, a common word in medieval trade, has a long history, being recorded in various forms, Late Latin, French, Low and High German and Dutch, and Old Norse. The word is originally Teutonic. The specific association with herring makes it most likely that the word came directly into Scots from MDu *mese*, but the earlier evidence necessary for certainty is wanting.

> *Fifteenth century: copill*, a measure of cloth, which DOST associates with MDu *coppel*, a leash, band; *grotken*, a gross (MFlem *grootken*); *kinkin*, a quarter-barrel (MDu *kintken*). Halyburton; the one measure which persisted practically to within living memory is the *mutchkin*, three-quarters of a pint (Du *mudseken*, which may be originally a diminutive conflated from *mutse* (see *mutch* above), and *mudde*, a liquid measure); *waw*, a measure of weight, twelve stone, also found in Northern ME (MDu *wage*).

COINAGE

In a country so chronically short of specie as Scotland foreign coins seem to have been pressed into service as currency and were of course much in demand for foreign exchange. And naturally some of these were Dutch, as:

> *Fifteenth century: gulden*, both in its sense of a Flemish gold coin of the fourteenth century and later of the silver Dutch coin (1542), called in Eng *guilder*; *lew*, the gold lion of Flanders (MDu *leeuwe*), which was in fact legal tender in Scotland by various Acts of Parlia-

ment from 1467–75; *plack*, a coin of James III, worth four pennies Scots or somewhat less than a halfpenny, taking its name from a copper coin of Flanders (*placke*) of the fourteenth and fifteenth centuries. The word survived the Union in the sense of something of very small value, like *farthing* in English; *rider*, a gold coin of James II, whose queen was Dutch, and who did much to foster trade with the Netherlands, was with little doubt borrowed from the somewhat earlier Flemish and Dutch *rijder*, which had the figure of a horseman on the obverse, also copied by the Scots; *steke*, a coin, piece of money (West Flemish *stik*, MDu *stuk*) is used specifically of Dutch money, beginning with Halyburton.

Sixteenth century: doit, a Dutch coin of very small value which had a wide unofficial currency in Scotland and found its way with regrettable frequency into church collections in the seventeenth and eighteenth centuries is of course MDu *duit*.

GAMES

A sure indication of the close and cordial relations existing between the Netherlands and Scotland appears in the various names for games which the Scots borrowed chiefly in the fifteenth century and in one instance at least appropriated for good.

Fifteenth century: cache, and later the combination *cachepell*, tennis, are MFlem *caetse(-spel)*; *golf* (MDu *kolf*, a club, *kolven*, a game with clubs), despite the disbelief of some Scottish devotees, is too well illustrated in Flemish painting to be anything else than of Dutch origin, however it may have been developed or modified in its adopted country; *kylis*, ninepins (MDu *keghel*, *keyl*, a ninepin), the word still being used for a New-Year-day game resembling skittles at Kirkcaldy; *speeler*, an acrobat (MDu. *speler*, a player, actor, juggler), suggests that the common Scottish word *spiel*, to climb up a rope, wall, etc, is originally Du *spelen*, to play, perform tricks, applied specifically to gymnasts, trapeze artists and the like.

Sixteenth century: The word *spiel* also occurs in *bonspiel*, a match, contest, now specifically at curling, the first element being obscure; *dool*, a goal, may also possibly be from Du *doel*, a target, but phonological considerations point rather to LG *dole*.

SEA AND SHIPS

As might be expected from the constant to-and-fro over the North

Sea in ships, nautical terms are likely to bulk fairly largely in the borrowings from Dutch. Though most of the early trade seems to have been carried in Dutch bottoms, many of the words date from the sixteenth century when the Scottish merchant marine was established.

Fifteenth century: lek, a bolt-rope, appears to be Du *lijk*; *mers*, a round-top on a mast (MDu *merse*).

Sixteenth century: bome, a boom in a harbour (Du *boom*) is recorded from Aberdeen a century before its appearance in England; *bowkdenning*, the planking of a ship's hold (Du dialect *buikdelling*); *boyart*, a one-masted vessel (MDu *bojert*); *boyrape*, a buoy-rope (Du *boeireep*); *cowbrig*, orlop-deck (Du *koebrug*); *coy*, a bunk (Du *kooi*); *dworce*, athwart a ship (Du *dwars*); *fanikin*, a pennant, banner (MDu *vaenken*); *flaw*, *flag*, a blast of wind (MDu *vlage*); *handspake*, handspike, appears to follow the Du by-form *handspeck*; *helmstok*, tiller (MDu *helmstoc*); *lek*, leak, n and v, with its short vowel contrasting with the Eng form, points to derivation from MDu *lec(ken)*, though LG is another possible source; *nock*, the tip of a yard-arm (Du *nok*); *reid*, a roadstead, an alternative to the more usual *raid*, seems to be Du *reede*; *steven*, the stem or prow of a vessel (MDu *steven*).

Seventeenth century: caper, a privateer, is a direct adoption of Du *kaper* during 'the warris betwixt the Inglisches and Hollanders', *ie* during the Cromwellian regime; *capraven*, a spar (Du *kapraven*).

WAR AND WEAPONS

The sixteenth and seventeenth centuries were the ages of war as far as the Netherlands were concerned and in so far as the Scots were also, as we have seen, involved, the bulk of the Dutch words dealing with military matters, which found their way into Scots, belong to these centuries.

Fifteenth century: First however is the important word *wapenschaw* (*-ing*), which Bense plausibly ascribes to the contemporaneous Du *wapenschowe, – schouwinc*, a part of the routine military drill of the burghers of Holland, which James I sought to impose on the Scots at the expense of the more popular diversion of football.

Sixteenth century: cranniken, a part of a crossbow (Flem *kraaneken*, diminutive of *kraan*). See *cran* above; *flas*, a powder-flask (Flem *flasch*), the first quoted instance (1541) in Scots also including the word *lunt* below; *fyane*, enemy (Flem *fijan*), of rare occurrence, twice only in the Aberdeen records, suggests a borrowing from some official diplomatic formula; *galya*, a safe-conduct, *might* be Du *geleide*, but as it first refers to a Dantzig merchant it is more likely to be of Hanse origin from Low German, or perhaps Danish; *letdecamp*, a camp-bed, though obviously originally Northern French, is connected by DOST on the strength of some by-forms, *liticant*, etc, with MDu *lytedecamp*, *lydecant*. It may well have been mediated through Flanders; *lunt*, a match for a gun (Du *lonte*), still surviving as a puff of a pipe, a smoke, is no doubt to be attributed to the excellence of artillery production in the Netherlands, which the gun Mons Meg in Edinburgh Castle attests to this day; *slang*, a culverin (MDu *slange*) may be another instance of this.

Seventeenth century: braveer, to swagger (Du *braveeren*); *cartow*, a small cannon (Du *kartouw*); *frezel*, a steel for striking fire from flint, probably originally in a musket, conjectured by DOST as a corrupted form of Du *vuurijzer*, 'fire-iron', is perhaps more easily recognisable in its Aberdeenshire forms *fleerish*, *furison*, used a couple of generations ago by smokers to light their pipes; *hoff-quarter*, headquarters (Du *hoofdkwartier*); *huskew*, which DOST regards as a misprint and derives from Du *huysken*, *huizeken*, a case, sheath, shell, or the like, is applied in Scots to some part of a scabbard; *ratt*, a file of soldiers, platoon (Du *rot*, with Scots alteration of the vowel), survived into the early nineteenth century in the *Toun Rats*, a nickname for the rather unpopular Town Guard of Edinburgh, gaining added opprobrium from confusion with the name of the animal.

MISCELLANEOUS

So much for words that illustrate one or other of the specific aspects of Dutch–Scottish relations. But there are many more of a miscellaneous affiliation not easy or convenient to classify. Sufficient to say that they touch almost every kind of activity in ordinary life.

Fourteenth century: crag, the neck (Flem *kraghe*); *kit*, a small tub (MDu *kitte*, water vessel); *lak*, disgrace, is a derivative meaning of *lack*, deficiency, also found in MDu; *slop*, later *slap*, a gap in a wall, etc (MFlem *slop*, with Scots phonological development).

Fifteenth century: boyspikar, a long nail (MDu *boeispiker*); *crune*, to make a mournful sound (MDu *kronen*, *kreunen*), now in Standard English as *croon*; *cute*, the ankle (MDu *cote*). The phrase *not ane cute*, common in the sixteenth century, corresponds to the Du *niet een cote*, not a whit; *dorp*, a village, as contrasted with the native and rare *thorp*, suggests that the word was adopted in Scotland from Flemish weaver-settlements; *dwang*, to oppress, a kind of lever or crowbar, could be either MDu or LG *dwang*; *flindrikin*, a frivolous person, apparently a dim. form of Du *vlinder*, a butterfly, a philanderer; *forehammer*, a sledge-hammer (MDu *voorhammer*); *geck*, a gesture of derision (MDu *gek*); *hak*, a hook (Du *haak*); *hink*, to hobble (MDu *hinken*); *knap, knip*, to tap, snap, snip, may be onomatopoeic merely, but there are Du *knappen, knippen* with similar senses; *lence*, in the expression *not worth a lence*, in Holland's *Buke of the Howlat*, is directly from the contemporary Du *niet een lens* (a linchpin). Did Holland know Dutch?; *loun*, a low fellow, rascal (Du *loen*), though also in early Modern English, including Shakespeare, must owe its much greater frequency in Scotland to direct influence from Holland and it is still the ordinary everyday word in the North-East for a boy; *moy*, demure (Du *mooi*, pretty); *rachter*, rafter (Du *rachter*); *rumple*, a crease, wrinkle (Du *rompelen*), is found much earlier in Scots than in English; *skaillie*, slate (MDu *schalie*, originally French *écaille*, from Teutonic), is now obsolete except in the sense of slate-pencil; *smook*, smoke, n and v (MFlem *smuuken*); *smoor*, to suffocate, is first recorded in Scots about 1470, but if it is to be connected with MDu *smoren*, must have been in the language much earlier, to make the phonology explicable; *upmake*, to make up, supplement, construct. Bense adduces arguments to claim a borrowing from MDu *opmaken* in similar senses, though this may be mere coincidence. But the fact that Scots tends to use this type of compound, with adverb or conjunction prefixed, much more in the Continental manner than English does, may have been helped by the influence of the Flemings in Scotland. It is perhaps significant that Douglas (see below) has many examples, as *uphese, upset, upsprent, upwarp*, which have Du equivalents; *yuke*, to itch (MDu *joken*, etc), must again be an early borrowing, as in the case of *smoor* above.

Sixteenth century: begaik, to befool (MDu *beghecken*). *Cf: geck* above; *flok*, snowflake (Du *vlok*); *groff*, rough, coarse (MDu *grof*); *houff*, a courtyard, specifically the original garden, later used as a burial ground, of the Greyfriars Monastery in Dundee, and in later Scots a place or popular resort in general (Du *hof*); *mannikin*, a small statue or lay figure, the original sense, from the vocabulary of

Dutch painters (MDu *manneken*); *mow*, a grimace, jest, joking matter, is phonologically nearer to MDu *mouw*, than to OF *moue*, of the same meaning and probably of the same ultimate origin; *pingle*, to wrangle, to do fine sewing (Du dialect *pingelen*, in both senses); *platfoot*, flat-footed (MDu *platvoet*); *scaff*, to scrounge, is referred by Bense plausibly to Flem *op schaaf loopen*, idem, and MFlem *schaeven*, to sponge, beg; *skink*, shin-bone soup (Du dialect *schink*); *spacier*, to stalk about (Du *spaseeren*).

It is worth noting that the first source of a number of our words is to be found in Gavin Douglas's *Aeneid*, partly no doubt as a result of his explicit policy of borrowing, and obviously Dutch would be particularly useful in providing a vocabulary for the sea and the nautical scenes in which he revels. So we have *bolm* (see *bome* above), *cowbrig*, *flag*, *flaw*, *helmstok*, *lek*, *nock*, as well as *bucht*, in Douglas. Other Dutch words are *bel*, a bubble (Flem *bel*); *brack*, salty, brackish (Du *brak*); *fordel*, precedence (MDu *voordel*, prerogative), in the sense of 'advantage' also English, and later developing the meaning of a reserve stock; *prig*, to importune, haggle, may have come by way of cant usage, like so many more cant words, from MDu, *viz: prigen*, to strive, resist; *prop*, a plug or wedge (MDu *proppe*, a plug, bung); *scone*, a flour cake, the best-known of them all (Flem *schoon(broot)*), fine bread, as opposed to the coarser oatmeal bannock); *spile*, a splinter of wood (MDu *spile*); *stake*, to place, MDu *staken*. There is no evidence of Douglas having been in Flanders. Did he learn these words from the Flemish colony in Edinburgh, when he was provost of St Giles?

Seventeenth century: doup, the bottom of an egg-shell, the eye-socket, later and modern, the posterior (MDu *doppe*, an egg- or nut-shell); *fize*, a screw (MDu *vise*), corresponding to English *vice*, from French; *plot*, originally to pluck wool or feathers, and because this involved plunging the skin in boiling water, later to scald, soak in hot water, is apparently MFlem *ploten* (*de wolle*). The first Scots plotter officially recorded seems in fact to have been a Dutchman from Leyden who settled by invitation of the Convention of Burghs in Ayr in 1601; *slank*, lean, thin (Du *slank*); *stopple*, pipe-stem (MDu or Flem *stapel*, a stalk or stem in general).

Many more Dutch words are to be found in Modern Scots from 1700 onwards of which a large number had very likely been in the language earlier though not recorded and the dates of those in the latter part of the alphabet are provisional where DOST or SND is not available. Shetland words are dealt with separately below.

Eighteenth century and later: besle, to talk nonsense (Du *bazelen*); *cookie*, a little cake or bun (Du *koekje*); *cowk*, to retch (Du *kolken*); *crannie*, the little finger, an extended usage of *cran*, a tap (see under TRADE above); *crappit heid*, a stuffed cod's head (Du *kroppen*, to stuff (the crop)); *cud*, a cudgel (Flem *kodde*); *doss*, a tobacco-box (Du *doos*, box); *faan*, a vane (Du *vaan*); *fozie*, soft and rotten, as of wood or vegetables, empty-headed, insipid, derives its root and meanings from Du *voos*; *kae*, pooh, pooh! (Du *ke*); *laffy*, soft, loose (Du *laff*, flaccid); *lill*, a bag-pipe stop (Du *lul*, a pipe, from which the commoner *lilt* is probably a derivative); *loll*, to caterwaul (Du *lollen*); *loy*, sluggish, lazy (Flem *loi*); *mattie*, a herring with roe (Du *maatjes haring*. An earlier form, in Ramsay, *matkie*, is LG *madikes*); *pinkie*, little finger (Du *pink*). Cf: *crannie* above; *rap*, still common in the West of Scotland for the plant *rape*, can best be explained as from Du *rap*; *ravel*, to entangle, mix confusedly (Du *ravelen*, with a by-form *rafelen*, which appears in Orkney *raffle*); and its opposite, the word *redd*, to unravel, disentangle, tidy, is from Du (MDu *redden*, to make ready (a ship), Middle West Frisian *redden*, to settle a dispute, Du (now dialectal) *beredden*, Frisian *biredden*, Du *redderen*, to tidy); *reesle*, to crackle, clatter (MDu *rysselen*); *roup*, *roop*, to shout hoarsely, hoarseness (Du *roepen*, to roar); *runt*, an ox for fattening (MDu *runt*); *scow*, a kind of barge (Du *schouw*); *scowp*, a ladle (MDu *schoppe*); *scribble*, to card wool (apparently from a Flem variant *schribbelen* of Du *schrobbelen*), first recorded in the accounts of the New Mills Cloth Company at Haddington which did a large trade with Holland at the end of the seventeenth century; *slinger*, to swing, roll (Du *slingeren*); *slock*, a draught, drink (Du *slok*); *spartle*, to sprawl (Du *spartelen*); *strule*, to make water (East Du dialect *struilen*); *swack*, active, nimble (Flem *zwak*); *trap*, a short stair or flight of steps (Du *trap*), appears first in Mrs Calderwood's *Journal*, who records its Dutch origin; *trackpot*, a teapot, still occasionally heard in North-East Scotland, is Du *trekpot*, from *trekken*, to infuse, which survives in Shetland as *trekk*; *wintle*, to roll, stagger (Du *wentelen*); *winze*, a curse (Flem *wensen*, to curse, or a reduced form of Du *verwensen*, idem), the last two Scots words being, curiously enough, from Burns's *Halloween*, which is full of archaic words.

Perhaps a word may be added about the Scots diminutive suffix -*ie* which became common in the seventeenth century, about the same time as the Du -*je* (< -*tie*, -*kje*, -*ken*), especially in Protestant Holland. While the two are etymologically distinct, the use of the one may well have helped the currency of the other, among the Scots who knew Dutch.

4 Shetland

The one part of Scotland which has had continuous close and direct contact with the Dutch in the last three hundred years is Shetland. For the Dutch as pioneers of the herring fishery, Lerwick was an important base early in the seventeenth century and continued as such with only a few intermissions during the Anglo–Dutch wars until within living memory. Indeed there were several naval engagements fought off Shetland between Dutch warships protecting their fishing-fleet and Spanish and French vessels sent to attack them, and it was the market provided by the Dutch fishermen for food and drink, especially the latter apparently, that induced the people of Scalloway, the old local capital, to set up another town at Lerwick, which ultimately superseded it. At the end of the seventeenth century we learn from a sociologist of the time that many people in Shetland could speak Dutch fluently[9] and hence quite a number of words have become current in Shetland speech, including a few mentioned above, like *bugdalin* (*bowkdenning*), *burgess* (*birges*), *coy*, *dwars* (*dworce*), *gilder* or *gudling* (*gulden*) which have survived, though now obsolete in mainland Scotland. Others include *alikruki*, a kind of whelk (Du *alikruik*, specifically in Zeeland and obviously from fishermen's vocabulary); *blöv*, to die (Du *blijven*, earlier *bleven*, to perish especially at sea); *crank*, weak, feeble, possibly from Norwegian, but the usage suggests rather a slangy adoption of Du *krank*, ill, with similar extensions of meaning; *dulhoit*, a stupor, lethargy (Du *dolheid*, mental disorder); *kardoos*, a fine-cut tobacco (Du *kardoes*, cartridge-paper in which snuff was wrapped); *kracht*, strength, energy (Du *kracht*); *krook*, a jar, especially one of Dutch make (Du *kruik*); *lar*, a fisherman's long sea-boot (Du *laars*); *leppel*, a horn spoon (Du *lepel*); *maat*, a chum, pal (Du *maat*); *pell*, tuft of hair, tatter (perhaps from Du *pel*, skin, fleece, husk); *peer*, a sand-worm (Du, or perhaps LG, *pier*); *pram*, to press, squeeze, stuff (Du *pramen*); *rook*, to smoke a pipe (Du *rooken*); *slacht*, a race, family (Du *geslacht*); *steeple*, a pile of dried fish, which corresponds to Du *stapel*, a heap of goods piled in layers, the form being however irregular and possibly to be explained rather as from West Frisian *steapel*; *sture*, any small coin, a penny, a reduced form of Du *stuiver*, which was equivalent in exchange to the penny; *yagger*, the ship which followed the herring-fleet to bring supplies and buy the catch (Du (*haring-*) *jager*), developing the meaning of one who dealt in fish and other commodities, a broker, and finally a pedlar or hawker.

5

Incomplete as these lists are, enough has been said to show the great and lasting influence of the Low Countries, especially Flanders and Holland, on the speech and culture of Scotland, an influence which still lives on to our mutual advantage and enrichment, and to which the Flemish scholar, in whose honour this was written, made his own kindly, generous and distinguished contribution.

Notes

1 On Flemish mercenaries under William the Lion, see A. C. Lawrie, *Annals of the Reign of Malcolm and William*, Glasgow, 1910, *pp* 130, 157.
2 See W. Hunter, *Biggar*, Edinburgh, 1867, Chap. xxii; R. L. G. Ritchie, *The Normans in Scotland*, Edinburgh, 1954, *pp* 374–7.
3 G. F. Black, *Scottish Surnames*, New York, 1962, s.vv. It is not absolutely certain that *Rakstra*, despite its appearance, is a Frisian name. C. M. Matthews, *English Surnames*, London, 1966, *p* 156, assumes it to be English.
4 *The Register of the Great Seal of Scotland*, AD 1306–1424, new edn, ed J. M. Thomson, Edinburgh, 1912, Appendix 1, no 128.
5 C. Gross, *Gild Merchant*, Oxford, 1890, Vol 1, *pp* 199*ff* and footnotes; W. M. Mackenzie, *Scottish Burghs*, Edinburgh, 1949, *pp* 36–8; J. A. Fleming, *op cit* (see *p* 159), Chap. xii; N. Trivet, *Annales*, ed T. Hog, English Historical Society, no 9, London, 1845, *p* 344.
6 *The Acts of the Parliaments of Scotland*, Vol 3, 1814, *pp* 507*ff* (1587, *c* 119). There was a similar Act of the Privy Council in 1600 (*The Register of the Privy Council of Scotland*, Vol 6, Edinburgh, 1884, *pp* 123–4).
7 Quoted in *Session Papers, Petition J. Boyd*, 1755, *p* 5 (Signet Library, Edinburgh).
8 *Cf* C. Gross, *op cit*, Vol 1, *p* 199 note.
9 Quoted in R. Sibbald, *Description of the Islands of Orkney and Shetland*, Edinburgh, 1845, *p* 16.

A. J. Aitken
Editor, A Dictionary of the Older Scottish Tongue

Variation and variety in written Middle Scots

1

According to Gregory Smith, 'Middle Scots was, more exclusively than any companion phase in the languages of north-west Europe, the special affair of literary habit, as distinguished from the spoken dialect.' 'Not only is Middle Scots a literary speech,' he proceeds, 'but it is the common medium of every writer during a century when Scottish literature was at its best. Despite certain internal differences, which we shall see were less idiocyncrasies than the sporadic effects of influences from without, the uniformity in the practice of Middle Scots is one of its most striking features.'[1] In the Introduction to his edition of Robert Henryson's *Poems*, H. Harvey Wood restates this theme with still greater emphasis: for him Middle Scots 'is not a spoken, historical dialect of the Scottish language at any period; but an artificial, created, "literary" language, used, for almost a century, by writers of very different locality and degree, with an astonishing measure of uniformity'.[2]

As will appear below (*p* 198), Middle Scots possessed a somewhat loosely defined standard of spelling which was generally followed by those writers with some pretensions to literacy. It is also possible to detail certain common tendencies and usages at other linguistic levels which characterise, at least in their most dignified passages, literary prose, the principal records and most other official writings, and some of them also serious verse: a general tendency to hypotactic rather than paratactic structure and towards the use of certain constructions, such as the Latin-derived 'accusative plus infinitive' construction, which were perhaps not normal to unstudied vernacular speech; a fondness for passive and impersonal constructions; a free use of loanwords of Latin or literary French origin in addition to, or instead of, equivalent vernacular expressions; in the later writings, the sporadic use of English-derived forms as alternative to their native cognates; the employment of *quh* forms of the relative where vernacular usage more probably had *that* or the 'zero-form';[3] the (more or less sporadic) habit of inflecting certain adjectives in plural concord;[4] and the avoidance of certain constructions and of certain words which apparently had specially strong colloquial overtones.[5] In these respects such writers conformed to a literary standard. But this standard was itself far from uniform and even within it variety of usage remains a notable feature. Hence the reader of Gregory Smith's 'The Main Characteristics of Middle Scots'[6] will find as many indications of variation and inconsistency as of homogeneity and uniformity; phenomena are 'common' or 'frequent', seldom 'exclusive' or 'universal'. And by no means all texts conform to such standard as there was. Many of the departures apparently reflect dialect and colloquial forms and usages of which we should otherwise have little contemporary indication. There is an abundance of evidence of this kind among the minor Middle Scots record sources, only awaiting collection and (cautious) interpretation.[7]

For many items of Middle Scots vocabulary indications of regional distribution may be observed in the relevant entries in the *Dictionary of the Older Scottish Tongue.*[8] Apart from the interest of these words as early instances of dialect usage, they also occasionally serve to confirm localisations of authors and texts. Thus John Knox's connections with Haddington are confirmed by his sharing with the Haddington burgh records the item *lowand-ill*, and Father James Dalrymple's possible Ayrshire origins by his use of *clachan* and *inspreth*; one or two such items also provide clues to the localisation of the authors of works of verse.[9]

The dictionary likewise provides useful indications of the stylistic distribution of items of vocabulary, that *knaw* and *pas*, for example, may have functioned as the literary 'translations' of the vernacular *ken* and *gang* or *ga*, that the three members of the set *hound, dog* and *tyke* had quite different overtones, that items like *cummer* (female crony), *gully* (large knife), *juggis* (lees of drink), *lug*, *bony* (bonny), *scunner*, as well as some others which are recorded only in comic verse, such as *gane* (face), *kyte* (belly), *larbar* (impotent), *lounge* and *queir*, had quite restricted spheres of use at the opposite pole from that of many of the 'exquisite termis quhilkis ar nocht daly vsit . . . , dreuyn or rather to say mair formaly reuyn fra lating' (*Compl.* 16).[10] Intensive investigations of the distributions of the elements of the Middle Scots vocabulary from some such point of view as this would certainly enhance greatly our appreciation of the subtleties of its literature.

We are even less well informed on the distribution of the elements of the syntax of Middle Scots. Almost everything remains to be done here – ranging over every point of the stylistic spectrum, from the structurally complex syntax of the most dignified literary and official style down to the paratactic, parenthetic and elliptical structures which mark the raciest kind of narrative (common in John Knox and his successors) and the passages of dialogue and direct speech abundant in these narratives and also in the court records. It would be of great interest to have a reliable account of the distribution of certain minor constructions which appear (on a purely impressionistic judgment) to be specially favoured in contexts of the latter kind and in certain other writings which bear traces of lack of sophistication in other ways: elliptical constructions like *I will in and se quhat thai ar doing* (1567 *Criminal Trials*, I, 495), *tha mecht never getin sa gud ane tym* (*p* 200 below), *he begowd rakein owp ane selder quhissell* (*p* 201 below), inverted constructions of adverbs or adverbial phrases with verbs of motion or action (*West about goes it, for doun goes the croses, of goes the surpleise*, Knox I, 259, 260), and rhetorical questions on the pattern *Quha . . . but . . .* (*and who was thare to led the ring but the Quein Regent herself?*, Knox I, 259). For the same reason one would like information on the commonness or otherwise in different types of text of the narrative present tense. In these and other respects the great stylistic variety of Middle Scots offers material for interesting and fruitful study, so far almost wholly neglected.

Even on simpler matters such as the distributions of variant features of the 'accidence' of Middle Scots we are still remarkably ignorant. It would be possible to assemble a lengthy list of alternative forms of expression at this level, of the distributions of which we have at present only the haziest notions: variant forms of the plurals of certain nouns (like *brether, bretherin, childer, childering*), inflected and uninflected plural forms of certain nouns (especially numerable nouns of measure[11] and personal surnames[12]), uninflected and inflected possessives of personal names and nouns of relationship,[13] the alternative possessives of *it* (*thairof, of the samin, of the self, of it, it*), certain anglicised forms of pronouns and verbs (*eg: these, thais, those* beside *thir* and *tha*, or present tense verbs in *-est, -ist* and *-eth, -ith*, beside the native equivalents in *-is*), uninflected and inflected past participles of Latin derived verbs (*creat, deput, disjunct,* etc), the alternative negative adverbs (*na, ne, nocht, not, no*) and other variable types of negative expression (*nor, na; nocht-, not-, non-*), the conjunctions *na, nor* and *than,* the presence or absence of enclitic *that* or *at* after conjunctions or relatives (*gif that, quhen that, quhilk that,* etc), and pairs or sets like *my* and *mine, thy* and *thine, na* and *nane, to* and *till, in, into* and *intill.*[14]

Variety of usage in such matters was certainly much greater than the quotations given at the outset of this paper might lead one to suppose. Another linguistic level at which 'uniformity in the practice of Middle Scots' can hardly be said to apply is that of orthography. In what follows I shall consider in necessarily general impressionistic terms some problems of distribution of certain types of variant spelling in Middle Scots. As well as possessing the interest due to them as an essential part of the general description of Middle Scots usage, these also possess, in their Middle Scots setting, the same kinds of dialectological and stylistic interest as do some comparable phenomena in Middle English which have been attracting much attention in recent years.

It is less likely that anyone would attribute uniformity of practice to such variant scribal practices as letter shapes, ligatures and the like or to 'different forms' ('allographs') of 'the same letters' ('graphemes'), such as, in Middle Scots, the several clearly distinguishable forms of 'the letter *s*', or to variations in frequency or contextual incidence of these or of abbreviations in manuscript and print. Clearly these and related palaeographic matters deserve to be studied for Middle Scots as much as for any other medieval language. So far this too has, however, been scarcely attempted, but I shall not attempt to pursue it further in this essay, confining myself to that level of orthographic usage which is treated in dictionaries and glossaries and for which some, albeit as yet very incomplete, information is available.

Nor is this essay intended to be a contribution to the evolving theory of 'graphemics'. No doubt the concepts and terminologies of this theory will feature largely in the further, more detailed studies which this aspect of Middle Scots deserves.[15] But for my present purpose of a broad survey of the Middle Scots situation as a whole, an approach from a fairly traditional standpoint using as far as possible a more traditional terminology seemed to be adequate.

My examples have been drawn mainly from my own reading over a wide range of Middle Scots texts and my tentative judgments about distribution and comparative frequency are mainly impressionistic or based on the selective evidence presented in DOST or in the few word-lists available at the time of writing. Though they will therefore require revision and massive amplification when the necessary detailed and rigorous studies of these phenomena have been carried out, it is hoped that they will meantime be tolerated in a preliminary exploration of this kind. I have confined my attention to the main Middle Scots period, from the fifteenth to the early seventeenth century, though similar questions naturally arise for the periods before and after this. Since verse texts present many special (though analogous) problems peculiar to themselves I have, except in one instance (*pp* 196–7), concerned myself chiefly with the evidence of the prose sources and only incidentally with the verse, ignoring entirely such verse peculiarities as the much earlier occurrence there of 'anglicised forms'.[16]

I have also confined myself to those prose texts which seemed to me to be in the main Scottish tradition. Thus I leave out of account Scottish copies of English works such as some of the contents of the Loutfut MS and MS Arundel 285 and Murdoch Nisbet's copy of Purvey's New Testament, and likewise those works of the later sixteenth century, including the statements of faith and discipline of the Scottish Reformed Church, and the printed prose of the seventeenth century, in which the spelling habits conform to English, not traditional Scottish, principles. These and other exceptionally heavily 'anglicised' writings of the sixteenth century no doubt present problems interesting enough in themselves but capable of largely separate treatment.[17]

For this general and preliminary survey (consisting largely of a lexicographer's impressions and gleanings) I have perforce relied on the best editions and manuscript transcripts which were available, though it is clear that for detailed work on these and related questions more complete and trustworthy texts of many of the sources will be needed.[18]

2

From the general viewpoint of the lexicographer surveying Middle Scots over its whole chronological, regional and stylistic range, the spelling system of Middle Scots was a perhaps extreme example of a common medieval European type, in which free variation was a prominent and important feature. Some of these variations,[19] with other features of the system,[20] Middle Scots simply inherited from Middle English. Others were it seems largely its own. Among the consonants the latter included *ʒ* and *y; v* and *w* and also, in non-initial positions, *v, w, f* and *ff*; a largely interchangeable set consisting of postvocalic *th, ch, tht, cht* and superscript *t*; intervocalic and occasionally morpheme-final *-m(m)-* and *-mb-*; intervocalic and morpheme-final *-k, -ck, -kk* and often *-ct* (as well as *-que* and *-cque* in many but not all of the same words); *-p* and *-pt; -x* and *-xt*. Similarly, by the sixteenth century one finds the members of the following sets interchanging more or less freely: *i(-e), y(-e)* and *yi; e(-e), ei, ey* and, in some words only, *ie, ye; a(-e), ai, ay; u(-e), ui, uy, wi, wy* (and in some words *o, oi, oy* are added to this set); and a number of other sets of interchangeable vowels and vowel-digraphs. One characteristic Scottish variation is typified by the interchange under certain conditions (before *k, p, t*) of *au, aw, al,* and (before or after *b, f, m, v* or *w*) of *a, au, aw, al: bahuif, bawhuif, balhuif; chamer, chawmer, chalmer; wapin, wawpin, walpin; hauk, hawk, halk; faut, fawt, falt.* Among a few prefix and many suffix syllables, sets like the following occur: *a-* and *e-; -is, -es* and *-s; -ill* and *-le; -ioun, -iown* and *-ion; -our* and *-or; -ure* and *-our, -or; -ar, -are, -air* and *-er; -y, -ie* and *-e*.

Free variation of this sort was then no less prominent a feature of Middle Scots than of Middle English. One difference from Middle English as a whole, however, was that in Middle Scots only a few spelling variants can be assigned to definable regions. Most variants, including all of those mentioned, were, so far as we at present know, current in comparable Scottish writings of every region. Throughout the period, too, the general trend was towards a proliferation of variants of this kind, as further items were assigned to particular variant sets. And, though one can observe considerable changes in the course of time in the relative frequencies of occurrence of the different members of some of the individual variant sets (particularly some of the sets containing digraphs in *-i* and *-y*, in which the latter became increasingly 'popular'), this seldom resulted in the total obsolescence of the less favoured variants; the only notable loss of a variant of this kind was the disappearance of *yh* and *ʒh* after the early sixteenth century, leaving *ʒ* and *y* as the only members of the set in question. In the second half of the sixteenth century the already considerable body of sets of alternative spellings in Scottish use was further supplemented by the introduction of graphemes which had till then remained largely or entirely confined to Tudor English (to the exclusion of Scots): *sh* was now added to *sch; tch* to *ch* (corresponding apparently to /tʃ/ in the spoken range); *gh* to *ch* (corresponding to (only postvocalic) /x/);

ea, ee to *e(-e)*, *ei, ey; oa* to *o(-e)*, *oi, oy; oo* to *u(-e)*, *ui, uy; -ed* to *-it, -yt*. And though, in the course of the seventeenth century, the native spelling system largely gave way to a much less variable 'English' system, the old tolerance of spelling variation has continued in writings in modern Scots vernacular down to the present day.

The dictionary record manifests this continuing tolerance of spelling variation in the fact that virtually every common Middle Scots word of more than one syllable possessed numerous alternative spelling forms, many of them contemporaneous, and most monosyllabic words at least several, resulting from the permutations of different members of the variant sets concerned. Among the 'vowel' spellings only *e* was in certain words (those probably which had the /ĕ/ phoneme in speech) fairly invariable throughout the period. Variation was a good deal less general, of course, among the 'consonants' and 'consonant' digraphs and combinations (particularly in the word-initial position), so that a few words like *bend* or *lent* do exist which (if we ignore the possibility of adding 'mute' *e*) were possessed of only one spelling. But these form only a small minority of the total.

Though free variation, fluctuating in these ways according to the vagaries of fashion, is a striking aspect of Middle Scots spelling practice viewed as a whole from the standpoint of the lexicographer, we need not expect that it will be present to the same degree when we turn to the orthographic practice of single texts or writers – to single orthographic 'idiolects'. At the same time it would be surprising, since presumably all writers of Middle Scots had access to this general varying system, if any one text or writer proved to possess a completely consistent practice with one and one only spelling for each of his 'words' – with a 'fixed' spelling system of his own. As a glance at any full glossary to, or description of, a Middle Scots text will show, few, if any, Middle Scots scribes (or, for that matter, printers) are wholly consistent in their spelling habits in this way. Some degree of free variation was normal in the spelling practice of individuals as well as over the system as a whole. And some scribes, like the writer of the Laing MS of Pitscottie's Chronicle,[21] are indeed highly inconsistent, varying freely between different spellings of single items, sometimes in quite short stretches of text, in what, to us, may seem a curious and striking manner. Without this habitual tolerance of spelling variation, the changes in popularity of particular variants and the introduction of new variants, including the 'anglicised' spellings common in later sixteenth-century texts like the Pitscottie, could of course hardly have occurred. The reader may like to work out the consistencies and in-consistencies of spelling of the following fragment of early sixteenth-century Scots:

> and yis maist ewill & crewall pepill & generacioun sall no*ch*t pas one
> to ye tym of ye antechrist neir*e* ye end of ye warld & ya*n* yai sall be
> extendit our all ye warld for yai ar sa mony yai may no*ch*t be numerit
> nor tald for multitud nor yar na pepill may resist to yam bot yar sall
> cum ane fyr fra ye hewyne sall suelli yai*m* be hi*m* quhilk is till iuge
> bat*h* queik & deid Alsua yar is ane p*a*rt of ane desert quhar ye Sandy
> see is ane pepill quhilk has round feit as ye clwis of ane hors and ya
> men hes na wawpynis bot yai teyll ye erd and yai ar gud teillme*n* bot
> yai ar werry crewall and yar habitacioune is ry*ch*t stark and yai ar
> subdeit till ws and one ye tothir part of ye desert yar is ane land callit
> ye veme*n* land quhar yair is na man nor na ma*n* dar byd our*e* ane
> ʒeire and yis land lestis xl days jurnay one baitht ye sidis in ye quhilk
> land yar is thre quenys w*i*th owt vthir greit laides yat haldis grett
> citeis & tovnys strenthes and castellis and quhen yai pleis till rid one
> yair*e* i*n*imeis yai ar ane hundretht thousand ridand ladeis w*i*thout
> yame y*a*t passis on fut w*i*th carrag*is* & metis and yai ar werray stark
> and cruell.[22]

It is nevertheless true that all writers of Middle Scots seem also to display some greater or lesser degree of consistency in some at least of their spelling habits. Gilbert Hay (1456) has, in one of his works, only two examples of *mair* to 221 of *mare* (more), and sixty-six of *maist* to one only of *maste* (most); and his spellings of *maidin* and *maister* are (according to the available edition) invariable.[23] In the choice between initial *v* and *w* (in words which apparently had either the /v/ or the /w/ phonemes) some scribes, like Alexander Wood of Old Aberdeen, copyist of Q. Kennedy's *Breif Tracteit*, have a strong preference for *v*- (spelling, *eg* both *veill* (veal) and *veill* (well), or *vile* (vile) and *vile* (wile)), others, such as some of the scribes of the Boyndlie MS of Bellenden's *Livy* and the copyist of the fforde MS of Kennedy's *Breif Tracteit*, prefer *w*-, some, like Gilbert Hay (1456), the scribe of the Advocates' MS of Bellenden's *Livy*, and James Dalrymple (1596), have a 'modern' distribution of the two letters, some seem merely in-consistent, like the scribes of John of Irland's *Meroure* and of the ver-sion of Pitscottie mentioned above (and there is one instance of an invariable preference of *u* to either *v* or *w*, in the person of King James VI).[24] No doubt all writers had access to the general variant system; but each made his own personal and idiosyncratic selection from the alternatives available to him.[25]

In these circumstances it would be highly improbable, in view of the very large number of different possible combinations within the system as a whole, that any two writers should coincide over the whole range of their spelling habits. The few brief and highly selective lists of spelling peculiarities of single texts[26] which have been published certainly do not contradict this: in the aggregate all differ widely from each other. Thus a writer's individual assemblage of spelling-choices could be just as distinctive of him as his 'handwriting' – his idiosyncratic habits in forming and connecting his written symbols – is generally accepted to be; as indeed was recognised in one celebrated trial at law when five unsigned, treasonable letters were brought home to an alleged author on just such grounds: "ffirst, that he newir vseit to wrytt '3' in the beginning of ony word, sik as '30w', '30uris', '3eild', '3ea', and siclyk; bot ewir wrait 'y' in steid of the said '3'; that he wrait all wordis begynning with 'w' with ane singill 'v'; and quhan that letter 'v' fell to be in the myddis or end of ane word, he wrait ane doubill 'w'; that quhen he wrait 'quhen', 'quhair', 'qlk' or ony sik word quhilk vsis to be written and spellit be vtheris with 'quh', he wrait onlie 'qh', 'qhen', 'qhair' and siclyk; quhaneeuir ane word began with 'con', he newir wrytt 'con' at lenth, bot with ane '9'; quhan euir 't' fell to be in the end of ane word, he wraitt it without ane straik throw the 't'; and did the lyk quhan ewir 't' fell in ony pairt of ane word."[27] No doubt the same was also true of 'sub-graphemic' or 'allographic' writing habits – the habits of preferring particular letter-forms in particular word-positions – and habits in respect of abbreviations, punctuation, capitalisation, word-division and so on, as is also recognised in the passage just quoted.

Unfortunately none of the existing studies of Middle Scots spelling peculiarities covers more than a fraction of the total lexicon of each text and the selections of lexical items are mostly not the same. Thus while we are on safe enough ground in making assertions about differences in general habit, we are as yet in no position to set about assessing general and particular *resemblances* between roughly contemporary texts. But the possibility clearly exists of studying numerically the habits of individuals in these matters – of identifying those habits in which each writer is consistent, those in which he shows strong preferences and those in which no preference is visible – and thereafter of matching and comparing writers one with another.

What correspondences would emerge from this we have no present means of telling. *A priori* it seems likely that pupils would share at least some of the preferences of their teachers, especially, no doubt, writing-teachers, so that 'schools' of spelling-tradition would exist, each of these sharing a common 'dialect' or 'style'. If this were so, in principle it should be possible to allocate individual writers between such 'schools' by procedures similar to, though doubtless much more complex than, those of the dialectologists of medieval languages. Conversely, however, it is just possible that the tradition of free choice in the matter of these variants did indeed overrule any tendency for one writer to imitate the preferred choices of another. This is apparently what is at present commonly assumed. If this proved to be so and no more than chance similarities in practice emerged, it would in itself be interesting. But until someone has tried to find out, we are in no position to prejudge it. For this and other purposes we need fully comparable accounts of the spelling habits of a number of Middle Scots texts of different types, beginning preferably with the available holograph texts.[28] Editors of texts could assist this by providing exhaustive rather than selective word-lists – something which so far only a very few of them have done.[29]

Comparative investigations of the spelling habits of Middle Scots writers could be carried out without reference to the phonemic level of Middle Scots at all, treating the spellings simply as phenomena in their own right, independently of whatever spoken forms they might be thought to 'represent'.[30] For this purpose, the language could indeed be viewed as 'the special affair of literary habit, as distinguished from the spoken dialect'. The least general procedure, which might nevertheless prove profitable, would be a simple comparison between various texts of the distributions of variant spellings of individual words. But it might prove convenient, and doubtless also revealing, to group together those words which proved to share the same variant sets or perhaps those which not only shared the same sets but also used the different members in roughly the same proportions. (For some texts, for example, it would turn out that the relative frequencies of *a-e, ai, ay* in, on the one hand, *lare* (lore) and *mare* (more), and, on the other, *lair* (resting-place) and *mair* (sheriff's officer), were strikingly different.) In this way we could assemble a system of orthographic variant and single member sets with a lexical inventory for each one.

This orthographic system could then be related to a phonemic system or systems reconstructed at least partly on other grounds – such as general rhyming practice, etymology and the modern dialect reflexes. Such a phonemic system for Middle Scots has been used and set out in outline by C. Kuipers in his *Quintin Kennedy: Two Eucharistic Tracts*, Nijmegen, 1964, *pp 76ff*. To detail its reconstruction is beyond the scope of this essay but it is assumed in what follows.

In the past some such relationship between the orthographic system of Middle Scots and its presumed phonemic system(s) has always apparently been taken as axiomatic (with a few exceptions such as the so-called 'artificial' spelling of the pre-consonantal indefinite article *ane*). To argue a case for this assumption would take us well beyond the intended confines of this essay, but it is perhaps not an impossibility. In general, much that we know of Middle Scots spelling and phonology does seem to square with a belief in a reasonable 'fit' between the orthographic and phonemic systems over a good deal of their area.

Many of the patches of 'misfit' which we can detect at certain stages are apparently due, as we should expect, to a tendency to retain established orthographic arrangements after the phonemic arrangements which they formerly reflected had ceased to exist. Though the early fifteenth-century coalescence of the segments /al/, /au/ and certain allophones of /ā/[31] is soon reflected in spelling under the conditions indicated on *p* 182, it is much less generally and immediately reflected in, for example, word-final conditions, so that *hall* (hall) and *haw* (livid) and *quha* (who) continue in general to be so distinguished in spelling throughout the period. Conversely, the emergence of Middle Scots doublets in /ē/ as well as in /ī/, in words like *dede* (dead) and *dethe* (death) which had /ę̄/ in early Scots,[32] is partly 'concealed' by a persistent preference of most writers for the traditional *e-e* or *ei, ey* spellings (which in Middle Scots frequently equate with /ī/), in contrast with the rare and tardy occurrence of the *a-e, ai, ay* spellings (which do indeed imply the doublets in /ē/).[33]

In what follows it will be assumed that, with qualifications such as those instanced in the previous paragraph, an equation can be made between the general or overall orthographic and phonemic systems of Middle Scots at the different stages of its development. It will further be assumed that individual writers of that language could, if they so chose, and in practice often did, evolve their own spellings or establish their spelling habits according to the 'rules' of equivalence so constituted. It will however appear that some writers applied these 'phonetic' principles more freely than others; and, as we have just seen, this 'phonetic' motivation was by no means the only one which controlled Middle Scots spelling practice.

3

Once we have mastered the rules of spelling variation discussed in the previous section it becomes possible to predict for every common word all the variant spellings which we may expect to meet in the majority of Middle Scots texts, the less numerous 'aberrant' texts of the type discussed in Section 6 only excepted. Morpheme-final *-k* has its limited set of normal variants (including, most commonly, *-ck* and *-kk-*). The sequence *a* followed by a single consonant followed either by final *-e* or by another syllable varies, up to about the mid-sixteenth century, only with *ai, ay* and, less commonly *e*; in certain cases (where the consonant is *f, l, t* or there is a second syllable) the three last may be followed by either a single or a double consonant, with or without a following *e* (*eg* in *hale, hail, hayl, haile, hayle, haill, hayll, haille, haylle, hel, hell,* (whole)); and this set apparently correlates with the phoneme /ē/ in speech. In other words these variations operate regularly and within predictable limits throughout the whole of the Middle Scots lexicon, accompanying their particular corresponding phoneme or phonetic segment in every word in which it occurs.

Middle Scots also however possesses a large number of words which appear to display more than the normally predictable range of variant spellings. These words constitute a substantial minority of the items in the dictionary. One of them is the verb 'to make', which appears in the variant spellings, all of frequent occurrence, *mak, mack, makk-,* and *make, maik, mayk*. The first of these subsets of three variants reminds us of the set of common variants for 'back' (*bak, back, bakk-*), and of part of those for 'act' and 'fact' (*ak, ack, akk-,* but also *act,* and *fak, fack, fakk-,* also *fact*); the second subset may similarly remind us of the common variants for 'oak' (*aik, ayk, ake,* also, but only rarely, *ak*). We may also recall that the spelling system as a whole includes a majority of instances in which *a* followed by a double consonant and *ai, ay* are mutually exclusive (*eg* in *hatt* 'hat' and *hait, hayt* 'hot' and 'to hate', or in *capp* 'cap' or 'cup' and *caip* 'cope', or in *call, kall* 'call' and *caill, kaill, kayll* 'cale, cabbage'). Or, to put this differently, we have seen that the spelling *a* followed by a double consonant regularly corresponds to a reconstructed /ă/ phoneme for Middle Scots, which was in contrast with the reconstructed /ē/ phoneme with which the *ai, ay* spelling frequently corresponds. To return to 'to make', we may also note that the modern Scots dialects contain reflexes both of a Middle Scots type /măk/ and of a Middle Scots type /mēk/ for this word: these would rhyme respectively with /ăk/ *ak, ack* (act) and /ēk/ *aik, ayk* (oak). This would seem to imply that Middle Scots possessed not one but two distinct synonymous morphemes for 'to make', which were similar but not identical in spoken form, and that each of these was spelled 'regularly' according to the normal 'rules' of the system.

By parallel processes of reasoning we are led to infer the existence of a large number of other similar sets of (apparently) synonymous doublets or morphemic variants in Middle Scots. Besides *mak* and *maik*, we have also *blak* and *blaik* (black), *lak* and *laik* (lack), *tak* and *taik* (take), *brek* and *breik* (break), *spek* and *speik* (speak), *glad* and *glaid*; and we have other sets like *sic* and *sa* beside *swilk* and *swa*, *waik* and *tway* beside *wauk*, *walk* and *twaw*, *giff* and *liff* beside *geve* and *leve*, *mekill* and *sekir* beside *mickill* and *sicker*, *abuif* and *abuin* beside *abouf* and *aboun*, *chese* beside *chuse*, *lese* beside *los*, *warld* and *warldly* beside *wardill* and *wardly*, *seildin* beside *seindill* (seldom), *brin* and *thrid* beside *birn* and *third*, *brander* and *hunder* beside *brandreth* and *hundreth* (and *houndreth*), *broder* and *fudder* beside *brother* and *father*, *bus* and *mers* beside *busk* and *mersk*, *nar* beside *nere*, *neist* beside *nixt*, *nerrest* and *narrest* beside *nerest*, *heich* and *hey* (high), *laich*, *lauch* and *law* (low), multiple sets like the various forms of 'great' (*grett*, *greit*, *gritt*, *gryte*, *gert*, *gart* and *girt*) and a similar set for 'grass'. One very numerous group exists among the principal parts of most 'strong' and some 'weak' verbs, where analogical processes supplemented the simple phonological and morphological causes which gave rise to the variants already instanced. Still another group exists in those verbs of Latin origin which had doublet forms borrowed respectively from the Latin present and past stems, like *dispone* and *dispose*, *expreme* and *express*, *promit* and *promeis*, *posseid* and *possess*, *include* and *incluse*. Each part of DOST provides evidence of scores of these sets, consisting of several segments which were constant and only one which varied, so that the near-identity of all the members is evident (and indeed is commonly assumed by modern readers). In all they must be numbered in thousands. Though this phenomenon is an important fact of life for the student of Middle Scots, its existence has so far gone virtually unnoticed and has hardly ever received separate comment.[34]

A few of the variants of this type were only partly synonymous, and this raises semantic problems which it is unnecessary to treat here.

Thus *lak* and *laik* (lack) coincide over the whole of the semantic range of *laik*, but *lak* has quite distinct additional senses not found for *laik*. Again, *laich* and *lauch* (low) occur chiefly in the 'literal' senses of this adjective; only the cognate *law* is at all common in the 'figurative' ones. But even if we exclude such instances and those others, like *laich* and *law* itself, or *droich* and *dwerch* (dwarf), where the variation extends over more than one segment so that the formal relationship is less obvious, we are left with a large majority of synonymous variants of the sort being considered. Nor is the number greatly reduced by excluding those instances in which the uncertainties or ambiguities of the spelling system leave room for doubt whether we are justified in regarding the contrast as potentially 'phonemic' or merely 'orthographic', as with *ak* and *act*, *effek* and *effect*, *temp* and *tempt*, *count* and *compt*, *nummer* and *number*.

Many of these variant sets clearly existed as phonemic variants before the beginning of the Middle Scots period: a considerable number (such as *mak* and *maik* or *heich* and *hey*) can be seen, for instance, to return to the twelfth or thirteenth centuries. But some others, like *gritt* and *gryte* beside the older *grett* and *greit*, and some of the variant past tense and past participle forms of verbs, as well as other sets to be mentioned below,[35] arose within the Middle Scots period itself. The general trend was plainly towards the accumulation of a larger and larger number of variants, only partly offset by the obsolescence of items like *ȝude* (went) to leave only *ȝeid* (itself later superseded by the analogical *gaid*) or *hevid* beside *heid*. As with the simple orthographic variants, the habit of tolerating this sort of variation perhaps provided a suitable condition for the ready acceptance, in the later sixteenth century, of a massive number of additional variants of English derivation like *oath, more, most, quhom, quhich, so, only, owe, kingdom, much, either, any, from, if, would* as occasional or frequent alternatives to the native *aith, mare, maist, quham, quhilk, sa, anerly, aw* or *aucht, kinrik, mekill, owther, ony, fra, gif, wald.*

Variants of this type are of course not unknown in other dialects and languages (including Middle and Tudor English). Middle Scots, however, seems to have been quite exceptional in possessing an extremely large number for which, at present, no regional or other specialisation of distribution is apparent – which co-existed as free variants over extensive regions and often in single, including some holograph, texts. Instances like the occurrence in close juxtaposition of *greit* and *grett* in the text quoted on *p* 184 are quite frequent.

It is of course not at all impossible that variant pronunciations of synonyms of this type existed in the same areas and even the same spoken idiolects, and that thus both variant spellings of this type 'genuinely' reflect a feature of the writer's or his community's speech. Instances of this are common enough in modern Scottish speech, not only as between a speaker's 'English' and 'Scottish' forms, such as *two* [tuː] and *twae* [tweː], but also, in some areas, between doublets of native origin, like *twae* [tweː] and *twaw* [twǫː].[36] Perhaps we may take it as a reasonable working hypothesis that at least in holograph texts written variants of this type do often imply that the writer either used himself or was familiar with the particular spoken form or forms to which, by the normal spelling 'rules', these written variants correspond; that, for example, a writer who wrote *greit* and *grett* (great) in fact knew the spoken forms /griːt/ and /grɛt/ in his own or his neighbours' speech.

This is reasonable enough as a working assumption; and we can perhaps be nearly certain that at least the *originators* of variant spellings of this type were familiar with (and probably used themselves) the particular spoken forms apparently implied (that, for example, the sixteenth-century *gritt* '/grɪt/' and *gryte* '/greit/' were indeed when first written genuine reflections of their original writers' pronunciations). But we cannot of course guarantee, even for holograph texts, that this was invariably the case once these spellings had come into established use. What were 'phonemic' variants for one writer may conceivably sometimes have been merely 'orthographic' for another. Thus whereas spelling *innovations* are quite likely to be 'phonetic', *established* spellings on the other hand may conceivably reflect the pronunciations of others than the writer, or former phonemic arrangements which no longer applied in any contemporary speech.[37]

Indeed, some quite clear instances exist of scribal defiance of 'phonemic' principles of spelling in cases of this sort. Most north-eastern scribes fairly consistently prefer 'standard' spellings like *quhare* or *quhair* when, as is likely, their own local pronunciation would have been less ambiguously rendered by *for* or *fair*, which indeed (see *p* 195 and note 41) a few of them also have as 'occasional' spellings. We may imagine, too, that in writing 'English' forms like *oath, if, from, would,* writers of the later sixteenth century were similarly 'misrepresenting' their normal speech-habits (in which, it is probable, they mostly used '*aith*' /ēθ/, '*gif*' /gɪf/, '*fra*' /frē/, '*wald*' /wald/ or /wăd/). The spelling *neixt* (next) of a Selkirk scribe of the 1520s and 1530s and of John

Wallwod (see *p* 200) is perhaps an orthographic blend of the phonemic variants *nixt* and *neist* and thus quite indeterminate as to its writer's preference between these two as spoken forms.

Though this uncertainty about the exact implications of variants of this type exists, it need not discourage us from studying their distributions and patterns of incidence as spellings. The results of this are bound to be interesting and revealing even if we are often not certain whose favoured pronunciation is being revealed to us – that of the writer himself, his writing teacher, those writers who set the national 'standard', or some other.

Some variant pronunciations of this type are involved in another kind of uncertainty, for a somewhat different reason – that of ambiguities inherent in the basic system of phoneme-grapheme equivalence itself. In Middle Scots, as in other orthographic systems of a similar type, individual symbols or 'graphemes' commonly participated in more than one orthographic set. Thus the graph *a* participated both in the set *a, a-e, ai, ay* /ē/ and in the (in this case single member) set *a* /ă/, so that such a spelling as *lard*, out of context, is completely ambiguous as between /lărd/ (lard) and /lērd/ (laird). With non-synonymous instances of this sort, of course, the ambiguity will nearly always be resolved in the usual way by the linguistic context at other levels than that of orthography. With synonymous variants of the type we have been considering, however, forms like *mak* may well remain ambiguous in some instances; since *a* participates both in the set (/ă/) *a* plus double consonant, *a* plus single consonant, on the one hand, and also (/ē/) *a-e, ai, ay* and also, though rarely, *a* plus single consonant. Similarly *gret* may be ambiguous, though *grett* /grĕt/ and *grete, greit* /grīt/ are (as a rule) not. Equally the commonest spellings for 'two' and 'who', *twa* and *quha*, fall uncertainly between the sets *a, ai, ay* /ē/ and (in a labial context) *a, au, aw* /ā/; the 'unambiguous' spellings *tway* and *quhay* are rather less common; and the 'unambiguous' spellings 'representing' the other doublets, *twaw* and *quhaw*, are rare.[38] By studying the specific habits of individual scribes some of these may be resolved: thus some scribes regularly exclude *a* plus single consonant from the *a-e, ai, ay* set. But this will be defeated if the scribe is at all inconsistent in his habits and no doubt a large residue of unsolvable 'ambiguities' will remain.

As against such considerations, however, we may also take note that, although many individual Middle Scots scribes do employ more than one variant from particular sets of the 'phonemic' or *quasi-*

phonemic type we have been considering, it is also evident that many of them had at least some individual preferences and more or less consistent habits. That copyists could often be more loyal to their own habits in this respect than to their author's apparent intentions is shown by the fairly numerous cases when it is necessary to 'restore' an alternative variant to make a verse line metrical or to provide a rhyme. The rhymes of the Maitland MS copyist's version of *King Hart*, for example, require a number of emendations of this kind (for *betrayid* (line 382) read *betraysit*, for *suppleit* (390) *suppleid*, for *dunt* (537) *dint*, for *glaid* (554) *glad*, and for *iustifeit* (574) *iustifyid*); similar examples from many other poems could easily be collected.[39] And, of course, different recensions of the same original often show consistent differences in their choice of variants of this kind (just as much as in the orthographic variants considered in the previous section). Whereas the copyist of the Edinburgh MS of Barbour's *Brus* regularly has *gan* (the auxiliary verb), *gres* (grass), *hundir* (hundred) and *leawte* (loyalty), his contemporary of the Cambridge MS as regularly prefers *can*, *gyrs*, *hundreth* and *lawte*, *laute*.

As yet we have little enough information on the detailed incidence of such variants even in literary texts. Besides these, we need also detailed studies of the distributions of some of the variants of this kind over limited chronological periods, based at least partly on the localised and holograph writings. Until all this is done we have no means of knowing what the detailed distributional patterns were and how these correlate, if at all, with chronological, regional, stylistic or personal factors. The possibility exists that patterns might emerge which would serve to 'date' and 'place' more accurately than we now can some of those Middle Scots literary texts whose origins and dates are at present quite indeterminate, as well as providing further insights into the nature of our available copies of all literary texts. In any case, in its possession of numerous variants of this type Middle Scots presents us with an interesting phenomenon which deserves detailed study for its own sake and for its potential implications for historical phonology, albeit the precise nature of these implications is at present not as obvious or as straightforward as might be wished.

4

Although most variants of the type considered in the last section can not as yet be seen to have been regionally distributed, others either

certainly or probably were. It is the present writer's impression that
the two variants of 'wake' (*waik* /wēk/ and *wauk, walk* /wāk/) had a
similar distribution to those of their modern dialect reflexes, *ie* /wēk/
in the south and south-east and /wāk/ elsewhere. A similar suggestion
for the distribution of the variant *maik, mea(c)k* (as against *mak*) has
been made in DOST s.v. *Mak* v. Perhaps the three variants of 'water'
(*watter* /ˡwătĭr/, *waiter* /ˡwētĭr/ and *wawter, walter* /ˡwātĭr/) may turn
out similarly. It might also prove that in these cases the boundary area
was, as it now is, within the Central Scots region, from which many of
the texts come, which would account for the comparative commonness
in record of all of the variant types.

It seems very probable (in view of the well-established normal correlation of the spellings *ȝ-* and *y-* with the /j/ phoneme) that the following spellings do indeed reflect early instances of pronunciations with
prosthetic /j/ which, though now only characteristic of Central and
Southern Scots speech, appear to have been more widely distributed in
Middle Scots: *yane* (=one) (1527 *Prestwick B. Rec.* 52) and *ȝown*
(=*oun*, oven) (1517 *Wigtown B. Ct.* 64a), and *ȝaikin* (=oaken) (1578–
9 *Elgin Rec.* I, 153), *yetling, yetlit* (*ettil* to try) (1606 *Inverness Rec.* II,
42, 47, 57, 59);[40] as well as the still more widespread *ȝake, ȝaik* (to
ache), *yerl* (earl), *ȝerd* (earth), which are common in all classes of text.

A noticeable and apparently regular habit of the clerk of Wigtown
Burgh Court in the early years of the sixteenth century was that of
writing *t* or less frequently *d* where his contemporaries wrote *th* or
postvocalically *tht* or superscript *t*: as *tyrd* (*f* 8a), *clat* (9a), *a towsand
v hundyrd* (9b), *tre hundyr bollis* (*Ibid*), *tolboud* (10a), *triys, triis* (12a),
hunderet (14b), etc. Here, in view of the coincidence of the locality, it
does seem possible to compare Andrew Symson's remark in his *Large
Description of Galloway, 1684*, repr. 1823, *p* 97: 'Some of the countrey
people, especially those of the elder sort, do very often omit the letter h
after t, as ting for thing, tree for three, tacht for thatch, wit for with,
fait for faith, mout for mouth.'

Another group of variant spellings whose phonological implications
seem reasonably certain are those which apparently reflect north-
eastern dialect features of pronunciation. In contrast with the last
example, some of these are very rare indeed in their incidence, as very
occasional aberrations from more or less standard spelling-practice:
thus, at least on the evidence of the printed record, the *for* spelling in
the 1539 quotation below is a unique exception to this scribe's otherwise regular *quhar*. Nevertheless, the coincidence in regional distribu-

tion with the modern spoken reflexes encourages the belief that we have here genuine reflections of dialect speech. In the quotations the variants in question are italicised:

> And the *quyntray* was dangerfull throw this plage of pestilence; 1500 *Aberd. B. Rec.* I. 68. That na burges . . . sal haue nay forstaller vnder him to pas in *quintray*; 1507 *Ibid* 435. In calling of hir commond vyld freris huyr that scho wes that hes ane pek of lyis betuix thi shoulderis. I sell leid the to the place *for* the freir swewyt the quhar thou tynt the pendace of thi belt in the hie publict gett; 1539 *Ibid* 159. Ane *phingar* (= quhingar, whinyard); *Ibid* 161. To heid the blokhouse with faill and to put ane fulse *rief* thairon, thykit with faill; 1542 *Ibid* 184. Dauid Anderson, maister of wark to the *stein* wark of the sayme gable of the parish kirk; Cullen, *Chron. Aberd.* 33. And thair efter I paist to Dunnotter *fair* I beheld his grace at his supar; *Ibid* 53. Swa that *neyn* belewit his lyif; 1596–7 *Misc. Spald. C.* I, 85. Beand gryt *wymb* with barne; *Ibid* 92. *Wytit* on be the cummer; *Ibid*. And quhow *sein* the woman spak of God, that ewill spreit vaniest away withe ane rwmleng; *Ibid* 100. In the forme of ane four futit beist, and speciallie lyk ane *futret*, and sum tyme lyk ane catt; *Ibid* 148. *Futherit; Ibid.* Seing he wes ane man so guidlyk and ritche . . . and scho ane vgle harlot *quyne; Ibid* 178.[41]

5

Still another class of occasional 'phonemic' variant spelling exists in which the distribution of the implied spoken forms was apparently by 'register' rather than by region. This is most obvious with certain items of that group of words which underwent phonetic reduction by the loss or assimilation of intervocalic or final consonants, resulting in the emergence of 'reduced' and 'unreduced' doublets, such as *aw* and *all*, *deil* and *devil*, *mow* and *mouth*, and so on. In every case both doublets persisted at least as orthographic variants. Since many of them are still represented in the modern Scots dialects of today by spoken doublets, it seems that for Middle Scots most of them can also be classed as 'phonemic' variants. As well as in the spellings to be considered below the 'reduced' members of these variant sets are evidenced also in 'reverse' spellings like *ewine* for *ein* 'eyes' (after *evin*, *ein*, 'evening') (*Leg. S.* ii, 557) or *send* for *sen* 'since' (after *send*, *sen*, 'send') (Cullen, *Chron. Aberd.* 50), and in innumerable instances in rhyme in (chiefly particular classes of) verse, like *evin* (evening) with *wene* (*Kynd Kittok* 12) or *send* with *den* (Henryson, *Fab*. 556).

Some examples of this sort of variant show no obvious tendency towards specialisation of distribution. It appears, for example, that *hauch, bow, how, know, row* and *gouff* were as common in all classes of text as *halch, boll, holl, knoll, roll* and *golf*, and *fouth* and *stouth* seem to have completely superseded *fulth* and *stulth*. *Clais* seems to have been as widely and freely used as *clathis; ill* and *evill*, though unrelated, were perhaps regarded as variants of this kind and indeed interchange freely (for example, in different recensions of the same text) and neither form appears to have been any more specialised in distribution than the other; and the specialisation of *fow* (as opposed to *full*) is apparently by 'meaning' rather than by dialect or 'register'. With sets like *aboun, abone* and *abovin, abuvin* and *lesum* and *leve-, leifsum*, the reduced variant is much the more common, without any evident specialisation of distribution of either alternative.

But, when all these have been excluded, there remains a large residue of sets of this class whose 'reduced' members seem either certainly, or, pending a full investigation, possibly to have been restricted in their distributions: *a, aw* (beside *all*), *caw, kaw* (beside *call*), *faw, fa* (beside *fall*), *staw* (beside *stall*, stole), *fas* (beside *fals*), *haus, hasse* (beside *hals*), *hauf* (beside *half*), *bowtt* (beside *bolt*), *stown, stoun* (beside *stolin*), *wow* and *woune, wone* (beside *woll* and *wollin*), *pow* (beside *pull*), *cowtter, kutir* (beside *culter*), *deil* (beside *devil*), *ein, eining* and *ʒistrein* (beside *evin, evining* and *ʒistrevin*), *hairst* (beside *harvest*), *ge* and *gein* (beside *geve, geiff* and *gevin, geiffin*), *him-, ʒoursell* (beside *-self*), *twell* (beside *twelf*), *a* and *ha* (beside *have, haiff*), *mow* (beside *mouth*), *no* (beside *nocht*), *uncow* (beside *uncouth*), *sen* (beside *send*), *Iis, ʒeis* (beside *I sall, ʒe sall*), *Ile, Iill* (beside *I will*), *yeil* (beside *ye will*). In his 'Reulis and Cautelis to be observit and eschewit in Scottis Poesie' King James VI specifies such 'cuttit schort' forms, as he calls them, exemplifying them by '*Iis neir cair*' for '*I sall neuer cair*,' as specially appropriate for 'flyting and inuectiues' and adds that in 'loue or tragedies' 'ʒour wordis man be drawin lang quhilkis in flyting man be short' (James VI, *Poems* I, 75/22*f*). In rhyme these reduced forms are indeed frequent only in certain specific genres of verse: comic and satiric verse of every kind and certain narrative poems, such as Hary's *Wallace*, the Asloan MS *Sevyne Sages*, Douglas's *Aeneid*, Stewart's *Chronicle* and Rolland's *Seaven Seages* (many examples could be assembled from the relevant entries in DOST); but in serious lyric or didactic verse and in courtly narrative (like Douglas's *Palice of Honour* or Dunbar's *Goldyn Targe*) they are rare or absent. As spellings (in other than rhyming positions) these forms seem to occur only in the same comic and narrative poems. They are also a prominent feature of the colloquial Scottish speech of the Jockies and Jamies of some English dramas of the Elizabethan and Jacobean period, *eg* in *Ays* or *I'se* (=I shall), *thouse* (=thou shalt), *I'll* (=I will), *deel* (=devil) and *our sell* (=ourself).[42] With the other distributional problems we have been considering, their incidence in Middle Scots prose requires further study: but they do appear to be much commoner in certain less conventionally spelled texts of the sort we shall briefly consider below (*pp* 199*f*) than in those whose spellings are more 'standard' (*p* 198): a few examples are *kaw* (=call, 1438 *Ayr B. Ct.* 32b), *sydwawdyk* (=side-wall-dike, 1462 *Peebles B. Rec.* I, 147), *thayr sell* (1497 *Dunferm. B. Rec.* 77), *gein* (=given, 1521 *Selkirk B. Ct. f* 89b), *eining* (=evening, 1561 *Edinb. Old Acc.* II, 121), *eyne* (=evening, 1600 *Glasgow B. Rec.* I, 101), and others may be sought in the appropriate DOST entries.

In general it looks as if, in this matter of these reduced and unreduced variant sets, the 'standard' spelling practice favoured the more traditional or conservative unreduced variants whereas the reduced variants are chiefly specialised to the particular classes of text suggested. It may also prove that *'d*, as the reduced and voiced variant of *it* (see DOST s.v. *'D*), had a similar distribution to these other reduced variants. It is possible also that some, though clearly not all, of the items of the class of 'aphetic forms' which are such an obvious and well-known characteristic of the Middle Scots morpheme system may have a similar distribution: this may turn out to be so with *chete*, *cheit* (beside *escheit*) and *tach* and *tachment* (beside *attach* and *attachment*) (*eg* 1456 *Peebles B. Rec.* I, 115), though apparently not with *fect*, *feck* (beside *effect*), *levint* (beside *elevint*, *alevint* (eleventh)) or *mendis* (beside *amendis*).

6

A dictionary such as DOST records all the variant spellings found in its collections for each of its word entries. In a somewhat crude way it also makes clear that some variants were much more common in their incidence and widespread in their distribution than others. What the dictionary record already shows crudely a more exhaustive study would no doubt confirm. It appears that the great majority of Middle

Scots texts at each chronological stage adhered fairly regularly to a
variant spelling system which included only the more common and
widespread variants just mentioned and in general excluded the rarer
variants. Conversely, there also existed a minority of texts in which
these less common variants were rather profusely used. But the boundary between these two classes of texts is somewhat indeterminate,
since one is apt to meet an occasional uncommon variant even in texts
which generally conform to the more limited system and since there
are also texts whose practice falls between the two extremes of somewhat limited variation and the free use of uncommon variants. Nevertheless it is already possible to specify those texts whose spelling practice is noticeably 'regular' (*ie* which have a more limited range of
variation) and others, less 'regular', in which the less common variants
are clustered.

Perhaps the narrowest limits of variation in this way will prove to be
those adhered to in some of the printed prose and verse of the later sixteenth century, as if the Scottish printers were moving, like their English opposite numbers, towards a 'fixed' spelling; this movement, if it
existed, came to an end when, early in the seventeenth century, the
Scottish printers abandoned the native spelling tradition altogether
for an imported English one. Among the sixteenth-century manuscript
sources, however, the great national registers (of Parliament, of Privy
Council, of the Great and Privy Seals) and almost all the existing
copies of the major literary texts in prose and verse, also conform to
comparatively narrow limits of variation (as exemplified in Sections
2 and 3 of this paper). And much the same range of variants is adhered
to by many other writers of that century, including local clerks, minor
officials and the writers of private records. If we assume that it was
writers like these royal and literary clerks who were likely to have set
the standards of spelling and of other literary usages, then we may regard this limited, majority practice as the 'standard' form of written
Middle Scots. That there was a contemporary belief in the possibility
of some such standard is implied in the frequent complaints of or
apologies for 'wrang ortographie and fals spelling' (Charteris, *Pref. to
Lyndesay*) or 'many incorrect errouris in . . . the ortographie' (James
VI, *Poems* I, 99/16), which occur in sixteenth-century Scottish writings.
A number of other instances, from 1549 (*Corr. M. Lorraine* 316) to
c 1608 (*Elphinstone Chart.* 181) will be quoted in DOST s.v. *Ortho-
graphie*.

But, as we have noted, the boundaries between this standard system and the less conformist system of spelling was neither sharply defined nor immutably fixed. Occasional 'irregular' or 'substandard' spellings, of the types exemplified in the previous section and in the following pages, do turn up in otherwise 'correctly' spelled texts, like *thua* (two) and *bethuix* (betwixt) in one early MS of Bellenden's *Boece*, and *staw* (p.t. of *stele* to steal) in another.[43] Even so, the rarity of these is itself strong 'proof' of the general 'rule' of the standard spelling: *staw*, for example, appears to be recorded only once in a MS of over 300 folios (the Pierpont Morgan Bellenden's *Boece*) as against the commoner *stall*. The available glossaries to other literary prose[44] are equally unproductive of these irregular spellings, together yielding only a handful. The highest single yield, that from the Laing Pitscottie, includes *schoissin* (chosen), *schyre* (chair), *staw* (p.t. of *stele*), *stowin* (p.p. of *stele*) and *schowne*, *shone* and *sowun* among the variants of 'soon,' in each case only as a unique or a much less common variant of the 'regular' spelling or spellings (*choissin*, *chyre*, *stall*, etc). But as more word-lists become available it may turn out that there were others among the late sixteenth- and early seventeenth-century literary and official scribes and men of letters who, as well as enlarging their limits of spelling variation with the new anglicised spellings (*pp* 182–3 and *p* 190) were also relaxing some of the traditional Scottish prohibitions. With spellings like *ga* (gall) and *stowin* (stolen), *blaithe* (blithe) and *whait* (white), *swyt* (sweat), *sweik* (= *swilk* or *sic*, such), *schosin(e)* (chosen), *lainthe* (length) and *strainthe* (strength), Rev James Melvill[45] is at least one instance of a highly literate writer of late Middle Scots who was no longer conforming strictly to the earlier 'rules' of 'correct' orthography.

For the seventeenth century we may have to assume a number of different traditions or different standards: of the printed literature in, virtually, English; of more or less regularly spelled and rapidly anglicising official registers, such as those of Parliament and Privy Council, and literary works circulating in manuscript, like Spalding's *Memorialls of the Trubles*; and of the miscellaneous mass of minor records and private writings, also increasingly anglicised, but in addition displaying a much wider overall range of characteristically Scottish spelling variation on similar lines to James Melvill's practice described in the preceding paragraph. A clearer picture will only emerge after much detailed study of the kind suggested in Section 2.

Meantime however it is of course possible to identify impressionistically those texts which are most irregular in their spelling-practice and thus lie at the opposite pole of this di-polar situation from the 'regularly' spelled texts which we have tentatively thought of as representing 'standard' or most generally approved practice. Writers of texts of this strikingly 'substandard' category include a number of local clerks (for example, certain of the burgh clerks of Aberdeen, Ayr, Dunfermline, Elgin, Inverness, Peebles, Selkirk, Stirling and Wigtown) and some writers of private documents,[46] such as letters or accounts, but, so far as my observations go, few others.[47] Their spelling-practice is typified in the following passages:[48]

1 It is statut and ordanit that na persoun nor personis woucht ony maner of clais at the toune bouirn within the Barrasyet or aboun, for fyling of the bourn, undir the pain of viij s. vnforgevin and brekin of the weschal that tha wous with (1522 *Stirling B. Rec.* I, 17). It was fundin be the said assis that Robe Murra and Jame Mur had thiftusly stouin ane gryne clok, ij syourds, ane sertane of sarkis, courcheis and colaris, vij pair of schoun, ane pair of hois, ane buklar (1525 *Ibid* 24).

2 Als sua I beseik your grace to caus my son and all uder Scottis men that ye ma forga to cum in this cuntre, for ther welbe besyns about this toun or ellis in som uder pairt in this cuntre. The French men that wes heyr cald not agre with the capeden wes sent to tham and said to hem they aucht na servis to the king and we haf caussit hem to send for uderis and pout them away. This last rad was mad in Ingland has doun na gud bot maid our inimeis harde and quhill it be mendit the Inglis men well never trast to geit skath. Your grac maun be vere scherp batht on the Franch men and on the Scottis men or it will nocht be weill; yet ader to do as aferis to tham or let it be, tha mecht never getin sa gud ane tym. Pardon me that writtis sa hamly to your grac for in gud feth it cumis of ane gud hart as than that loifis bath the honour of Scotland and Frans. Forder, God keip you grace. Writin of Hom, the ix day of Merch be your gracis servetour Marion Lady Hom. (1548–9 *Corr. M. Lorraine*, 292).

3 Item for owr lledein of collis awcht skor and awcht pownd quhilk was to yowr payrt 21 lib. Item quhane we came bak to Dondei was bocht mell and elle and canwes that sormontit to 26 lib. 10s quhilk is to yowr payrt 3 lib. 4s. Sua gaid I till y cam to Engelland one and warrit 15 lib. 15s quhilk was in Inglis monnay 37s 6d. Item bocht sex payr wone schankis cost 5s the pair quhilk was for sex payr 30s (John Wallwod, supercargo of the 'Grace of God' of Dundee, in 1600

Misc. Hist. Soc. x, 67). Thane it came that he grantit to llend ane hownder and fowrtei crownis to the mayrschand and that he begowd rakein owp ane selder quhissell that the mayrschand hid promeist him or the scheip sowld go to the sei and some dray fisch that he gif the mayrschand to wettell the schip withall. And y gif the hell monney that y sowld hawe send yow for the proffeit was gowd gif we haid 'gottein it quhilk was fowrttei of the hownder (Idem in 1602 *Ibid* 73).

Some of the spellings employed by writers such as these are so unusual as to be unique or almost unique: John Wallwod's habit (following a simple orthographic analogy) of doubling his initial *ll-* in *eg: lledein* (leading or loading) and *llend* (1600 *Misc. Hist. Soc.* x, 67) or his unique spelling of 'silver' as *selder*[49] (1602 *Ibid* 73) or the practice of the Stirling clerk of writing *sy-* for normal *sw-*, *eg* in *syourd* (=sword), *syene* (=swine), *syoerne* (=sworn) (1525 *Stirling B. Rec.* I, 24, 25) or the same clerk's *kt* for normal *cht* in *slaktir* (1526 *Ibid* 26) or his quite logical (but unique) *lujene* (for *luging*, lodging) (1525 *Ibid* 23), or Skipper Morton's unique 'phonetic' spelling of 'narrow' as *nawrye* (*a 1600 Skipper's Acc.* (Morton), 48a).

More often, however, these irregular or 'substandard' spellings conform to recurrent patterns common to this group of writers as a class. It was apparently chiefly writers of this kind who were given to writing *sch-* where standard spelling prescribed *ch-* (as *schallans* (=*chalange*), *schairge* (=*charge*), *schertee* (=*cherite*, 'charity'), *scheis*, *schosing* (=*chese*, *chosin*, choose, chosen, etc), and, though apparently less frequently, the converse of this in *eg: chep, cheip* (sheep) (1468 *Peebles B. Rec.* I, 157, 1503 *Dunferm. B. Rec.* 132, 1557 *Iverness Rec.* I, 10) and in *fycht* (as well as *fysche*) (1519–20 *Stirling B. Rec.* I, 3) and *flecht* and *flechour* (as well as *flescheir*) (1520 *Ibid* 15) and *feych* (=fish) (1532 *Selkirk B. Ct.* 160b).[50] A similarly widespread tendency in many of these texts is to interchange *th* and *t* spellings in *eg: tha tyngis* (14. . *Liber Calchou* 449), *efter the theching of this trethis* (*Ibid* 451), *qwath anwallis* (1456 *Peebles B. Rec.* I, 113), *at thwa termis* (*Ibid*), *his thachment* (*Ibid* 115), *bethwen* (1457 *Ibid* 122), *ragrathing* (1520 *Stirling B. Rec.* I, 7), *scheit* (for 'sheath') *makar* (1520–1 *Ibid* 14), *flything* (*Ibid*), *thwa siluer ringis* (1540 *Elgin Rec.* I, 49), *thwyching* as well as *tweching, twyching* (=touching, concerning) (*Ibid* 52), *outout* (=*outouth*, outwith) (1541 *Ibid* 65), *thalch* (=*talch*, tallow) (1542 *Ibid* 73), *schait* (=*scaith*, injury) (1543–4 *Ibid* 79), *the*

tain . . . the thother (*Ibid*), *thechyt* (1546 *Ibid* 89).[51] Other recurrent
'substandard' variants are *i, y* for 'standard' *e, ei, ey* (/ī/) (*eg* by our
Stirling clerk or by Mary Queen of Scots), *ou, ow* for 'standard' *u*
(either /ŭ/ or /ȳ/) (in, *eg: hourt, goud, soun, schoun* (= shoes)), and *e* for
standard *i* (/ĭ/), (in, *eg: meln, mestour, begit* (= *biggit,* built), *kel* (= *kill,*
kiln), etc) (1456 *Peebles B. Rec.* I, 115*f*), *well* (= will), *hem* (= him),
mecht (= might) (by Lady Home, above, *p* 200), *selder* and *wettell*
(= victual) (by John Wallwod, above, *p* 201)). In addition, some rather
more widely distributed variants, like *ai, ay* as an addition to *i, y, yi*
/ei/ or *-ene, -ein, -eyn* as an addition to *-ing, -yng, -in, -yn* for the verbal
noun-ending (*cf: lledein, p* 200, and *lujene, p* 201), and *ra-* beside
re- in *eg: ragratour, ralef, raward,* are especially common in recognis-
ably 'sub-standard' contexts.

Some of these variations are no doubt 'phonetic' in origin. Evi-
dently, like some illiterate spellers today, these 'substandard' spellers
were given not only to apparently inexplicable idiosyncratic modifica-
tions of the general spelling system (like the Stirling scribe's *sy-* symbol) but also to 'phonetic' innovations, to 'improvements' in the
standard spelling system in the direction of greater 'phonetic' consistency. These spellings thus reflect idiosyncratic or dialectal or even
generally distributed phonemic or allophonic variant pronunciations
which the more stable and conservative standard spelling fails to reproduce.

This 'explanation' and the consequent 'interpretation' of the spellings can often be applied with some confidence (as in the externally
supported instances listed in Section 4). The variant *-ene, -ein* of the
verbal noun ending, for example, bears, according to the normal pho-
nemic-orthographic 'rules', a clear relationship to a morpheme /-īn/
of which we have abundant confirmation in modern speech and early
rhyme; it may well have been, in spoken use, more common than its
doublet /-ĭŋ/ which the 'standard' spelling *-ing, -yng* on the face of it
'represents'.

But of course in the absence of external confirmation of this kind we
must be much more cautious. It may be that the interchange of *sch* and
ch noted above originally arose from an assimilation in some or all
positions of /tʃ/ to /ʃ/ in some dialects or idiolects and that all the spellings noted either directly imitate this or follow as 'reverse spellings'. A
similar phonemic levelling might be advanced in explanation of the
interchange of *th* and *t* also exemplified. This explanation would have
an advantage in accounting for the tendency of these spelling habits to

recur in widely dispersed texts of this type. At the same time I do not see that we can exclude the possibility that we are dealing with purely orthographic phenomena such as the interchange of *v* and *w* mentioned above (*p* 182) may also represent. If this were so the recurrence of these habits in texts which, so far as we know at present, have no local or other points of contact, is harder but not necessarily impossible to explain.

7

This essay must at least have shown that the old concept of Middle Scots as an 'artificial' and highly uniform language should now be discarded. At every linguistic level it is marked by variety of usage rather than uniformity. The fact of this variety and its particular manifestations are clearly enough displayed in DOST. But there is a need to proceed beyond what the Dictionary presents and to explore the details of distribution, particularly regional and stylistic, of the numerous variant phenomena. Few contributions towards this as yet exist.[52] Even for such a commonly noted feature as the occurrence of the indefinite article *ane* before consonants, no attempt has ever been made to show how it and its variant *a* were comparatively distributed.[53] From all this we may expect illumination of every aspect of the history of the language, notably in its dialectological and stylistic aspects.

Not the least varied and complex of these manifestations of varied usage of Middle Scots is its orthography. Only the merest beginnings to a proper account of this as yet exist in the 'phonologies' of various poets and one or two prose writers.[54] At most these include only some minor contributions[55] to some of the questions raised in this essay. For this purpose a much more systematic examination of the spellings as such is needed – and not one which, as some of these works do, presents a hotch-potch of the spellings of a later copyist or even several later copyists as somehow 'representing' the pronunciation of an earlier author. Only one study, of rather limited value for the purpose suggested, has been provided for a holograph writing.[56] Nothing whatever has been written on the spellings of the major official records, which may well have predominated in the setting of orthographic standards. Only one minor work exists on strictly localised texts,[57] and this is dependent on fairly inaccurate editions. Private writings have been totally ignored.

We are then still at the very beginning of the study of this aspect of Middle Scots. One need at this point is for 'diplomatic' editions, which are also more reliable than those we now have, of many of the national and local and private record sources. Further study of some of the questions posed might well be assisted by computer techniques, based on an enlargement of the computer archive of Middle Scots texts on which a start has been made in Edinburgh[58] – once we have adequate texts to feed in to the archive.

Notes

1 G. Gregory Smith, *Specimens of Middle Scots*, Edinburgh, 1902, *pp* xi–xii.
2 H. Harvey Wood, *The Poems and Fables of Robert Henryson*, Edinburgh, 1933, *p* xxxi. The notion is carried to its ultimate extreme by M. W. Stearns who, in his *Robert Henryson*, New York, 1949, *p* 6, writes: 'The new (*ie* Scottish Chaucerian) poetry was written in Middle Scots, a literary language which was probably never spoken', though he adds elsewhere (*p* 129), 'Although the dialect of Middle Scots was never spoken, Henryson's verses, read aloud, would probably have been easily understood by his contemporaries at any social level.'
3 The relative constructions of Early Scots (to 1500) have been admirably studied in S. J. G. Caldwell's *The Relative Pronoun in Early Scots*, PhD Thesis, University of Edinburgh, 1967, unfortunately as yet unprinted.
4 Commonly only the adjectives (*fore*)*said*(*is, vther*(*is,* (*welebe-*)*lufitt*(*is* and the relative adjective and pronoun (*the*) *quhilk*(*is.* Gilbert Hay and John Bellenden and some others writing under the immediate influence of French or Latin originals also occasionally inflect some other adjectives, apparently only of Latin origin, often with the (French or Latin) inverted word-order for the noun-adjective phrases, as *instrumentis subordinatis* (Hay I, 76/30), *all vther thingis necessaris* (Bellenden, *Boece* (M) I, 25). The habit, never invariable in any text, is absent from most verse and some literary prose texts (for example, James VI's *Basilicon Doron*), and from many texts of the 'substandard' type discussed in Section 6 of this paper. No doubt it was indeed an 'artificial, literary' feature.
5 See below (*pp* 178–9) for a few examples of these.
6 In *op cit, pp* xvi*ff.*
7 Particularly interesting would be a study of the innumerable dialogue passages in the narrative prose of Knox and his successors and in the sixteenth-century court records. In the latter the wording of alleged statements by the accused as cited in witnesses' depositions is frequently evidential (*eg* in trials of treason or slander) and thus presumably plausible as to wording. Here is a reasonably reliable basis for a description of the colloquial, as distinct from literary, register of Middle Scots.
8 See, among many others (for Orkney and Shetland) *cloggand* or *clowgang, hafe-wrak, hallow, handband, heavie*; (for the north-east) *codrach, daker* v, *halfdisch* or *haddisch, kard* (n²), *leit* (n¹); (for central and south Scotland) *clour, herring-drave, hirst, holm, hope* (n²), *hurl* (to wheel), *idilteth, kimpill, lokman*; (for the south-west) *clachan, clat, inspreth, lime-craig, lime-holl*; (for the east coast) *likkarstane, linkis, lippie*; and more narrowly localised items like *inland* (inner portion of a tenement, Aberdeen), *cumling* (incomer, Perth), *greveschip* (precinct, Moray Firth burghs), *kirkmaister* (church-officer, Kirkcudbright), *kist* (fish-cruive, Inverness), *murement* (spoil, Sheriffhall coal-mine).

9 For Richard de Holland's 'Orkneyisms' see DOST s.vv. *Lang reid* and *Idy* (the latter in the Additions and Corrections to Volume III). At lines 734, 5 the author of *King Hart* (most recently edited by Priscilla Bawcutt in *The Shorter Poems of Gawin Douglas*, STS, 1967), employs two items now localised to the middle and the western border shires – *waile* (read *wyle*, 'thraw-cruik', rope-twister) and *rewle*, = (1) ravelling, (2) revelling (see G. Watson, *The Roxburgh-shire Word-book*, Cambridge, 1923, s.vv. *Wyle* and *Rewel*).

10 My abbreviated references are as prescribed in the *Dictionary of the Older Scottish Tongue*'s 'Combined Register of Titles of Works Quoted' in Vol III of that work (itself abbreviated as DOST).

11 Like *mark, pund, fute* (the plural of the noun of measure is *futis* or *fute*), *elne, mile, hour, 3eir, hors, schepe*.

12 As *Jhon and Andro Moffatis*, 1564 St A. Kirk S. 220.

13 Like *fader, moder, brother* (also *lady* and *maister*). For some examples also with personal names, see P. Müller, *Die Sprache der Aberdeener Urkunden des Sechzenten Jahrhunderts*, Diss. Berlin, 1908, *p* 121.

14 Perhaps, by the sixteenth century, some of these may turn out to be regionally distributed, as was guessed by J. A. H. Murray (*Compl.* cii–ciii). On the similar case of pre-consonantal *a* and *ane*, see note 53.

15 The seminal writing on this subject, with special reference to Middle English, is Angus McIntosh, 'The Analysis of Written Middle English', *TPS, 1956*, 26–55. The influence of this on my own view of the Middle Scots problems will be apparent in what follows. See also John C. McLaughlin, *A Graphemic-Phonemic Study of a Middle English Manuscript*, The Hague, 1963, for a first attempt to apply these principles to a specific Middle English text (reviewed by McIntosh in *AL*, 16, 1964, 78–80). For a brilliant demonstration of a methodology for analysing rigorously and objectively the kind of phenomena mentioned in the previous paragraph of the present essay, see W. Nelson Francis, 'Graphemic Analysis of Late Medieval English Manuscripts', *Speculum*, 37, 1962, 32*ff*.

16 On these see especially M. M. Gray, *Lancelot of the Laik*, STS, 1912, *pp* xxi*ff* and DOST s.vv. *Be* v. 1 and 2c, *Fro, Go*, etc.

17 For some general remarks on all this see M. A. Bald, 'The Anglicisation of Scottish Printing', *SHR*, 23, 1926, 107*ff* and 'The Pioneers of Anglicised Speech in Scotland', *SHR*, 24, 1927, 179*ff*.

18 One hazard run by the investigator of these matters at present is the normalisation practised by some editors, especially, but not only, historians editing record texts. For some avowals of this see Hamilton, *Cat.*, 1884, *p* xliii; Knox I, 1846, *p* xliii, note 1; *Reg. Privy C.* I, *pp* xliv*ff* esp. *pp* l–lii, and *Misc. Hist. Soc.* x, 28. In these and other similar cases the intention is only to modernise the treatment of *i* and *j, u, v* and *w, y* and *th, y* and *3*, to expand abbreviations without notice and to supply a modern punctuation. No doubt there is a more serious hazard in the lapses in accuracy which occur with greater or lesser frequency in many modern editions.

19 *Eg* interchangeable *i* and *y, au* and *aw*, and, under certain conditions, *y* and *th, c* and *s, c* and *t* (*nacioun, natioun*).

20 *Eg* the alphabet itself, many of the digraph and trigraph groups, the phonemic or morphemic correlations (see *pp* 186–7) of many of the graphemes, the usual restriction of geminate consonants to non-initial positions and by other conditions (as a rule only after 'short' simplex vowels and vowel-digraphs) and the tendency to restrict the combination simple consonant plus 'mute' *e* to a different set of conditions (on the conditions for single and double consonants see further *pp* 188 and 192).

21 As printed in the STS edition of Pitscottie: see Robert Lindesay of Pitscottie, *The Historie and Cronicles of Scotland*, i, STS, 1899, *p* lxxii on this MS, and the glossary of that edition for evidence of this statement.

22 From the fragmentary Middle Scots version of the Letter of Prester John in BM Royal MS 17 Dxx, *ff* 310*ff* (transcribed from photostats in the National Library of Scotland, MS 8494 (ii)). Though abbreviations are marked, other variations of the sort mentioned on *p* 180, between, for example, different 'forms of *s*', have not been indicated.

23 At least in the initial syllable: *maidin* also appears as *maiden* and *maidyn*. The source of these details is the computer-made word-list to Hay in the files of DOST: see *p* 204 and note 58 for further information on this.

24 For the Q. Kennedy texts see the edition by C. Kuipers cited on *p* 187, *pp* 84 and 107. For James VI see especially the STS editions of his *Basilicon Doron* and his *Poems* (both edited by J. Craigie) and also Vol 2 of the former *p* 120.

25 In her unpublished dissertation *Studies in the Language of Bellenden's Boece*, PhD Thesis, University of London, 1936, *p* 211, E. A. Sheppard writes: 'The complete orthographical independence of the sixteenth-century scribes is shown by a comparison of the *Boece* manuscripts. Each scribe has a characteristic and (more or less) consistent mode of spelling.' Subsequently (*pp* 230–1) she notes the inconsistency as between *v* and *w* of David Douglas, a notary practising mainly in Elgin, who was the scribe of the Pierpont Morgan MS (*c* 1531) of Bellenden's *Boece*.

26 For prose texts, C. Kuiper's edition of Q. Kennedy, *pp* 104*ff*; W. A. Craigie's edition, STS, 1903, of Bellenden's *Livy*, Vol 2, *pp* 330*ff*; and J. Craigie's edition of James VI's *Basilicon Doron*, STS, 1950, *pp* 118*ff*; and, for verse, F. W. Mühleisen's *Textkritische, metrische und grammatische Untersuchungen von Barbour's Bruce*, Diss. Bonn, 1913 (much the fullest and most self-consistent of these studies), and a brief comparison of some of the spelling details of two alternative prints of the same work (Douglas's *Palice of Honour*) in Priscilla J. Bawcutt, *The Shorter Poems of Gavin Douglas*, STS, 1967, *pp* xxiii–xxiv. All of these – and they are unfortunately all we possess – are concerned with alternative scribal copies of common literary originals: *cf* note 28.

27 From 'The Summons of Treason and Forfeiture of the Memory and Estaites of the deceased Robert Logane of Restalrig, June, 1609', in R. Pitcairn, *Criminal Trials in Scotland*, Edinburgh, 1833, Vol 2, *p* 288 (also 1609 *Acts* IV, 423/1).

28 So far this question has been approached only in the few comparisons of different scribal versions of literary works listed in note 26. The scribes of copied texts of this sort may be presumed sometimes to belie their own spelling habits by imitating some of the spellings of texts they are copying rather than those which they themselves otherwise favour. The resultant mixing of spelling practices thus introduces a further complication to the comparative study of Middle Scots orthography which to begin with we might do well to avoid, concentrating instead on holograph texts.

29 For Middle Scots prose, so far only C. Kuipers in his work on Q. Kennedy cited on *p* 187.

30 As proposed (for Middle English) by Angus McIntosh, *loc cit*: see note 15.

31 Schematically, as follows:

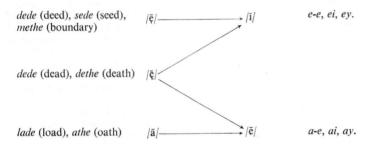

EARLY SCOTS   MIDDLE SCOTS

eg: hall   /al/

au ⟶ /ā/

eg: haw   /au/

In labial contexts,
eg: quha, twa, water   /ā/

In other contexts,
eg: ga (go), *ta* (toe),   /ā/ ⟶ /ē/
mater (matter)

The divergent arrows represent divergent developments, resulting in 'doublets', in different dialects and idiolects.

32 Schematically, as follows:

EARLY SCOTS   MIDDLE SCOTS   SPELLINGS

dede (deed), *sede* (seed),   /ē̦/ ⟶ /ī/   *e-e, ei, ey.*
methe (boundary)

dede (dead), *dethe* (death)   /ē̦/

lade (load), *athe* (oath)   /ā/ ⟶ /ē/   *a-e, ai, ay.*

The divergent arrows represent divergent developments, resulting in 'doublets', in different dialects and idiolects.

33 Both of these developments and the resulting sets of doublets (on which see further *pp* 188*ff*, especially *p* 191) are fully attested in rhyme and in modern reflexes (which appear to be regionally distributed but with areas of overlap: *cf p* 191 and note 36.)

34 Instances are occasionally noticed in passing, generally as resolving some phonological crux, in some of the studies mentioned in note 54 below; the fullest list, which is nevertheless, even for this one work, by no means complete, could be extracted from F. W. Mühleisen, *op cit* (see note 26) and another from P. Müller, *op cit* (see note 13). But nowhere is there any attempt at sustained comparative study.

35 *pp* 195*ff*, and see also *p* 187 above.

36 See the distributional map for the similar case of 'who' in Angus McIntosh, *An Introduction to a Survey of Scottish Dialects*, Edinburgh, 1952, *p* 117.

37 Compare *p* 187.

38 See note 31 for the phonology of these doublets.

39 Perhaps it was this kind of thing that Gavin Douglas had in mind when he
   wrote:

> ȝhe writaris all and gentill redaris eik,
> Offendis nocht my volum, I beseik,
> Bot redis leill and tak gud tent in tyme
> ȝhe nother maggill nor mysmetyr my ryme,
> Nor alter not my wordis, I ȝou pray.
>
> (Douglas, STS, IV, 194/21 *ff*).

40 And *yin* inscribed for the indefinite article, apparently by confusion with the
   numeral *ane*, on a gravestone in Monkton, Ayrshire: Heir lys yin vary honrible
   mon Davit Blair of Adamtoun spouse to Marget Hamiltoun quo decesit Sep.
   1577 (quoted in Kirkwood Hewat, *A Little Scottish World*, Ayr, 1908, *p* 84).
41 Alexander Wood of Old Aberdeen has three instances of *for* for 'where' in his
   copy of Q. Kennedy's *Breif Tracteit*: see Kuipers, *op cit* (*p* 187), *p* 84 and s.v.
   in the Glossary. For some further examples of these and other north-eastern
   forms, see DOST s.vv. *Correll, Cort* n[2], *Cuntra(y* n (*quintra*) and *Cuntré*
   n 3a (*quentre, cuintrie*), *Fayte, Folp, Forl* and *Fow* adv, and *Fedill* n. Several
   other examples are cited (without exact reference) by R. McKinlay, *The*
   Speech of Scotland prior to the Eighteenth Century, Peterhead, 1914 (reprinted
   from *The Transactions of the Buchan Club*, 1914), *pp 8ff*.
42 See E. Eckhardt, *Die Dialekt- und Ausländertypen des älteren Englischen Dram-*
   as, Louvain, 1910, especially 'Die schottische Mundart in den einzelnen
   Dramen', Vol 1, *pp 91ff*. Eckhardt provides a full account of the individual
   word-forms and items of vocabulary with respect to their Scottish provenance.
   But he takes no account of other aspects of the language (*cf*, for example, the
   word-order of "that sall I, mary" and the 'ellipsis of "have"' (*cf p* 179) in
   "mary, I wad full faine heard some question tween you tway", in the Scottish
   captain's speeches in Shakespeare's *Henry v*, III, ii); and he is naturally unaware
   of the stylistic implications of his material. I owe thanks to my colleague, Dr
   J. A. C. Stevenson, for reminding me of this source and bringing Eckhardt's
   work to my notice.
43 According to E. A. Sheppard, *op cit* (see note 25), *pp* 211 and 236.
44 *Viz*, Irland *Mir.*, Bellenden *Livy*, Gau, *Compl.*, Hamilton *Cat.*, Q. Kennedy,
   Winȝet, Pitscottie, Fowler, Dalrymple, James VI *Basil. Doron* and Bisset.
45 An important writer who deserves study from this and many other points of
   view, including the literary and the stylistic. The forms quoted occur on *pp* 125,
   423, 126, 270, 137, 170, 128, 317, 157, of the Wodrow Society edition (1842) of
   The Autobiography and Diary, quoted in DOST as Melvill. Most of these and
   others like them, however, appear in Melvill's personal narrative; in copying
   official documents and formal declarations, including those originally composed by himself, his spelling standards were perhaps less relaxed.
46 Collections of private correspondence, such as *Corr. M. Lorraine* ('The Scottish Correspondence of Mary of Lorraine') and the many published collections of family letters, provide a good many specimens of this sort of thing.
   Another example is an apparently holograph letter of King James v, printed
   in *Misc. Spald. C.* II, 193. The highly idiosyncratic Scots spellings of the holograph writings of his French-educated daughter, Mary Queen of Scots, are
   doubtless a special case.
47 For one very minor literary text containing a number of 'irregular' or 'substandard' spellings, see H. H. Meier, 'A Pre-Reformation Biblical Paraphrase', *Innes Review*, 17, 1966, 11*ff*, espec 21. The majority of the 'irregularities' in the separate Dunbar collection now incorporated as *pp* 3–18 and

339–42 of the Maitland Folio MS are of the type discussed in the previous section of this essay and in keeping with the comic character of the poems copied (*cf pp* 196–7 above); otherwise, despite W. A. Craigie's remark (*The Maitland Folio Manuscript*, Vol 2, STS, 1927, *p* 6) that these fragments 'have a very unconventional and almost illiterate spelling of many words', they largely though not entirely conform to the 'standard' limits of variation.

48 Another instance occurs in note 40.

49 Apparently to be explained thus: '*silver*' had become, colloquially, '*siller*', by normal reduction of *-v-* in this position; in a number of words dialect or colloquial /-l/ was represented in standard spelling as *-ld* (*eg: cauld, auld, ȝeild*); and Wallwood is one of those (see *p* 202) who frequently have *e* in place of standard *i*.

50 P. Müller, *op cit* (see note 13), has some further examples on *pp* 110 and 112.

51 For other examples of coincidences between northern and southern usage, see the spellings in *y-* and *ȝ-* cited on *p* 194, and, at the lexical and morphemic levels, DOST s.v. *Landimer* and *Milve*.

52 A useful beginning is Mrs S. J. G. Caldwell's study of the relative pronouns: see note 3 above. C. Kuipers and E. A. Sheppard both provide useful data on the lexis and syntax of the texts studied by them: see *p* 187 and note 25.

53 The practice of writing the indefinite article as *an* or more often *ane* before consonants as well as before vowels first becomes common in the second half of the fifteenth century, though an instance occurs (till an michty lord; Slater, *Early Sc. Texts*, No 2) as early as 1379. Many sixteenth-century writers, such as those quoted on *pp* 184, 185 and 200 above, as well as some others who have been mentioned (*eg* the copyist of the Laing MS of Pitscottie's Chronicles: see note 21) strongly favour *ane*, though seldom to the complete exclusion of *a*. Others, such as George Bannatyne or the copyist of the Cotton MS of Buchanan's *Chamaeleon* (Buchanan *Wr*. 42*ff*), vary freely between these two. On the other hand some, but not all, of the copyists of the 1566 MS of John Knox's *History*, follow what was and is the normal English practice, and had been that of early Scots, of writing *a* before consonants and *an* or *ane* before vowels. Around the turn of the sixteenth century the ministers James Melvill and James Carmichael have the same usage. But sporadic instances of *ane* before consonants continue to occur in Scottish official and legal writings down to the eighteenth century (see L. E. C. MacQueen, *The Last Stages of the Older Literary Language of Scotland*, Edinburgh University Thesis, 1957, *p* 397 and Glossary s.v. *Ane*). That this was a quite conventional and 'unphonetic' or 'artificial' symbol for whatever form of the indefinite article the context required is indicated, *inter alia*, by usages like *ane levin, ane mendis* (=*amendis*) and *ane mis* (=*amis, amiss*): see DOST s.vv. *Ane-levin, Mendis* n 2 and *Mis* n 6.

54 Consisting for the most part of German doctoral dissertations of the late nineteenth and early twentieth centuries. They are listed in part in W. Geddie, *Bibliography of Middle Scots Poets*, STS, 1912, and most of the remainder in J. S. Woolley *Bibliography for Scottish Linguistic Studies*, Edinburgh, 1954.

55 Most of these which have something to offer have been mentioned in previous notes.

56 By J. Craigie on the language of James VI's *Basilicon Doron*: see note 26.

57 By P. Müller: see note 13.

58 See A. J. Aitken and Paul Bratley, 'An Archive of Older Scottish Texts for Scanning by Computer' in *English Studies*, 48, 1967, 61–2, and *Studies in Scottish Literature*, 4, 1966, 45*ff*.

W. F. H. Nicolaisen

Associate Professor of English, State University of New York at Binghamton; formerly Reader in Scottish Studies, University of Edinburgh

Early spellings and Scottish place-names

1

It is taken for granted in modern place-name research that, in addition to the recording of the local pronunciation of each name, all early spellings in written documents, both printed and manuscript, should be collected and used as a basis for its phonological, morphological and semantic analysis. The shortcut from the modern map-form via the dictionary to a proposed etymology is no longer permissible. Consequently, recent literature on the methods of onomastic research in England has emphasised the importance of this essential principle in one way or another, using more or less identical, or at least similar, phraseology: W. J. Sedgefield in his article on 'Methods of Place-name Study', says that 'the first step to be taken by the investigator is to collect all early forms of the place-name',[1] because 'the first thing that will strike even the untrained eye is that in a very considerable number of cases the earliest recorded form of the name is very different from the modern form and reveals at once its original meaning'.[2] Eilert Ekwall, in the introduction to his remarkable *Dictionary*,[3] points out that 'it is the first principle of place-name etymology that there must be early name-forms on which to found the explanation' for 'in general it would be useless to try to explain place-names on the strength of the modern name-form alone'.[4] When counselling intending collaborators on the collection of material, A. H. Smith remarks that 'the material on which the survey of English place-names is based consists chiefly of early spellings of place-names found in documents of all kinds';[5] he therefore suggests that 'as complete a list as possible of early spellings of the names in a county should be prepared at once'.[6] P. H. Reaney also insists that 'the student must first make as wide a collection as possible of the early forms of each name',[7] and Kenneth Cameron states that 'unless early spellings of a place-name are available we can never be absolutely certain of its original meaning' because 'for the most part ... the present spelling of a place-name either gives an entirely wrong idea of its original meaning or else is completely meaningless';[8] he later repeats categorically that 'the study of place-names is based on an analysis of the early spellings of names in the light of the historical development of English sounds'.[9]

Although there are no pronouncements of a similarly authoritative nature with regard to Scottish place-name research, it has naturally – and as we think, with justification – been thought that there is no basic difference in the proper handling of the Scottish toponomastic material in this respect. It is therefore the main task of the Scottish Place-Name Survey in the School of Scottish Studies of the University of Edinburgh to bring together at this stage centrally and, if possible, comprehensively, the early spellings of Scottish place-names and to file them systematically for the use of all accredited scholars. In the realisation of this project it has always been silently understood that, compared with England, Scotland is indeed much poorer as far as early spellings are concerned and that the proportion of names which will at the end of the day remain unexplained or at least difficult to interpret will therefore be higher than in England. The question arises whether this tacit assumption has a basis in fact or whether one is allowed to be more optimistic about the ultimate results of the Survey's work. In fact, we are really confronted with two questions: Firstly, is the general documentation of Scottish place-names really so very much later than its English equivalent? Secondly, how seriously does – real or hypothetical – lateness impair the satisfactory interpretation of names? Following up this second question one has perhaps to probe even more deeply and ask what such qualifications as 'early' and 'late' mean in terms of place-name documentation, when both epithets are obviously relative in any given context and not absolute chronological descriptions.

This essay is intended to examine some of these problems and their possible effect on Scottish place-name research. As its raw material it will use evidence presented in the three PhD theses produced in the University of Edinburgh while O. K. Schram, to whose memory this volume is dedicated, was a member of staff in its Department of English and able to bring to bear on the teaching of English linguistic history his own intimate knowledge of English place-names and onomastic research. The choice of these three theses seems to be appropriate when the Scottish Place-Name Survey, although having amassed more than one million early spellings over the years, is not yet in a position to provide systematic historical coverage of individual names. The dissertations in question are: Angus Macdonald, *The Place-Names of West Lothian* (1937);[10] May Gordon Williamson, *The Non-Celtic Place-Names of the Scottish Border Counties* (1942);[11] and Norman Dixon, *The Placenames of Midlothian* (1947).[12] From these three titles it is at once apparent that geographically our choice will be limited to areas in the Scottish south-east, with a strong preponderance of English names and only little Gaelic influence, although West Lothian will at least convey some of the flavour of Gaelic place-nomenclature. What might at first look like a drawback may, however, suitably be turned into an advantage when it is remembered that our primary concern is to compare the English and Scottish situation from the point of view of early place-name spellings. In this respect, the three dissertations supply excellent basic material, quite apart from the fact that there are not many Scottish county surveys which have collected and set out the early forms in such reliable and systematic fashion (more or less adopting the method of the publications of the English Place-Name Society).

2

Let us first of all look at the general applicability, to Scotland, of the notion that early spellings help us to arrive at a proper etymology for a name when the modern form would have been quite misleading. A small number of examples will suffice to make our point: Oxton in Berwickshire (BWK)[13] is by such forms as *Hulfkeliston* and *Ullfkeliston* 1206 (*c* 1320) *Kel. Lib.*[14] and *Ulkilstoun c* 1220 (16th) *Dryb. Lib.*, shown to contain the Scandinavian personal name *Ulfkell* and not the word *ox* (Williamson, 31). Leadburn in Midlothian (MLO) is not a compound of *lead* and *burn*, as the modern name might suggest, but turns out to contain Gaelic *leac* 'stone' and the personal name *Bernard*, because of such early spellings as *Legbernard c* 1128 *Holy. Lib.*, *Lekbernarde* 1459 *RMS*, *Leckbernard* 1653 *Retours*, etc (Dixon, 267–8). Similarly Moorfoot MLO (Dixon, 296) is shown to be Old Norse *mór þveit* 'moor place' rather than Old English *mōr fōt*, by a number of spellings contained in *Newbattle Registrum*, like *Morthwait* 1140–53, *Morthwayt* pre-1153, *Morthweth* 1174, *Mortwait* and *Mortwath* 1361, and others.

There is therefore no doubt about it that there are many Scottish place-names which, mostly due to a process of full or partial re-interpretation, are superficially misleading when no attention is paid to their historical spellings.

Not quite so common are names which have no meaning whatsoever when only their modern form is taken into account but become meaningful when earlier spellings are consulted. Again, only a few representative instances can be given in this context: Pinkie MLO (Dixon, 207) makes little sense as it stands but early spellings like *Pontekyn* and *Pontekin* both pre-1198 *Dunf. Reg.* point towards a compound of Welsh *pant* 'valley' and *cyn* 'wedge'. Hiltly West Lothian (WLO) (Macdonald, 59) allows one or two guesses but only *Hildecliue* 1296 *Inst. Pub.*, *Hildeclive* 1296 Stevenson, *Documents*, *Hildeclyve* 1296 and *Hildeclife* 1336–7 *CDS* permit a satisfactory etymology, such as 'at Hild's cliff'. Heriot MLO (Dixon, 197) may serve as a third example, for only the spelling *Hereget* of 1198 *CDS* reveals it to be derived from OE *here-geat* which refers to a gap (in the hills) through which an army might pass, although OE *here-geatu* 'wergeld' has also been suggested.

Sometimes an earlier name for the same settlement or geographical feature is revealed. This is perhaps not so much a question of an earlier spelling being more useful than later ones but rather a complete name change which is not apparent from modern evidence alone. The name Temple MLO (Dixon, 293), which came into existence when the place to which it was applied became the property of the Knights Templar must have existed side by side with, and later replaced, a Gaelic name *Baile nan Trodach* 'settlement of the warriors' which is evidenced from the *Ballentrodoch* of 1237 *Newb. Reg.* right into the eighteenth century. In the same county, the parish-name Colinton (Dixon, 146), recorded as a name since the fourteenth century (*Colbanestoun* 1319 *RMS*), superseded an earlier *Hala c* 1150–3 *Dunf. Reg.*; *Halis* 1329 *ER*, *Haillis* 1561 *Dunf. Reg.*, etc, which derives from the plural of OE *halh*, dative *hale* 'nook, haugh'. In Foxhall WLO we have what Macdonald (*pp* 41–2) called 'an instance of mistranslation from dialect into Standard English'. The earlier forms are *Toddishauch, Todhauch* both 1539 *St A. Rent.*, ie a compound name containing Northern English *tod* 'fox' and Old English *halh* 'corner, angle, flat land beside a river', unless the first element is the personal name *Todd*. *Tod* was replaced by Standard English *fox* and *haugh* was confused with *hall*, roughly from the middle of the eighteenth century onwards.

15—E.S.E.S.

These three categories of names – and there are other groups – the re-interpreted modern form, the meaningless modern spelling, and the replaced name prove without any shadow of a doubt the value of the collection and examination of early spellings in the Scottish place-names of the region covered by the three theses in question and – we may safely say – of the rest of the country as well. Scotland therefore in no way differs from England in this respect, as we had suspected any-how. In all these cases, the modern spelling (and pronunciation) would have been misleading, to say the least, but in all nine instances there were sufficiently early recorded forms to help us out. Does this mean that, as in England, our records start early enough to assist us in solv-ing our etymological problems? How early are, in fact, our earliest main sources?

In answer to this last question it must be stated straight away that Scotland has nothing to compare with England's *Domesday Book* of 1086, that invaluable source of English place-name spellings. There is also nothing to rival the Anglo-Saxon Charters and Rolls of pre-Norman date which on the first page of Ekwall's *Dictionary* produce such early dates as 972 for Abberton, *c* 730, 811, 931 and 961 for Abington and 855 and 899 for Ablington. On the same page, eight other names (Abberley, Abberton, Abbotsham, Abdon, Abinger, Abney, Abthorpe and Aby) are first recorded in Domesday Book, five names (Abbotsbury, Abbotstone and three Abingtons) have early spellings going back to eleventh-century sources other than Domesday Book, seven names (Abberwick, Abbotsley, Aberford Abergavenny, Abinghall, Abram and Abson) are first found in the twelfth century, and two names (Abbotstoun and Abridge) have their earliest spellings surviving from thirteenth-century sources. This may not be typical of the whole of Ekwall's *Dictionary* but it nevertheless underlines the fact that our earliest recorded Scottish tradition is centuries later than its English equivalent, for neither state documents nor monastic chartularies and registers begin much before the twelfth or, more often, thirteenth centuries, and fourteenth- and fifteenth-century spellings are quite frequently our earliest evidence. This will become clear in the main body of our examples and can therefore be stated here in advance in this summary form.

3

If the absolute beginning of our written place-name tradition is so much later than in England, does it follow that we have little hope of getting near the truth as far as the derivation of the majority of Scottish place-names is concerned? How early does a spelling have to be to be of value in the elucidation of the morphological and semantic origin of these names? Here it may be said that we get very little help from the writers on English place-names whom we quoted at the beginning as insisting on the collection of early spellings as an essential part of modern onomastic research. Sedgefield only implies that he is thinking of pre-fifteenth-century sources when he advocated that, because they might be copies of earlier documents, 'spellings of fifteenth century and even much later documents must not be disregarded'.[15] He seems to regard fifteenth-century sources as quite late. Ekwall is a little more precise but also more pessimistic when he states that 'if good name-forms from Domesday Book or texts from the twelfth or early thirteenth century are available, a fairly safe etymology can generally be attained. But even then the etymology of many names remains more or less doubtful'.[16] Smith and Reaney[17] do not have any specific information as to what constitutes an acceptable early spelling, but Cameron points out that 'though so many English place-names originated before 1066, comparatively few spellings of them from pre-Conquest times have survived', and 'as a result of this most of the early forms come from the Middle English period, which linguistically extends from roughly 1150 to about 1500'.[18] According to him, the most prolific period for early forms of English place-names appears to have been the twelfth, thirteenth, fourteenth and fifteenth centuries – not necessarily for the earliest forms, however, which – if the first page in Ekwall is anything to go by – may frequently be of eleventh-century provenance or even earlier.

Again looking at that much quoted first page in Ekwall's *Dictionary*, it becomes clear that of the spellings listed only two pre-Domesday ones, three Domesday ones, and two other eleventh-century ones are vital to the proper etymologisation of the names concerned, whereas otherwise four twelfth-century spellings, twelve thirteenth-century ones and one fourteenth-century one suffice to provide an acceptable etymology. In these latter cases, where earlier spellings exist these are a welcome addition to our knowledge, very often confirming later spellings, but they are not essential. Does this give us new heart for the investigation of the place-names of Scotland where the documentary evidence begins just about the time when these English forms prove so decisive? In order to arrive at a more factual picture, we shall examine two groups of names more closely within the chosen geographical area – those ending in OE *hām* and those in OE *tūn*. The first category is amongst the earliest English names found in Scotland and should therefore help us to throw some light on what might be termed the Scottish equivalent of the English pre-Domesday group of names which according to Cameron is quite numerous. Those ending in *-tūn* will cover a much longer period, as some of them might be almost as old as the names in *-hām*, whereas others may have been created as late as the seventeenth century. They should therefore be good material for an assessment of the relativity of the term 'early spelling'.

4

All the names in *-hām* are in the so-called Border Counties covered by Miss Williamson: Berwickshire, Dumfriesshire and Roxburghshire (but not in Selkirkshire). They also occur in East Lothian for which we do not possess any sufficiently detailed study; two of the three oldest English names in Scotland can therefore not be included – Tynningham and Whittingham, but the third – Coldingham BWK – is well documented in Williamson, 4. If our documentation were to go back no further than the thirteenth century, we would still know from the spelling *Goldingeham* in *Scalachronica* that a vowel has dropped out between the particle *-ing-* and our word *hām*. The preceding century would tell us that this vowel was *-a-* for *c* 1125 the name is recorded as *Coldingaham* in *CDS*. Coldingham is therefore undoubtedly an *-ingaham*-name, containing the genitive *-inga-* of the plural suffix *-ingas* 'the followers of, etc'. In the same century, about five years earlier than this entry, MS E of the Anglo-Saxon Chronicle mentions for the year 679 the name *Coludesburh*, a parallel formation to our own name. This reference completes the story by giving us the clue to the authentic form of the first element which must have been *Colud* and the original form of our name **Coludingahām* 'village of the settlers near *Colud*'. Admittedly the Anglo-Saxon Chronicle draws on earlier material, but nevertheless our written tradition does not have to go any further back than the early twelfth century to provide us with all the phonological and morphological material necessary for an authoritative etymology. We can in fact ignore as an unnecessary luxury the fact that our name is also mentioned as *Collingaham* at the end of the eleventh century (*ESC*) and in its parallel tradition even goes back to Bede's *Coludi urbem* and *Coludanae urbs* (*c* 730). These supply confirmatory evidence, no more; otherwise our twelfth-century records are quite sufficient for a satisfactory morphological and semantic solution.

If Coldingham can be assigned to the second or third quarter of the seventh century, the names in simple -*hām*, without the -*inga*- particle, were probably not much later. Most of them undoubtedly existed before the eighth century was over. Not one of them, however, is recorded before at least three hundred years later. This group of names is therefore particularly good testing ground for the worth of our Scottish place-name documentation. There are ten of them altogether. The first of these, Birgham BWK for which Williamson, 14, notes the modern pronunciation ['bɜːrdʒəm] is revealed as late as *c* 1300 *Cold. Corr.* through the spelling *Briggeham* as having undergone metathesis (which by the way appears to have started to develop by the middle of the twelfth century, as the spelling *Birgham(e)* 1165 (1434) *Cold. Cart.* indicates). The palatalisation of the last consonants of the first element, still preserved in the modern pronunciation, is also apparent – if the spelling means anything – in the form *Bricgham* of 1095–1100 (15th) *ESC*; in spite of its interest for the phonological evolution of the name, it is hardly necessary for the establishment of the etymology of the name which must be OE *Bryċġ-hām* 'bridge settlement'. Two other forms recorded before the *Briggeham* of *Cold. Corr.* are also not required to establish this etymology although they are fortunately available. If we examine a second name in -*hām*, Ednam ROX (Williamson, 12), we find that the late twelfth-century spelling *Hedenham* 1165–1214 (*c* 1320) *Kel. Lib.*, although misleading in its initial consonant, shows our name both to be a -*hām*-name and to have been disyllabic in its first element at the time (*Eden*-). A little earlier – *Ednahim* 1165–77 (*c* 1500) *Melr. Lib.* – we find a reflex of the inflexional ending of the first element which is clearly the name of the river Eden on which Ednam is situated. This is *Edene* 1178–98 (*c* 1320) *Kel. Lib.*, a spelling which fills a gap in the history of our settlement name, for in the compound of the river-name with *hām* the former never appears in its trisyllabic form but always with either the vowel of the second or the third syllable missing. During the second half of the twelfth century the form our name took must therefore have been something like **Edene-ham.* Our written documentation begins at the beginning of the same century and does not help us any further. As far as the etymology and the meaning of the name are concerned, we are left in no doubt whatsoever by the spellings which have survived. Our Scottish documentation is in this respect quite satisfactory although no pre-twelfth-century spelling has come down to us. Only if we want to follow up the phonological development of the river-name in order to establish the exact form which our name may have had when first created in, let us say, the eighth century, do we have to look across the Scottish border to Cumberland and Westmorland where the identical river-name Eden, also recorded as *Edene* in the twelfth century, was fortunately included in Ptolemy's second-century account of Britain as *Itouna* which according to Ekwall 'became *Iduna, whence OE *Idune and with *u*-mutation *Iodune, Eodune* and later *Edene*'.[19] We can assume with some certainty that the original form of our name must have been *Eodune-hām or *Eodene-hām, but not on the strength of our native Scottish documentation. Semantically close to Ednam is Edrom BWK (Williamson, 14), for it contains the river-name Adder as its first element, as the thirteenth-century spelling *Hederham* 1262 *Chron. Melrose* shows, at the same time establishing *-om* as a reduction of *-ham*. Spellings like *Edirham* and *Ederham* which are available as far back as the last decade of the eleventh century do not help us any further. Again, one might investigate the phonological history of the first element further but the derivation of the whole name is clear.[20]

For Kimmerghame (House) BWK, Williamson, 15, notes the modern pronunciation ['kimərdʒəm] which alerts those who know the history of Birgham in the same county. We have to go back to 1332 *ER* to retrace the unassimilated *-b-* in the spelling *Kymbirgame*; two years earlier in the same source the form *Kymbridgeham* preserved the middle element perfectly, and in 1296 *CDS* the spelling *Kynbriggeham* permits us to restore the *-n* of the first syllable. However, only the *Cynebritham* of 1095–1100 *ESC* gives us the right to postulate an OE *cȳna-bryċġ-hām* 'village at the cows' bridge' as the original form of the name. If the singular *-britham* of this spelling has any significance, one might, of course, have to look for a completely different origin for the part preceding *-hām*. Miss Williamson thinks of a hypothetical OE **Cyneberhtinga-hām* 'village of the followers of *Cyneberht*' but this seems to be difficult to prove. In Kimmerghame we definitely have a name for which one would like to have pre-eleventh century evidence to clear up any doubts which might still exist with regard to the proposed etymology. Nevertheless the spellings we have get us very close to the truth, one would imagine. Leitholm BWK (Williamson, 15) only requires the thirteenth-century spellings *Lethame c* 1230 and *Letham c* 1200 (1434) *Cold. Cart.* and the knowledge that it is situated on the Leet Water to add it to the category of *-hām*-names and to suggest a straightforward meaning 'village on the Leet (Water)'. A spelling identical with the last also occurs in 1165–1214 *Melr. Lib.* but does not add anything to our knowledge. For Midlem ROX (Williamson, 13) the fifteenth-century *Myddilham* of 1429 *HMC* (Drumlanrig) is sufficient to indicate the identity of both elements, although earlier forms are available back to *c* 1120 (*c* 1320) *Kel. Lib.* (*Middelham*). The name quite obviously means 'the middle village'. Similarly, the etymology of Oxnam ROX (Williamson, 13) is solved by the *Oxenham* of 1354 *Kel. Lib.* That it is OE *Oxena-hām* 'village of the oxen' is confirmed by the two spellings *Oxeneham* and *Oxanaham* of 1152–3 (15th) in the *Whitby Cart.* Both Smailholm ROX (Williamson, 13) and Smallholm DMF (Williamson, 15) share with Leitholm the re-interpretation of the last element as -*holm*, as the spellings *Smailhame* 1465 *Dryb. Lib.* for the former, and *Smalehame* 1429–30 *RMS* for the latter demonstrate. For the Roxburghshire name the *Smalham* of *c* 1300 *Cold. Corr.* and for the Dumfriesshire one the *Smalham* of 1374–5 *CDS* remove all doubt about the first element, and both names must be interpreted as OE *Smælhām* 'small village'. Any further proof from earlier spellings is not required. Lastly (Town and Kirk) Yetholm ROX (Williamson, 14) is exposed as another -*holm* < -*ham* candidate by the spelling *Yetham* of 1335–6 *CDS*. This is paralleled in earlier records. The forms *Yatheam* 1214–43 *Melr. Lib.* and *Gatha'n c* 1050 (12th) *HSC* help to identify the first part as OE *gæt, geat*, probably in the meaning 'pass' rather than 'gate', but are not strictly needed.

As far as our ten names in -*hām* are concerned, it can be claimed with confidence that the early Scottish spellings which have survived are quite sufficient to establish convincing etymologies. Although only Birgham and Kimmerghame preserve the basic element in a clearly recognisable form, the -*holm* of Leitholm, Smailholm, Smallholm, and Yetholm, the -*am* of Ednam and Oxnam, the -*em* of Midlem, and the -*om* of Edrom are quite clearly shown to be of the same origin. With regard to the explanatory elements only Kimmerghame leaves an element of doubt; in the case of Ednam even the trisyllabic form of the river-name can be reconstructed, and for Oxnam and probably Kimmerghame reflexes of the OE genetive plurals *oxena* and *cȳna* have survived. This is also true of the *Coldinga-* in Coldingham which has the additional good fortune of having the pre -*ing* part established as *Colud-*, by a parallel tradition. For this very early group of English settlement names in Scotland one can therefore state that our early spellings, although in many respects later than those for their English

counterparts, are early enough to permit the establishment of a satisfactory meaning and an acceptable etymology for each name. It is
undeniable that, mainly for the phonological aspects of the history of
the names, one would like to have even earlier spellings available, but
otherwise a certain amount of optimism is permissible with regard to
the worth of the relevant place-name documentation.

5

The second category of Scottish place-names to be examined, those
compounded with the basic element -*tūn*, is so numerous that it would
be impossible to deal with all of them in the same detailed fashion as
those in -*hām*. Only selected examples can be investigated but these, it
is hoped, will be adequately representative of the whole group of names
involved. As indicated above, names in -*tūn* (-*ton*) more or less span the
whole period of English-speaking Scotland, some of them being as
early as -*hām*-names, some as late as the seventeenth century, whereas
most of them appear to have been created some time in between these
two limits. The relativity of terms like 'early' and 'late' is therefore
more obvious here than in the previous category because for names
coined in the seventeenth century contemporary seventeenth-century
spellings are naturally early enough (*cf* the three Dumfriesshire names
mentioned by Williamson, 36: McCheynston which is *Makchymstoun*
and *Makchynestone* in 1618, indicating the 'farm of the MacCheyne
family'; McCubbington, first recorded as *Makcubbeintoun* in 1645
and owned by a family named MacCubbin at the period; and McMur-
dostown, first mentioned as *Macmurdiestoun* in 1625 when the farm
was owned by John MacMurdie; all spellings are from the index to the
Register of Sasines for Dumfries, etc.) whereas they must be considered
almost too late to be valuable for names given in the Early Middle
Ages.

Amongst the earliest names in -*tūn* are those containing the element
-*ing*-. At least some of them are likely to have existed when -*hām*-names
were still being created, and the problems are consequently not dissimilar. Carrington MLO although recorded in a number of slightly
varying spellings (*Caringtoun*, *Caryntoun*, *Karingtoun*, *Keringtone*,
Keryngtoun, etc) right back to the early thirteenth, and possibly the
late twelfth, century (see Dixon, 118) remains obscure as to the proper
form of its first element. Dixon suggests a personal name **Cēnhere* on
the strength of Keresley (Warwickshire) and Kearsley (Northumber-

land) but their recorded spellings, too, do not begin until approximately the same time as the ones for the Midlothian name[21] and do not allow any convincing conclusion as to the first part which is possibly, but not necessarily, a personal name. The form *Cēnheringatūn which Dixon postulates is therefore hypothetical; our written tradition is simply not good enough. The name Duddingston occurs in both Midlothian and West Lothian (Dixon, 186, and Macdonald, 15). Their phonological and chronological sequences of early spellings is almost identical; both have parallel traditions of -ing-forms (MLO: Duddings-, Dudings-, Duddyngs-, Dudyngs-, Dodyngs-, Dodings- back to 1214–49 Holy. Lib.; WLO: Duddings-, Dudings-, Dodyngs- back to 1219 Inchcolm Chrs.) and -in-forms (MLO: Duddins-, Dudins-, Duddyns-, Dodyns-, Dodines- back to 1153–65 Kel. Lib.; WLO: Dudins-, Dodins- back to c 1370–6 Inchcolm Chrs.), as well as a late development of spellings – and pronunciations – without the -ng- (MLO: Duddis-, Dudis- and Dedis- in the sixteenth and seventeenth centuries; WLO: Duddis-, Dudis-, Diddis- and Didis- in the second half of the sixteenth and in the seventeenth century). In the case of the Midlothian name, the Du-spellings go back to 1328 Holy. Lib., whereas Do- is found from 1412 back to 1153–65 Kel. Lib.; similarly the West Lothian name has Du-spellings as far back as 1432 Laing Chrs., and Do-forms from c 1390 to 1219 Inchcolm Chrs. Both Dixon and Macdonald derive the name from Dudda + ing + (genitive singular) -s- + tūn: 'farm of Dudding' who must originally have been the 'follower of Dudda', but the earlier Do-forms seem to point to Dodda rather than Dudda, especially as the former is also on record in such English place-names as Doddenham (Worcestershire), Dodbrooke (Devon), Dodcott (Cheshire), Dodwell (Warwickshire), and particularly a number of Doddingtons, although some of these – like the Kent and Northamptonshire examples – may contain Dudda rather than Dodda (DEPN, pp 146–7). The only two twelfth-century spellings available – villa dodin 1166–1214 Holy. Lib. and Dodinestun 1153–65 Kel. Lib., both for the Midlothian name – must weight the evidence heavily in favour of an original *Dodin(g)s-tūn, probably without the -g-, as the very man who gave his name to Duddingston is mentioned in connection with the last entry as Dodin de Dodinestun and also appears in the Latinised genitive Dodini[22] in the phrase villam de Trauerlen [the old name of Duddingston] et terram Dodini in Berewyco 1165–74 Kel. Lib.[23] If our early spellings might be overrated in their implication that the -ing-forms are secondary in our two names, they appear to establish the Do- > Du- sequence with some certainty. Similarly, if we ignore the -*g*-lessness of the earliest spellings for Edington BWK (*Hadynton* 1095 (15th) *ESC, Edintun* 1165–82 *Melr. Lib.*), these simply confirm our name as containing a first element *Ead(d)a* or the like which occurs as a personal name in such English identical equivalents as Addington in Berkshire, Kent, Northamptonshire and Surrey.[24] The eleventh- and twelfth-century spellings for these four names are exclusively *g*-less, as in the case of the Scottish name under discussion. For this we do not really require any early spellings although if they did not exist we might be less sure in our interpretation of its first element.

   A clear example of an early name in -*ingtūn* is Edrington BWK (Williamson, 7) which must be compared with the other Berwickshire name Edrom, analysed above (see *p* 218), for both contain the river-name *Adder* as their first element, and are situated on the river of that name. The spelling *Ederington* of 1330 *ER* establishes the -*e*- of the second syllable of the river-name, and the much earlier *Hadryngton* 1095 (15th) *ESC* gives us a glimpse of the phonological development of the stem-syllable.[25] Our spellings are easily early enough to show Edrington to be ' the *tūn* of the settlers on the river Adder', if such proof were necessary. For Hassington BWK (Williamson, 8), the sixteenth-century *Hawsintoun* 1516–17 *RMS* draws attention to the earlier vowel quality of the first syllable, and the fifteenth-century *Halsyngton* 1406 *RMS* proves this to have developed – as expected – from -*al*-. Earlier forms, which do exist, are not any more helpful and rather misleading. With Miss Williamson we must therefore leave the question unanswered whether our name contains Old Northumbrian **hals* 'neck' (here probably in its topographic meaning of 'a small valley') or the tribal name *Haelsing(as)*; if the latter, Hassington would, of course, be an extremely important name from a historical point of view, but we must realise that our evidence is not good enough to confirm this importance. Livingston WLO (Macdonald, 75–6) only needs a correction from -*i*- to -*e*- in the vowel of the first syllable to reveal its etymology. We find the form *Levingston* as late as 1688 in the Livingston Kirk Session Records and from there right back to the Latinised *Uilla Leuing* of 1124–52 *Holy. Lib.* As Macdonald points out, 'the Leving in question . . . appears in several charters of the reign of David I'; our written tradition therefore goes back to his own lifetime. Mersington BWK (Williamson, 8) is an instance of a name which has practically never changed its spelling since first recorded, and the *Mersington* of 1291 *Inst. Pub.* does not help us any further in our quest for an etymology. Ekwall claims a personal name *Mǣrsa for Mersham in Kent (*Mersaham* 858, 863; *Merseham* 1086)[26] and this may also be our first element but although our spelling tradition is so consistent, it does not begin early enough to allow definite proof. A name in the same category is Upsettlington BWK (Williamson, 9), for we derive no help whatsoever from a variety of spellings dating back to the last decade of the eleventh century, and an original OE *Upp(e)-Setling-tūn* '(upper) farm near the ledge' which none of them completely confirm but also none of them contradict, might as well be based on the modern map form. In contrast, the spelling tradition for Shearington DMF (also Williamson, 9) begins so late (*Sherington* 1570 *CSP*) that any equation with Sherington (Berkshire) which according to Ekwall[27] is 'the *tūn* of Scīra's people' must remain speculative although well within the realms of possibility. Even more doubtful is Thirlington BWK for which Williamson, 10, does not give any early forms, and it is questionable whether it contains as its first element the OE adjective *þyrel* which Ekwall[28] sees in Thirlwall (Northumberland), Thurlbear (Somerset), Thurlestone (Devon) and possibly Thirlmere (Cumberland), and which is, of course, also the first part of the Scottish name Thirlestane 'stone with a hole through it'.

6

The percentage of names in this group which cannot be satisfactorily explained on the basis of the evidence we possess or which do not need any early forms is perhaps rather high. With regard to some names we are not even quite certain whether they are compounded with *-ing-*, although it is very likely that they contain this particle. Much longer, however, is the list of those names which at one time or another appear in spellings containing *-ing-* but seem to have attracted this element by analogy, rather than as part of an organic phonological development. Names of this kind can be grouped under two main sub-headings: (*a*) those which in their present form contain *-ing-*, and (*b*) those which occasionally in their written tradition have *-ing-*forms but do not possess them now. In both cases, the question as to whether we are dealing with original *-ingtūn*-names can undoubtedly only be answered from our early spellings. In a way, these names are one of the best hunting grounds for those who want to demonstrate the necessity for the scrutiny and proper analysis of early name forms, for because *-ing-* has fulfilled so many morphological uses and grammatical functions

at all stages in the general history of the English language and because
of the many genuine names in *-ing, -ingas, -ingatūn, -ingahām*, and the
like, the forces of analogy have always been particularly strong with
regard to the substitution of this particular particle for similar sound-
ing elements. In addition, the dialectal and colloquial change from a
velar to an alveolar nasal, [ŋ] > [n], which produced an opposition of
-in in non-standard English against the *-ing* of the standard pronunciation, also led to the incorrect restitution of *-ing* in cases where *-in* had
not developed from *-ing* in this way. These three factors together produced quite a number of 'false' *-ington*-formations.[29]

The most instructive of these is probably Symington MLO which as
late as 1593 *RMS* reveals its true origin as *Symonstoun* (Dixon, 287)
and appears as *Symontoun* from 1584 *RPC* to 1664 *RMS*. If it seems
surprising that such a well known personal name as *Symon* should have
lost its identity and succumbed to the *-ingtoun*-analogy, it can be
pointed out in support that both the Symingtons in Lanarkshire and
Ayrshire have exactly the same origin and have shared the same fate.
For all three there are sufficiently early spellings to tell the story. Not
dissimilar appears to be Davington DMF (Williamson, 33–4) but its
earliest form *Davitoun* 1652 *Blaeu* is too late to allow the definite conclusion that this is 'Davie's farm'; it is also too late, on the other hand,
to permit the claim that our name is identical with Davington (Kent)
which in its twelfth- and thirteenth-century forms is *Dauinton*,
Davynton and *Davinton*, and on the strength of these is, rightly or
wrongly, interpreted by Ekwall[30] as 'the *tūn* of *Dafa*'s people', *ie* a
genuine *-ing*-name. A personal name of Scandinavian origin is involved
in Dolphington WLO (Macdonald, 6) which has this spelling and the
closely related *Dolfing-* of the first element in an uninterrupted tradition back to 1490 *ADC*; a spelling *Dolphingstoun* 1653 *Retours* shows
a possessive *-s-*. The disappearance of the *-l-* in pronunciation is signified by *Dauphingtoun* and *Daufingtoun*, both in 1692 in the Kirk Session Records of Dalmeny, and the *Doffyntoun* of 1540 *Prot. Bk.
Johnsoun* indicates in addition that the *-ing*-form was not necessarily
representative of the local pronunciation, as the source for *Doffyn-*
was probably closer to local usage and less indebted to official scribal
tradition. The West Lothian name is parallelled by Dolphinston ROX
(Williamson, 20) and others.[31] The Roxburghshire example has a
Dolphingston for 1475 *HMC* (Roxburghe) and a *Dolphington* for 1434
in the same source: the modern name has, however, reverted – as far as
its official spelling is concerned – to a more original form, as demon-

strated by the *Dolfynston* of 1354 *Kel. Lib.* and *Dolfinestone* 1296 *CDS*. The personal name involved is quite clearly ME *Dolfin* from ON *Dólgfinnr*, and the *-ing*-forms of both names are spurious.

Another group of names with Scandinavian associations is represented by the two Bonningtons of Midlothian (Dixon, 122 and 275) and Bonnytoun of West Lothian (Macdonald, 56). Both Dixon and Macdonald regard these as genuine *-ing*-names and give their meaning as 'farm of Bóndi's people'. None of them is recorded before the fourteenth century, however, and although spellings with *-ing-* abound, there are many others in *-y*, *-i*, *-ie* and *-yn*, quite apart from *-yngs* and *-igis*, and in the case of the West Lothian name the *-y*-form has, of course, won the day (no doubt at least partly by association or confusion with the Scottish adjective *bonnie*). For the latter name and for one of the Midlothian examples the spellings are early enough to show that *-nn-* derives by assimilation from *-nd-* (*Bondyng-* and *Bonding-* from 1586 *Dunf. Reg.* back to 1315 *Ms. Royal Charters*, and *Bonding-*, *Bondyng-*, *Bending-*, *Bounding-*, all in the fourteenth century, *RMS* and *CDS*, respectively). However, whereas the identity of the personal name involved is clear,[32] the written tradition seems to be too confused to allow a definite decision as to whether this is an *-ingtun*-name, or not.

Other names in this category must be dealt with more briefly: *Clerkington* MLO (Dixon, 294), although displaying this particular spelling as early as 1444 *Midl. Chrs.*, is proved by the earlier series of *Clerkin-*, *Clerkyn-*, and *Klerkyn-* from 1563–1338 *Newb. Reg.* to derive from a ME *clerkene tūn* 'farm of the clerics'. It belonged to the monks of Newbattle. *Lemington* BWK (Williamson, 29) must have joined the ranks of the *-ington* names at a fairly late stage for in Blaeu's Atlas of 1652 it is still *Lemminden*, and earlier forms like *Lemonkton* 1306 *Mel. Lib.*, *Lemontoun c* 1304 (*c* 1320) *Kel. Lib.*, and *Lematon* 1296 *Inst. Pub.* show it to have been OE *hleomoc-tūn* 'farm where speedwell grows' (compare Lemington in Northumberland). Milsington ROX (Williamson, 24) is *Milsintoun* in 1652 *Blaeu*. The fact that this is apparently the earliest recorded form of the name is not too much of a drawback, as it points to the ON personal name *Mylsan* (from Old Irish **Maelsuithan*?) as a first element which is probably also found in the Yorkshire Melsonby.[33] The reference in *Blaeu*, of course, is too late to be absolutely conclusive, but it at least establishes Milsington as a non *-ing*-name. For Mordington BWK (Williamson, 30) even a thirteenth-century reference would not have been sufficient to permit a satisfactory interpretation, for in *c* 1276 *HMC* (Wedderburn) the name is still spelt *Mordingtoun*. Fortunately the last decade of the eleventh century produced at least three different spellings (all in *ESC*) – *Morthyngton, Morthintun, Morttringtonam* – and a combination of these makes OE *morð-hring* 'murder ring' (possibly applied to a stone circle) the most likely basis of the first element. As a final example of false *-ington*-formations may serve Morrington DMF (Williamson, 36) which, according to the *Register of Sasines* was *Morringtoune* in 1671 but *Morreintoun* in 1628. The latter presupposes an owner of the name of *Morin*, a common surname in Galloway. The place-name itself is probably not very much older than its first written record.

Three paragraphs above we quoted Dolphinston ROX as a name which survived a period of false *-ing*-formation. There are a few more names of this kind, some of which only show a fleeting attraction to this prolific element. Colinton MLO (Dixon, 146) is frequently spelt *Colingtoun* and *Collingtoun* in the sixteenth and seventeenth centuries. The modern form is found as *Colintoun* as far back as 1488 *ADC* and continued to be used in a parallel scribal tradition when the two *-ing*-formations were introduced. The sequence *Colinstoun* 1531 *RSS* – *Colbyntone* 1506 *RMS* – *Colbantoun* 1479 *ADA* – *Colbanystone* 1406 *RMS* – *Colbanestoun* 1319 *RMS* proves the personal name *Colban* to have been the first element;[34] it also illustrates very well the strong points of the better type of written tradition in Scotland. The Dumfriesshire name Dalswinton (Williamson, 33) establishes itself in unbroken tradition back to 1290 *CDS*, when it is *Dalswynton*, as one of the most interesting names in the Scottish south because the later addition of Gaelic *dail* 'river-meadow' to OE *Swīn-tūn* 'pig-farm' is evidence of an early English and largely pre-Gaelic element in the population of that area. However, even this interesting and etymologically straightforward name is at least once recorded as *Dalswingtoun* in 1309 Robertson, *Index*. Rowieston [Lodge] BWK (Williamson, 32) makes a seventeenth-century appearance as *Rowingstoune* in 1654 in the *Commissariot Record of Lauder*, but is otherwise *Rowenstoun* in 1652 *Blaeu* and *Rowiston* in 1567 *Kel. Lib.* It is just possible that a family name *Rowan* is involved here but our evidence is not conclusive on this point. The only name which seems to go against this trend and contradict our argument is Renton BWK (Williamson, 9). It is *Rennyngton* in 1296 *CDS* and *Regninton* in *c* 1100 *ESC*. If these two forms are taken together, a hypothetical starting-point *Regningatūn* 'the *tūn* of *Regna's* people' may be assumed which Ekwall (DEPN *pp* 379 and

384) also suggests for Rainton (Durham; *Reiningtone c* 1170, 1228), Rainton (Yorkshire; *Reineton* DB, *Rennington* 1202, *Reynington* 1231), and Rennington (Northumberland; *Reiningtun* 1104–8, *Renninton* 1176, *Renigton* 1242). We know that in the last name **Regna* is short for *Reingualdus* but this does not mean that this also applies to the other three names because other names in *Regn-* are also possible, like *Regengār, Regnhēah, Regnhere*, which Ekwall mentions under Rainford (Lancashire) and Rainham (Essex).[35] There is no indication in the early spellings we have for any of these names, which longer name is represented by **Regna* but this is not too worrying as it is practically certain that only the short form was used in the naming of the places concerned. Apart from Rennington (Northumberland), all our names seem to have moved away from the *-ing*-form at an early stage, and the usefulness of early spellings is well demonstrated here. It is in a way gratifying to see that *Regninton* of 1100 for our Scottish Renton preserves the original form of the personal name best.

7

Despite certain disappointments, then, our Scottish written tradition seems to be not at all unsatisfactory in the elucidation of the specific problems arising out of place-names in *-ingtūn*. How does it fare, however, with regard to another question that is continually troubling investigators of names in *-tūn*: the ambiguity of the last element when preceded by an *-s-*? This problem becomes acute whenever the first part is a personal name in the possessive case, and there are at least eighty examples of the combination personal name $+ s + t\bar{u}n$ in the area covered by the three theses which form the basis of this article. Of these, eight (or ten per cent) have final *-stone* in their modern spelling and are only revealed as *-tūn*-names by a series of earlier spellings: Alderstone MLO (Dixon, 242) is shown by spellings like *Awdenstoun* 1535 *RMS* and *Awdinstoun* 1586 *Proc. Bar. Court* to belong to the *-tūn*-category. Edmonstone MLO (Dixon, 260) is well documented and from the seventeenth to the thirteenth century has spellings which prove that the last element is *tūn*: *Edmiestoun* 1557–85 *Dunf. Reg.*, *Eadmundstona* 1338 *Newb. Reg.*, and *Edmundistune* 1253 *Dunf. Reg.* are three of these. Groundistone ROX (Williamson, 21) is *Groundestoun* in 1535 *RSS*; Howatstone MLO (Dixon, 245–6) is *Howitstoun* in the Kirk Session Records for the parish of Midcalder for 1698; Johnstone DMF (Williamson, 35) is *Jonistune* 1194–1214 *HMC* (Drumlanrig); and

Malcomstone MLO (Dixon, 177) is *Malcolmstoun* 1538 *RMS*. In all these cases there are – often numerous – other spellings to corroborate the evidence of the samples quoted. For Philpingstone WLO (Macdonald, 32) the *Philpenstoun* of 1643 *RMS* is sufficient evidence to dispel any doubts about the last element, and *Watherstone* MLO and *Waterstone* WLO are clarified as to their etymology by such spellings as *Watterstoun* 1643 *RMS* (Dixon, 288) and *Waterstoune* 1670 *Kirk Session Records* (Ecclesmachan) respectively. Both are, of course, ' Walter's farm'.

Brotherstone BWK (Williamson, 150) and Brotherstone MLO (Dixon, 191), on the other hand, can easily be shown to be straightforward -*stone*-names, because both of them have early spellings in Scots -*stanes*, -*stanis*, -*stanys*, and -*stane* throughout. Similarly, Loanstone MLO (Dixon, 272) is *Lonestane* in 1614 *RMS*, but Flotterstone in the same county (Dixon, 195) is unrecorded and, although a minor name, leaves at least a doubt in one's mind. Names in modern -*stane* are usually unambiguous, like Bore Stane MLO (Dixon, 179), Caiystane MLO (Dixon, 149), Ericstane DMF (Williamson, 152), and Kellerstain MLO (Dixon, 278). Sometimes the fact that they are names of stones rather than of settlements is important corroborative evidence. Even in this group, however, there are exceptions, and if it were not for our written evidence, names like Brunstane and Rowlestane would certainly be interpreted incorrectly. Brunstane MLO (Dixon, 32), a transplanted name, is *Brunstoun* in 1654 *Laing Chrs.*, and the other Brunstane in the same county (Dixon, 233–4) is *Brunstoun* about the same time in 1655 *RMS*. For Rowlestane BWK (Williamson, 32) the spelling *Rollandstoune* of 1451–2 *RMS* gives a clue as to the nature of both the first and the second elements. For several other names our earlier forms reveal that confusion with *stone* (or *stane*) did take place at one time or another but did not lead to a complete replacement of elements. Some of these may serve as illustrative examples. Usually confusion may arise with the standard form *stone* as in *Dolfinestone* 1296 *CDS* for Dolphinston ROX (Williamson, 20), *Hawcarstone* 1453 *Laing Chrs.* for Halkerston MLO (Dixon, 112), and *Levingstone* 1301–2 *CDS* for Livingstone WLO (Macdonald, 75). However, two examples of -*stane* for -*stoun* occur. One is not surprisingly a third Brunston in Midlothian which is *Bruntstane* in the eighteenth-century Memoirs of Sir John Clerk of Penicuik. The other is Edgerston in Roxburghshire which occurs in Blaeu's Atlas (1652) as *Egyrstain*.

8

If our early spellings are of notable assistance in resolving such ambiguous alternatives, as to whether a name contains the element -*ing* or not, or whether the basic element is OE *tūn* or *stān*, they are, of course, of even greater importance in the interpretation of first elements, especially the proper forms of the personal names involved, and some of the more striking examples of this kind of usefulness are here quoted as the final section of our evidence. For Arniston MLO (Dixon, 110), the *Arnetstoun* of 1609 *RMS* establishes the dental consonant in the second syllable, *Arnaldstoun* 1507 *Laing Chrs.* reveals an earlier -*ld*-, and *Arnoldstoun* 1449 *Midl. Chrs.* shows us that this -*ld*- was originally preceded by an -*o*- and that the name means 'Arnold's farm'. Dingleton ROX (Williamson, 19) is still *Danyeltone* in 1682 *Melr. Recs.* and produces the possessive -*s*- in the *Danyellyston* of 1359 *ER* and similar forms. It is, of course, 'Daniel's farm'. Although the -*s*- of the first syllable is not preserved, the *Ileffeston* of 1329–71 *Melr. Lib.* and other spellings for Elliston ROX (Williamson, 20) get us quite close to the personal name *Ísleifr* involved. This may, of course, have developed into **Ill-leif* by this time so that a preserved -*s*- would have been anachronistic. Curious, in this respect, is the juxtaposition 'Johannes filius Yliff de Ylistoun' which is recorded *c* 1220 *Dryb. Lib.* Identical with Elliston is Illieston WLO (Macdonald, 42) which also has its -*f*- preserved in such spellings as *Illefston* 1335–6 *CDS* and *Ilvestune c* 1200 *HMC*. For Hermiston ROX (Williamson, 22), the *Hirdmanstone* of 1305 *CDS* is sufficient to point to OE *hiordemann* 'herdsman' as the first element. Other earlier forms are simply confirmatory. Similarly Hermiston MLO (Dixon, 175–6) has a number of spellings *Hirdmanstoun* and *Hirdmanestoun* from 1488 *ADC* back to 1214–26 *Mort. Reg.* to uncover its identical origin. The *Hirdmastoun* of 1494 *ADC* demonstrates that the -*n*- of the second syllable disappeared before the -*d*- of the first. The Berwickshire Lyleston (Williamson, 29) has a sufficiently good thirteenth-century tradition to enable us to establish the original bi-syllabic nature of *Lyle*- in the *Liolleston* of 1296 *Inst. Pub.*, while the fact that -*oll*- derives from -*olf*- becomes apparent in the spelling *Liolftoun* of *c* 1222 *Dryb. Lib.* The personal name involved is presumably ON **Ligulfr*, a name which appears in twelfth-century charters as *Ligulf*, *Lyulf* and *Liulfo*. Our place-name evidence is very close to that tradition. Oxton BWK (Williamson, 31) has already been referred to;[36] it is probably the most spectacularly convincing of all examples one can quote from our area for the necessity to take full account of early

16—E.S.E.S.

spellings when attempting to interpret and etymologise place-names. The very misleading modern form Oxton is exposed by the *Uxtoun* of 1652 *Blaeu*. Two hundred years earlier, the first part had still consisted of two syllables as shown by the spelling *Ugistoun* of 1463–4 *RMS*. That the first syllable of this element had contained an -*l*-, becomes clear from the *Ulkestoun* of 1273 *Dryb. Lib.*, and the same source shows that an -*l*- had also been part of the second syllable because it has *Ulkilstoun* about 1220, in a sixteenth-century copy. The true nature of the first element is finally brought to light by the spellings *Hulfkeliston* and *Ullfkeliston* of 1206 (*c* 1320) *Kel. Lib.*; it must have been the Scandinavian personal name *Ulfkell*. It is not often, of course, that one gets such an unbroken recorded sequence like this (*Ox-* < *Ux-* < *Ugis-* < *Ulkes-* < *Ulkils-* < *Ullfkelis-*) but when it does occur it is very satisfying. Compared with Oxton, our final example is probably rather tame but it is nevertheless also very reassuring to know that our twelfth-century forms *Ulvestona* 1165–1214 *Nat. MSS Scot.* and *Ulvestoun* 1147–52 *ESC* confirm the personal name involved in Ulston ROX to have been ME *Ulf* < ON *Ulfr*, a conclusion which otherwise one could only have reached by the consideration of analogical material elsewhere.

9

And so we come to the end of the task which we set ourselves at the beginning and we must ask ourselves what conclusions we can now reach on the basis of the material presented (and represented). Can we, in fact, dispel the doubts we raised at the outset about the value and competence of the available written tradition of Scottish place-names or do we have to reinforce the criticism of those who think that most of it is too 'late' to be really useful in search for etymologies and meanings? Let us answer our initial questions one by one: (*a*) How much later is the written documentation of Scottish place-names, in comparison with England? Scotland lacks such sources as the Anglo-Saxon Charters and Rolls of pre-Norman days, as well as the extensive eleventh-century coverage provided by Domesday Book, but otherwise the onset of the written tradition does not differ greatly in the two countries. (*b*) How much does the absence of the important English sources mentioned interfere with a satisfactory interpretation of Scottish place-names? Judging by the English evidence, pre-Norman documentation does not add greatly to our knowledge if we are concerned with the semantic origin of the name only. It is, however, of great value in tracing the detailed phonological development from the times a name was coined to the present day. This, of course, only applies to pre-Norman names because for later periods – at least as far as the area covered by the three theses is concerned – early spellings are just as plentiful in Scotland as in England. Difficulties about the etymology only arise when a name dating back to the pre-Norman times does not have any twelfth- or at least thirteenth-century documentation although, as we have seen, even this is superfluous or merely confirmatory in quite a number of instances. Obviously the written tradition is much better in the region under discussion than in other parts of Scotland where an obscuring process of Anglicisation of Gaelic names is parallelled by rather poor documentation, quite apart from the complex linguistic mixture of the nomenclature owing to the fairly rapid succession of languages, as for example in counties like Fife, Angus and Kincardineshire. Similarly, the Gaelicised versions of Norse names in the Hebrides and elsewhere have hardly any early documentary backing whatsoever, but just as we have, in the course of our argument, from time to time looked across to England for guidance with regard to early English names, so Norway, and sometimes also Iceland, provides excellent comparative material to make up for the lack of early spellings. (c) What is the relative value of terms like 'early' and 'late' when applied to toponymic documentation? A spelling may be called 'early' when it is close to the date at which a name is likely to have originated. 'Lateness', on the other hand is implied when no documentation is available within centuries after the creation of the name. This does not mean that 'early' spellings are necessarily better than 'later' ones, but as a general rule chronological 'lateness' also means deterioration in the absolute value of a spelling. This point is proved particularly by names for which early spellings exist which are contemporary with the creation of a name.

The writer as well as the reader of this essay would have liked to see this investigation based on a wider geographical area than the one covered by the three theses but, apart from Aberdeenshire, no comparable evidence is readily available from any other part of Scotland. One might also have preferred a more systematic approach linked with tabular summaries and statistics rather than the impressionistic results obtained from the presentation of selected evidence. We do, however, feel that this essay has been more than just a mental exercise and that the name material under discussion has shown that, when handled with adequate knowledge and caution, our Scottish place-name documentation can supply the answers to the majority of etymological quests, even if pre-Norman spellings are largely lacking. When treated in combination with the modern pronunciation and the relevant comparative material from outside Scotland, this documentation is assigned its rightful place in the study of Scottish place-names; and when all has been said and done the dictum with which we began still stands that in the interpretation of a Scottish place-name 'all early spellings in written documents, both printed and manuscript, should be collected and used as a basis for its phonological, morphological and semantic analysis'.

Notes

1 In *Introduction to the Survey of English Place-Names*, Cambridge, 1925, *p* 2.
2 *Ibid p* 3.
3 E. Ekwall, *Concise Oxford Dictionary of English Place-Names*, first edn, Oxford, 1936; here quoted from fourth edn, Oxford, 1960, hereafter abbreviated as DEPN.
4 *Ibid, pp* ix–x.
5 A. H. Smith, *The Preparation of County Place-Name Surveys*, London, 1954, *p* 11.
6 *Ibid, p* 12.
7 P. H. Reaney, *The Origin of English Place-Names*, London, 1960, *p* 17.
8 Kenneth Cameron, *English Place-Names*, London, 1961, *p* 17.
9 *Ibid, p* 25.
10 Angus Macdonald, *The Place-Names of West Lothian*, PHD Thesis, University of Edinburgh, 1937, published Edinburgh, 1941; hereafter quoted, from the 1941 edn, as Macdonald.
11 M. G. Williamson, *The Non-Celtic Place-Names of the Scottish Border Counties*, unpublished PHD Thesis, University of Edinburgh, 1942; hereafter quoted as Williamson.
12 Norman Dixon, *The Placenames of Midlothian*, unpublished PHD Thesis, University of Edinburgh, 1947; hereafter quoted as Dixon.
13 The county abbreviations in this essay are those used by the Scottish Place-Name Survey in the School of Scottish Studies. A complete list of these is found in *Scottish Studies*, 10, 1966, 225. The actual abbreviations employed are:

AYR	Ayrshire	MLO	Midlothian
BWK	Berwickshire	ROX	Roxburghshire
DMF	Dumfriesshire	WLO	West Lothian

14 The abbreviations for sources cited are those recommended in the 'List of Abbreviated Titles of the Printed Sources of Scottish History to 1560', Supplement to *SHR*, 42, 1963, also available as a separate reprint. Abbreviations used for additional sources not in this list are:
Blaeu Geographiae Blavianae Volumen Sextum quo Liber XII, & XIII, Europae Continentur, Amsterdam, 1662.

Commissariot Record of Lauder   *The Commissariot Record of Lauder*, Scottish Record Society, 1903.

HSC   Historia Sancti Cuthberti, by Symeon of Durham, Rolls Ser., 75, London, 1882–5.

MS Royal Charters   HM Royal Charters, HM General Register House, Edinburgh. 2 vols.

Proc. Bar. Court   Proceedings of the Baron Court of Calder Comitis, quoted in H. B. McCall, *The History and Antiquities of the Parish of Mid-Calder*, Edinburgh, 1894.

Whitby Cart.   Whitby Cartulary, 2 vols, Surtees Society, 1879–81.

15 *Op cit* (note 1), *p* 3.
16 DEPN, *p* viii.
17 See notes 5 and 7.
18 *Op cit* (see note 8), *pp* 19, 20.
19 DEPN, *p* 160.
20 For a detailed account of the river-name *Adder*, see W. F. H. Nicolaisen, 'Blackadder and Whiteadder', *Scottish Studies*, 10, 1966, 78–87.
21 DEPN, *pp* 273 and 269.
22 See DEPN, *p* 152, for English place-names containing this personal name.
23 See G. W. S. Barrow, 'Treverlen, Duddingston and Arthur's Seat', *The Book of the Old Edinburgh Club*, 30, 1959, 1–9.
24 DEPN, *pp* 2–3.
25 For details see Nicolaisen, *loc cit*, 82–5.
26 DEPN, *p* 323.
27 DEPN, *p* 417.
28 DEPN, *p* 472.
29 See also my discussion of Binning WLO, Crailing ROX, Simprim BWK, and Cunningham AYR in W. F. H. Nicolaisen, 'Celts and Anglo-Saxons in the Scottish Border Counties: The Place-Name Evidence', *Scottish Studies*, 8, 1964, 141–71.
30 DEPN, *p* 140.
31 See W. F. H. Nicolaisen, 'Scandinavian Personal Names in the Place-Names of South-East Scotland', *Scottish Studies*, 11, 1967, 228.
32 See also Nicolaisen, *loc cit*, 1967, 226–7.
33 DEPN, *p* 321.
34 On this name see further Nicolaisen, *loc cit*, 1967, 228.
35 DEPN, *p* 379.
36 See *p* 212 above.

John MacQueen

Professor of English Literature (Medieval and Renaissance), University of Edinburgh

The case for
early Scottish literature[1]

Present academic circumstances make it difficult to defend con-
vincingly the study either of a provincial literature or of anything
which seems to resemble a provincial literature. For such studies,
universities are the only possible home, and today university curricula
are over-crowded, and as a consequence almost as strictly delimited as
they were in the Middle Ages. In literary work, certain figures are presented as major, and every year it becomes more difficult to obtain a
hearing for any writer outside what is sometimes called the Great Tradition, a tradition which in English studies has come increasingly to
mean Chaucer, Shakespeare, Donne, Milton, Dryden, Swift, Pope
and Johnson – to come no nearer than the safe confines of the eighteenth century.

For opponents of this approach, one point to be noticed is its clever
inadequacy, which by defining itself as normative effectively closes the
possibility of useful critical discussion in other terms. Closed systems
are naturally self-preserving and self-perpetuating. For that reason I
hesitate to defend the study of early Scottish literature by maintaining
the counter-argument, in itself not wholly implausible, that the Scots
have a Great Tradition of their own, quite separate from that of the
English. No absolute separation of the two literatures is possible.
During the fourteenth, fifteenth and sixteenth centuries they inter-
link in a single development, which for more than a century the Scots
dominate. Shakespeare, for instance, in *Troilus and Cressida* was more
directly influenced by Robert Henryson than by Geoffrey Chaucer.

It is true that the past twenty years have seen a certain amount of
good critical and scholarly writing – especially that of C. S. Lewis[2] – on
early Scottish literature. Nevertheless, it is scarcely surprising that
when Langland and Spenser are merely tolerated, Henryson, Dunbar
and the other Scots scarcely gain admission at all. I do not say this with

any intention of belittling their comparative literary importance – they
suffer from inherent non-literary disabilities sufficient in themselves to
prevent the question of literary importance from ever being raised.
They wrote in a language which nowadays is usually and formidably
called Middle Scots, although they themselves simply called it *Inglis*,
'English', a language which for the twentieth-century reader has one or
two real, and many imaginary terrors. Nor does it help that we are
told over and over again that this Middle Scots was a purely literary
creation, never spoken by anyone – as if everyone at some time spoke
the language of *The Canterbury Tales* or *King Lear*. The works of the
poets and prose-writers are most readily consulted in the volumes of
the Scottish Text Society, volumes which retain a markedly nineteenth-
century format, and which appear to belong primarily to the more
remote and dusty shelves of our greater public and university libraries.
STS editors for the most part have been philologists and historians,
often amateurs, relatively unconcerned with literary values: in addition, several have failed to provide glossaries or notes to the texts for
which they were responsible. The poetry again is very much the product
of fifteenth- and sixteenth-century Scotland, and today, even in Scotland, comparatively few people are able to distinguish one of the seven
King James's from another, let alone comment in detail on the social,
political or cultural concerns of the verse.

   In literary histories, finally, these poets have come to be known as
the Scottish Chaucerians – a phrase suggesting that they owe to
Chaucer any merits they may happen to possess, and that only their
deficiencies are native to Scotland and themselves. How many
readers, I wonder, would have taken up Pope or Johnson if they had
come to be known as the English Drydenists?

   None of those obstacles is major, most are negligible, and all might
(and should) long ago have been removed by the efforts of Scottish
scholars and critics. Native scholarship, however, has been inhibited
by other, more subtle factors. It is well known, for instance, that fear of
English dominance is a powerful element in the Scottish character – a
fear only partly to be explained by the history of the two countries,
where on the whole the Scots have been well able to look after themselves. It is not English linguistic imperialism, but the Scots themselves
and general world circumstances which are responsible for the fact that
since the Reformation of 1560 and the Union of the Crowns in 1603,
Scots has ceased to be a respectable language and southern English
has become the normal method of spoken, and more particularly

written, communication in Scotland as a whole. Yet it scarcely helps
that as a consequence many Scots feel some sense of linguistic guilt
that they have allowed their own form of the language to slip so far
from everyday usage. The guilt feeling is compounded by another
factor. English in the form of Lowland Scots has never been the only
Scottish vernacular, and there is a common feeling that as the Scots in
the last four centuries have allowed southern English to become
dominant, so their more remote ancestors allowed Lowland Scots to
displace the true vernacular – Gaelic, that is to say, the Celtic language
now spoken by fifty or sixty thousand people in the western Highlands
and Islands.

It is often noted that the most famous Scottish authors of recent centuries, Robert Fergusson, Robert Burns and Sir Walter Scott, wrote at
their best only when they wrote Lowland Scots. Does it not follow
that earlier writers would have written at their best only if they had
written in *their* vernacular – in Gaelic? The phrase 'Scottish Chaucerians' undeniably suggests a group of poets who permitted nefarious
southern influence to overcome any talent which they might naturally
possess. Why should such poets be studied? Should not Gaelic poetry
receive our first attention? Such a position was once held by Hugh
MacDiarmid[3] and many of his followers.

Nor is this all. Gaelic is a difficult and subtle language which few
Scots have the time, the energy or the ability to master. And there is
finally the question of religion. The Reformation came late to Scotland, but it came in a doctrinally extreme form which dominated the
country for more than three centuries. For anyone brought up in the
Reformation tradition (and most Scots to a greater or less extent have
been so) it was extremely difficult to believe in even the possible value
of anything anterior to the Reformation – particularly anything belonging to the wicked centuries which immediately preceded it.
These were times of barbarism. William Wallace and Robert Bruce
admittedly lurked somewhere in the darkness: the ruins of Melrose
Abbey might be considered a pleasant place for a moonlight stroll –
but much, much better not to look too closely into the uncouth society
which had produced Bruce and Wallace and which had built rather
than ruined the abbeys. Enlightenment began with the murder of
Cardinal Beaton in 1547 and was completed by the expulsion of
Queen Mary twenty years later. In any case, literature and the arts by
their very nature were sinful.

Several of those arguments are self-evidently absurd; others may

require a little reasoned refutation. Gaelic, as has been well established, is no more native to Scotland than is Lowland Scots: the linguistic ancestors of both languages were imported at much the same
time, Gaelic in the fifth and sixth centuries AD from Ireland; Lowland
Scots in the sixth and seventh centuries AD from the Germanic-speak-
ing continental fringe of the North Sea. For centuries the two languages did not overlap, and there are parts of Scotland where Gaelic has
either never been spoken or has been spoken only by an invading
aristocracy who held an English-speaking peasantry in subjection by
right of conquest. There is no likelihood that Henryson or Dunbar
spoke Gaelic but wrote 'Inglis'. Walter Kennedy is the only early
Scottish poet of whom this may have been true.

In the second place, the natural achievements of pre-Reformation
Scotland in fields other than literature are easy to demonstrate: in
ecclesiastical architecture, for instance, one would single out the great
cathedrals and abbeys – St Andrews, Glasgow, St Magnus in Orkney,
Elgin, Dunfermline, Holyrood, Dryburgh, Jedburgh, Melrose,
Sweetheart, Dundrennan, Glenluce, Kilwinning, Paisley, Iona, to
mention only a few: in secular architecture, such castles and palaces as
Holyrood, Linlithgow, Stirling, Huntly, Falkland, Tantallon,
Dirleton and Caerlaverock. The musical accomplishment is less well
known, but does include such formidable names as that of Robert
Carver of Scone (1491–c 1550), of whose compositions five masses and
two motets have survived; Robert Johnson of Duns, whose dates are
uncertain, but who was an approximate contemporary of Robert
Carver, and spent much of his life in England; Sir John Fethy (?c 1480–
?c 1570), who was poet as well as composer; David Peebles (ob 1579)
who wrote the four-part canticle Si quis diligit me, much admired by
Thomas Wode, the post-Reformation vicar of St Andrews whose
manuscript Psalter preserved so much older Scottish ecclesiastical and
secular music, and finally Andrew Blackhall (1536–1609), who before
the Reformation was 'one of the conventual brethren of the Abbey
of Holyroodhouse', but who became a Presbyterian minister, and
spent the greater part of his life at Musselburgh near Edinburgh.
Blackhall wrote much, but is best known for his song 'The Bankis of
Helicon'. The work of those men and their contemporaries is admittedly little known and almost never performed, but it has enor-
mously impressed a number of distinguished musicologists. Sir Henry
Hadow, for instance, described Carver as 'this great forgotten master'
and others have been no less enthusiastic.

16*

Architecture has no necessary association with literature: music is associated only by way of song. The evidence is somewhat meagre, but enough has survived to show that poetry and song were memorably combined in the work of such men as Sir John Fethy and Alexander Scott. More obviously than either music or architecture, humanistic studies at the universities are linked to literary achievement, and in this field it is easy to show the importance of the three oldest Scottish universities, all founded in the course of the fifteenth century – St Andrews in 1411, Glasgow in 1451 and Aberdeen in 1495. It is rather surprising that so little has been made of the fact often enough noted that many of the better known Scottish literary figures – for instance, Henryson, Walter Kennedy, Dunbar, Walter Ogilvy, Hector Boece, John Major, Gavin Douglas, Sir David Lindsay, John Bellenden, Florence Wilson and George Buchanan – were university graduates, Henryson of a continental, perhaps Italian, university, Boece and Buchanan of Paris, Major of Cambridge and Paris, Kennedy of Glasgow, Wilson of Aberdeen, and the other five of St Andrews. The names listed fall into two categories; those whose main accomplishment was in Latin, generally of a humanistic kind – Ogilvy, Boece, Major, Wilson and Buchanan – and those who wrote in the vernacular. Another group of graduate humanists brilliantly utilised humanistic Latin for public affairs, usually as part of their diplomatic work in the royal secretariat of James III, James IV and James V – during the period, that is to say, 1460–1542. The most famous are Archibald Whitelaw, Secretary of State to James III, his colleague, John Reid of Stobo, who continued to serve under James IV, Patrick Panter, who was James IV's Secretary from 1507 onwards, and his nephew, David Panter, Secretary to James V, and afterwards Bishop of Ross. This is a remarkable sequence, and the work of those men has impressed everyone who has taken the trouble to study it.

The cultural vigour and enterprise of fifteenth- and sixteenth-century Scotland may thus, I hope, be taken as reasonably established. Those are qualities which often enough accompany a vernacular literature of distinction. Often enough, I say, but not necessarily always: a society which is vigorous and cultured in other fields may rest content with an almost entirely derivative literature. It is here that the phrase 'Scottish Chaucerians' becomes crucial. If it is properly applicable and means that the work of the early Scottish poets is more or less entirely derivative from Chaucer, that work is no more worthy of real critical and scholarly attention than, let us say, the poetry of Alfred

Noyes or Ella Wheeler Wilcox. The case is altered only for the worse if we change the phrase, as has occasionally been suggested, to Scottish Lydgateans. But I question whether the most prejudiced scholar would really hold that even *The Kingis Quair*, saturated as it is with reminiscences of Chaucer and Lydgate, should be considered as wholly Chaucerian and Lydgatean. The question is largely one of poetic *persona*. That of Lydgate is difficult to establish with any kind of certainty; however hard that of Chaucer may be to define, it is certainly not difficult to experience. That of James I is equally apparent, and quite unlike that of either of his predecessors. Chaucer in particular usually presents himself as the detached narrator, capable of sympathetic imaginative involvement, but equally of ironic or theological withdrawal. Despite its length, the *Troilus and Criseyde* comes nearest of his works to a fully lyrical narrative. The poem ends however in the affirmation of an order which reduces passionate love between man and woman to insignificance; by this far more than by the portrayal of Criseyde's faithlessness, the poem is the heresy against the doctrines of the God of Love which is denounced in the Prologue to *The Legend of Good Women*.

The *persona* adopted by James is entirely different: as narrator of *The Kingis Quair* he tells his story with the detachment only of a mature man looking back on the events of his youth. The entire poem is set in the first person singular. Third-person narrative qualifies and ultimately overthrows the lyricism of the *Troilus and Criseyde*. The first-person narrative of *The Kingis Quair* is unmodified by such externals and remains in full accordance with the eventual position reached by the poet when he is accepted into the cosmic dance of love. It is not surprising that *The Kingis Quair* was so influential in the development of the Scottish love-lyric in the later fifteenth and sixteenth centuries.

The paradox apparently inherent in this combination of detailed resemblance but overall difference is, of course, to be resolved in terms of the literary doctrine of *imitatio* which James shared with his predecessors and his successors. For James as for Lydgate and Chaucer (or for that matter Virgil and T. S. Eliot) it was an essential part of poetic technique to make reminiscence of classical authority contribute to novelty of effect. James almost certainly was less of a scholar than Lydgate or Chaucer, and so incapable of the range of reference open to them: for him they themselves came close to being the classics, although it should be remembered that he introduced Boethius into his poem with some originality of effect. The major Scottish poets, most notably Robert Henryson, worked with greater originality in a much wider area of reminiscence and reference.

The Testament of Cresseid, Henryson's greatest poem, and one of the great poems of the English language, is in a sense his most Chaucerian achievement in that it presupposes in the reader a knowledge of Chaucer's *Troilus*, and that for the most part it employs the *Troilus* stanza. Chaucer, of course, is by no means the only authority to influence the poem. The main point however is the way in which Henryson's imitation conveys an implicit criticism and correction of Chaucer's achievement. Henryson, in other words, follows the great masters by 'improving' as well as 'imitating' his predecessor.

Henryson makes five main criticisms of the *Troilus:*

1 In the latter part of his poem Chaucer inartistically concentrates the reader's attention on Troilus to the exclusion of Cresseid, of whom he had previously drawn a sensitive and sympathetic portrait. In human terms, the fate of Cresseid is more interesting than that of Troilus.

2 Chaucer avoids the realities of dirt, disease and death.

3 Chaucer's poem is long and over-diffuse in style.

4 Chaucer's treatment of free-will and predestination is unsatisfactory and on occasions downright clumsy.

5 The Christian epilogue is inartistically related to the remainder of the poem, not because it is Christian, but because the earlier part of the poem does not establish the opposition of the pagan gods and Christ which the epilogue so strongly emphasises.

Space does not permit me to show in detail how Henryson's poem embodies and answers each of those criticisms. He established the first by the mere fact that he wrote the *Testament*, still more by the psychological depth and delicacy of the portrayal of Cresseid. Cresseid's leprosy establishes the second. The third is to be deduced from the length of the *Testament* – 616 lines as opposed to the 8239 lines of the *Troilus* – and from the style which A. C. Spearing[4] has accurately characterised as high and concise, a style summarised by Henryson in a single line:

In breif Sermone ane pregnant sentence wryte.

Nothing could be further from the norm of the *Troilus*.

Henryson established his fourth and fifth points in a more indirect way. The poems differ strikingly in that Henryson unequivocally introduces pagan divinities. The planetary portraits form one of the most striking passages of the *Testament*, a passage which functions in at least two ways. The planets represent the destinal forces of the universe, the natural laws to which Cresseid as a material being is absolutely subject. At the same time they are the pagan divinities whom Chaucer set in opposition to Christ and Christian salvation. Henryson accepts physical determinism as exemplified by Cresseid's leprosy:

> He luikit on hir uglye Lipper face,
> The quhilk befor was quhyte as Lillie flour,
> Wringand his handis oftymes he said allace
> That he had levit to se that wofull hour,
> For he knew weill that thair was na succour
> To hir seiknes, and that dowblit his pane.
> Thus was thair cair aneuch betuix thame twane.

Even after the affliction of leprosy, however, Cresseid retains a rational free-will which is able to bring her from the position represented by her first ignorant outburst against the gods:

> O fals Cupide, is nane to wyte bot thow,
> And thy Mother, of lufe the blind Goddes!

to her final recognition of responsibility:

> Nane but my self as now I will accuse.

The poem contains no specifically Christian reference to counterbalance the presence of the pagan divinities, but a Christian interpretation remains a possibility, indeed a probability, in terms, first, of Cresseid's progression, despite the Gods, from ignorance to self-knowledge, and, secondly, of the narrative parallels between the *Testament* and the parables of the Prodigal Son, who returned to his father, and of Dives and Lazarus, the leprous beggar who attained salvation, while Dives, the rich man, was condemned. The combination of implicit Christian reference with a specific and historically appropriate pagan setting seems to me not only independent of Chaucer, but also a major triumph of controlled literary art.

E. M. W. Tillyard[5] was once so rash as to contrast the amateur quality of Henryson's poetry with the professionalism of Dryden's.

Dare I say that to me the truth seems almost the reverse? By comparison with Henryson, Dryden was a very uncertain artist – as witness, for instance, the botched conclusion of *Absalom and Achitophel.*

Henryson remains in a limited sense a Chaucerian. It is not difficult to point to works which stand completely outside the Chaucerian tradition. I have already, for instance, referred to the lyric poetry of the fifteenth, and more particularly the sixteenth century, which parallels and sometimes surpasses the work in England of Wyatt, Surrey and their contemporaries. The most important writer is the musician and poet Alexander Scott.

There is a probable immediate relationship between Scott's poetry and Sir David Lindsay's play *Ane Pleasant Satyre of the Thrie Estaitis in Commendatioun of Vertew and Vituperatioun of Vyce*, which was certainly performed in its entirety at Cupar in Fife on 7 June 1552, and at the Greenside in Edinburgh on 12 August 1554. The first act belongs, or at least refers, to the early or middle 1530s, and is a satirical and comic presentation of the relations between James v (King Humanitie) and his mistress, Margaret Erskine (Lady Sensualitie) whom he was still seriously thinking of marrying as late as 1536. Alexander Scott was probably a protégé of the same Erskine family, and the world of his poetry is by no means entirely separate from that of Lady Sensualitie.

Formally *Ane Satyre* is a morality play, but its primary concern is social and even political – the need for reform in Scotland, a need which receives, in a sense, historical treatment. The first of the two main acts deals with corruption at the centre of affairs in terms of the court of the young James v. Act II deals with the consequences – general corruption in the nation – in terms more applicable to the 1540s and 1550s than to the 1530s.

The play has four main characters, King Humanitie, Lady Sensualitie, King Correctioun and John the Commonweill. Partly as a consequence of the open-air stage for which it was written, the secondary characters tend to fall into groups, usually of three, thematically related to the four principals. Variations of dramatic and social importance receive expression: the two Kings occupied thrones on a platform: other characters of consequence – Sensualitie, the Thrie Estaitis, Gude Counsall and Veritie – had 'seats', which probably were thrones at ground-level, and figures of lesser social consequence were restricted to the central 'bent' or 'field'. The dramatic impact of a breach of those conventions might be considerable as for instance when at the beginning of the interlude which separates Act I from Act II Pauper, the poor man, climbed up to occupy the King's throne on the platform. In Act II John the Commonweill, obviously the major figure, begins by occupying neither platform nor throne: he enters from the audience (soaking himself in the process by falling into the water which divided spectators from actors), and dominates the action from the central 'bent'. Only towards the end does he receive visual recognition when he is clothed 'gloreouslie' and given a throne in company with the Thrie Estaitis.

Character groupings differ somewhat in the two main Acts. For the greater part of the first, the central figure is King Humanitie, the varying aspects of whose character are conveyed by his two groups of followers, the trio of genuine courtiers, Wantones, Placebo and Solace, and the more sinister and professional group, Flatterie, Falset and Dissait, who worm their way into the King's confidence by disguising themselves as Devotioun, the friar who becomes the King's father confessor, Sapience, who becomes his Secretary of State, and Discretioun, who becomes his Lord Treasurer. Real social differences are no doubt echoed when the first group involves the King with Lady Sensualitie while the second is more concerned with possession of his purse. Two of the latter group come to a bad end on the gallows. Lindsay's hostility towards the professional civil servant is very clear.

As courtiers, Wantones, Placebo and Solace are closely associated with music and song, a fact which links them in turn with Lady Sensualitie and her three followers, Hamelines, Danger and Fundjonet (this last apparently played by a professional woman-singer and entertainer). Lindsay however draws distinctions even in musical matters. Songs such as that sung by Sensualitie and her companions to Venus, corrupt and lull King Humanitie into the allegorical sleep from which he is awakened only by the arrival of King Correctioun. But other kinds of song do exist, and together with legitimate sports and pastimes appertain properly to the court of a king. It is Solace who makes this plea to Correctioun:

Sir wee sall mend our conditioun,
Sa ye give us remissioun,
   Bot give us live to sing,
To dance, to play at Chesse and Tabils,
To reid Stories and mirrie fabils
   For pleasure of our King

The reply is favourable:

> Sa that ye do na uther cryme,
> Ye sall be pardonit at this tyme,
>   For quhy as I suppois
> Princes may sumtyme seik solace,
> With mirth and lawful mirrines,
>   Thair spirits to rejoyis.

Lindsay is no mere blue-nose.

A somewhat different trio of secondary characters is that made up of Gude Counsall, Veritie and Chastitie. Their individual importance is greater than that of the others and receives correspondingly greater visual and dramatic emphasis. Gude Counsall and Veritie each has a throne, and while Chastitie enters as a homeless wandering exile, she too is promoted to a throne before the end of the act. Each as an individual is balanced against a group: Chastitie against Sensualitie and her followers: Veritie against Flatterie, Falset and Dissait. By way of those oppositions each in addition is contrasted with the entire Spiritual estate, Spiritualitie, that is to say, representing the bishops, Abbot and Persone. Gude Counsall provides the political counterbalance to Flatterie, Falset and Dissait; the three vices at line 977 hurl him away, and he does not reappear until King Correctioun comes on the scene at line 1572. It is by way of King Correctioun that at the end of Act I Gude Counsall, Veritie and Chastitie are brought into a proper relationship with King Humanitie.

In Act II the balance is very different. Gude Counsall, Veritie and Chastitie are enthroned and to some extent withdrawn from the main action. The central figure is now John the Commonweill, who appears as the principal plaintiff before the court of the King in Parliament. *Ane Satyre* in fact is one of the earliest modern plays to exploit the effect of a trial scene, and it is important for the reader to visualise the action in those terms. John stands at the bar in virtual isolation, directly supported as he is only by Pauper, the poor man, and equally directly opposed to the powerful Thrie Estaitis. He complains against each in turn, and the justice of his complaint is already established when at the beginning of the act the Estates make the slow entrance to their seats which a stage-direction so vividly describes – 'Heir sall the thrie estaits cum fra the palyeoun gangand backwart led be thair vyces.'

The Estates themselves are the three classes actually represented in the sixteenth-century Scottish parliament, the Lords spiritual, the Lords temporal, and Merchand, who represents the merchants and craftsmen of the burghs. Each of the second two is played by a single actor, but, as I have already mentioned, Spiritualitie is supported by Abbot and Persone. The weighting of the ecclesiastical order by comparison with the other two is significant, for in Act II as opposed to Act I Lindsay's satire is primarily directed at the corruption of the organised church. Lindsay, despite the fact that he was himself a graduate, had a strong belief in the efficacy of university education, and towards the end of the play three university graduates, a Doctor, a Licentiate or Master, and a Bachelor of Divinity (distinguished, one presumes, by their academic dress) are brought forward to supplant the corrupt Bishop, Abbot and Persone.

Each of the Estates is accompanied by its appropriate Vice or Vices (the term is used to denote the evil low-comedy characters of the morality plays as well as the abstract quality), and here again Lindsay weights the dramatic action against the spiritual Estates, which is palpably the most corrupt of the three. Temporalitie is led by a single figure, Public Oppressioun (who afterwards escapes the stocks and gallows): Merchand by two, Falset and Dissait, representing respectively the merchants and the craftsmen. Both are finally hanged. Spiritualitie however is accompanied by five followers, Abbot, Persone, Sensualitie, Covetice and Flatterie, disguised as Friar Devotioun. Nor is this all. When Temporalitie and Merchand have been separated from their vices, they are fit to play a full part in the King's council. Not so Spiritualitie: when the three churchmen are separated from their external vices, they remain as corrupt as before, and when as a consequence they are stripped of their habits, the motley of the professional fool is revealed beneath. When the Abbess is stripped of her habit, a prostitute's gown is revealed. A clear parallel emerges between the hierarchy as a whole and Friar Devotioun, who appears at first as Flatterie, dressed in cap and bells, afterwards disguises himself as a friar, and when he is finally revealed, escapes hanging only by agreeing to serve as hangman for his former friends, Falset and Dissait. Hypocrisy is clearly, in Lindsay's opinion, the ruling vice of the spiritual Estate. In the end, as has been mentioned, honourable university graduates are substituted for the corrupt clergy. Nunneries are altogether abolished.

Spiritualitie is Lindsay's first target, Temporalitie perhaps his second, but it is very noticeable that representatives only of the lower orders suffer the extreme penalty – a penalty the possibility of which is kept before the audience by the fact that the gallows on which Common Thift, Dissait and Falset are finally hanged, dominate the stage visually from the beginning of Act II. One reason for the exemption is certainly Lindsay's satiric observation that the less privileged orders are likely to be less privileged in death as well as in life. Executions always have a strong stage effect: in the present instance that of Falset must have been unusually powerful, particularly as it receives considerable oral and visual emphasis. Falset is the last vice to be executed, and his gallows-speech is much longer than that of Thift or Dissait. The moment too of his death is marked in an unusual way. Thift and Dissait die to a virtually identical stage-direction, 'Heir sal Thift / Dissait be drawin up, *or his figour.*' It seems likely, in other words, that each of those characters was hanged in effigy rather than in person. The final speech and death of Falset is punctuated by several stage directions: 'Heir sall he luke up to his fallows hingand': 'Heir sall they festin the coard to his neck with ane dum countenance'; and the final 'Heir sal he be heisit up, *and not his figure*, and an Craw or ane Ke [jackdaw] salbe castin up as it war his saull.' Here there is no question of a hanging in effigy.

One might well wonder why so elaborate a treatment should be given to a vice who after all represents only the craftsmen, a class of much less social consequence than the Merchants or the Temporalitie, and which in general receives from Lindsay sympathetic, if still satiric, treatment. His real importance is established by the last part of his gallows-speech. Falsehood is not restricted to a particular social class: the obvious relationship is not with craftsmen but with Truth – the Veritie of Act I whom Falset helped to suppress, and who remains throughout the latter part of the play in her throne on the stage. Indeed, all the corruptions attacked during the play have in a direct sense been corruptions of some aspect of truth, examples of falsehood, and one function of Falset's final speech is to pull into a single hempen strand the various threads which have gone to make up the overall action. Immediately before his execution, Falset summons his retainers to accompany him to Hell – wicked Kings, like Humanitie at the beginning of the play: Public Oppressors, like the second Estate: false Prelates, like the first: corrupted lawyers, like the ones who refused justice to Pauper: corrupt divorce commissioners, like the Pardoner in the first Interlude: termagant wives, like those of the Tailor and Souter who 'ding thair gudemen'. Towards the end, the speech relapses into farce, but one cannot miss Lindsay's purpose – to indicate the need of reformation on a scale even greater than that which he dared to present directly on stage. In the rest of the play Lindsay admits that the practical possibility of such a reformation is small; here he establishes that it is none the less a moral imperative.

I have demonstrated, I hope, that *Ane Satyre of the Thrie Estaitis* is a play of sophisticated technique and unusual range and relevance – a relevance no more limited to the Scotland of the middle sixteenth century AD than that of a comedy by Aristophanes is limited to the late fifth century BC. The parallel, in fact, between Lindsay and Aristophanes is striking. No one denies that Aristophanes deserves serious study and appreciation; it would seem to follow that the neglect suffered by Lindsay, and by the entire early Scottish literature of which his play forms a part, cannot be justified.

I do not recollect that anyone has drawn a significant parallel between Aristophanes and Chaucer.

Notes

1 This paper was delivered in November and December, 1967, at Michigan State University, East Lansing, Michigan, Moorhead State College, Moorhead, Minnesota, and the University of Texas, Austin, Texas. I am grateful to the audiences on those occasions for their comments and suggestions.
2 'The Close of the Middle Ages in Scotland', *English Literature in the Sixteenth Century Excluding Drama*, Oxford, 1954, *pp* 66–119.
3 See, for instance, the Introduction to *The Golden Treasury of Scottish Poetry*, edited by Hugh MacDiarmid, London, 1940.
4 'Conciseness and *The Testament of Cresseid*', *Criticism and Medieval Poetry*, London, 1964, *pp* 118–44.
5 *Five Poems 1470–1870*, London, 1948, *p* 49.